W9-CNF-466

Coleridge, Wordsworth,
and
Romantic Autobiography

Coleridge, Wordsworth, and Romantic Autobiography

Reading Strategies of Self-Representation

Sheila M. Kearns

Madison • Teaneck
Fairleigh Dickinson University Press
London: Associated University Presses

Associated University Presses
440 Forsgate Drive
Cranbury, NJ 08512

Associated University Presses
25 Sicilian Avenue
London WC1A 2QH, England

Associated University Presses
P.O. Box 338, Port Credit
Mississauga, Ontario
Canada L5G 4L8

The paper used in this publication meets the requirements
of the American National Standard for Permanence of Paper
for Printed Library Materials Z39.48-1984.

Library of Congress Cataloging-in-Publication Data

Kearns, Sheila M., 1955–
    Coleridge, Wordsworth, and romantic autobiography : reading
strategies of self-representation / Sheila M. Kearns.
        p.   cm.
    Includes bibliographical references and index.
    ISBN 0-8386-3546-6 (alk. paper)
    1. Coleridge, Samuel Taylor, 1772–1834.   Biographia literaria.
2. Poets, English—19th century—Biography—History and criticism.
3. English literature—19th century—History and criticism.
4. Wordsworth, William, 1770–1850.   Prelude.   5. Romanticism—
England.   6. Narration (Rhetoric)   7. Self in literature.
8. Autobiography.   I. Title.
PR4476.K43   1995   821'.709145—dc20   92-55128
                                                                                          CIP

With thanks and love
to my mother Rita S. Kearns,
and in memory of my father,
James M. Kearns.

Contents

Acknowledgments   9

Introduction   13
1. The Writing of Autobiography in Romanticism   18
2. The Subsidiary to Preparation   37
3. The Surface of Past Time   62
4. To Thee the Work Shall Justify Itself   81
5. The Sense of Before and After   108
6. The Passive Page of a Book   133
7. Perpetual Self-Duplication   156

Notes   168
Bibliography   191
Index   199

Acknowledgments

I wish to thank several friends, teachers, and colleagues who have taken an interest in my work and have generously assisted in the completion of this book. Homer Brown and John Carlos Rowe offered support and encouragement during the early stages of this project when I was a student at the University of California, Irvine. Andrew Cooper read early versions of several chapters and gave me his characteristically thorough and productive criticism and comments. Lance Bertelsen had much to do with helping me to refine the direction of the study and gave me editorial assistance for which I am very grateful. Theresa M. Kelley read and commented upon the manuscript at several stages in the course of my writing, and I am especially grateful for her expressions of support and encouragement, both public and private, during the last several years. Manda Rash provided invaluable help in the preparation of the typescript.

I want to express my gratitude to my family. Their love and support continues to sustain me.

The author gratefully acknowledges the following publishers for permission to reprint previously copyrighted material: Princeton University Press for *The Collected Works of Samuel Taylor Coleridge* (1969–   ); Cornell University Press for *Coleridge's Dejection: The Earliest Manuscripts and the Earliest Printings*, edited by Stephen Maxfield Parrish, reading text copyright © 1988; and W. W. Norton and Company for *The Prelude: 1799, 1805, 1850*, edited by Jonathan Wordsworth, M. H. Abrams, and Stephen Gill (1979).

S.M.K.

Coleridge, Wordsworth, and Romantic Autobiography

Introduction

Iᴛ seems that the study of autobiography will never be done with trying to define itself. From initial efforts to establish autobiography as a distinct genre, through the general effort to provide an account of autobiography's significance as a genre, up to the substantial challenges posed to the study of autobiography by poststructuralist theories of language and of subjectivity, those who study autobiographical writing continually seem to be at the point of announcing their ability to claim a stability or coherence for their field of study.[1] However, even as such claims to stability have been made, along have come problematic announcements such as the "death" of autobiography (at least as defined traditionally), and the need for those who study autobiography to come to terms with a "new" model autobiographer.[2]

Perhaps the most decisive element in the various challenges to the coherence of the field of autobiographical study has been the advent of poststructuralist theories of language and of subjectivity. In general terms, poststructuralist theories of language and their challenge to traditional notions of reference undermine the most basic, defining element of autobiographical writing, the stability of its referent and the general notion of the recoverability through language of an author's past.[3] Poststructuralist notions of the autoreferential character of language and the lack of any stabilizing "center" to hold in check the endless "play" of signification was/is in itself enough of a disturbance to traditional modes of literary/textual interpretation to create problems for those who have tried to define the field of autobiography. However, these theories posed even greater problems for those who study autobiography because of their implications to the effort to define the nature of subjectivity. While critics of autobiography have long defined their activity by their efforts to arrive at adequate or proper models for understanding how some essential self/world could be embodied in the autobiographical text, poststructuralism challenged that effort with the notion that the self or the world that constitutes its past is, itself, nothing more than another sign in the endless chain of signifiers; the self is as much a construct or a text as is the text through which autobiographers seek to represent themselves.

I am interested in this challenge to traditional notions of auto-biography for two reasons. First, it is within the context of this challenge that I wish to begin to define a way of reading, or perhaps negotiating with, the process of autobiographical representation. Toward this end, I will point out what I believe to be certain elements of poststructuralist theories of language and of subjectivity that are crucial to our understanding of autobiography. Second, and by far the more important reason for my interest in the way in which poststructuralism impinges upon the study of autobiography, is my belief that in the process of formulating their activity, Romantic autobiographers such as Wordsworth and Coleridge were facing challenges to "traditional" notions of selfhood and of self-representation that very closely parallel the challenge to "traditional" strategies of self-representation occasioned by the advent of poststructuralist theory.

The place of poststructuralist theory in the critical accounts of Romanticism of the last two decades can hardly be underestimated. Its influences can be traced not only in strictly deconstructive studies of Romantic texts but also in the elements of poststructuralism that inform much of New Historicist scholarship. Among the works of the many scholars that inform this study, the works of three key figures are perhaps most exemplary of the way in which I have attempted to both build upon and, at times, depart from a poststructuralist reading of Romanticism. Jerome Christensen's examinations of Coleridge's textual machinery provide important groundwork and a starting point for my account of the textual production of the self in Romanticism.[4] The matter of Wordsworthian self-division has long been a focus for Romantic criticism, and the work of Frances Ferguson has offered me some very important insights into Wordsworth's struggles with textual indeterminacy, particularly in *The Prelude*.[5] I have brought these readings of Wordsworth and Coleridge together with the material provided by Jon Klancher's recent study of Romantic reading audiences in such a way as to make the case that Romantic autobiography was very much formed by the author's concern with the way in which the reader

figures in the construction of the self in and through autobiographical writing.[6]

Wordsworth and Coleridge are apt subjects for making such a
case in that their primary autobiographical works, *The Prelude*
and the *Biographia Literaria*, are constructed in such a way as
to structure the process of reading not only for a general reading
audience, but also for the very real and present reading audience
that they constitute for one another. Recent studies by Lucy
Newlyn, Paul Magnuson, and Gene Ruoff have focused specifically on Wordsworth and Coleridge's literary relations and
have provided some significant readings of the intertextuality of
Wordsworth and Coleridge's poetic productions.[7] This study of
their autobiographical writings marks out a different area of critical investigation in that intertextuality is examined specifically
as a phenomenon of self-representation and in my account of
the way in which the reader figures in the production of the self
in writing.

I begin my exploration of these strategies of Romantic self-
representation in chapter 1 with an examination of recent theoretical approaches to the study of autobiography in general and
of Romantic autobiography in particular. This examination leads
to a formulation of a concept of Romantic authorship based on
Michel Foucault's concept of the "author-function."[8] Chapter 1
also examines Giambattista Vico's *Autobiography* as an example
of the shift in the nature of self-representation that occurs with
the development of print-culture during the Romantic period at
the end of the eighteenth century.

Chapter 2 focuses primarily on Book 1 of *The Prelude* and
examines Wordsworth's efforts to define the nature of his autobiographical project. Prominent elements in Book 1 such as
Wordsworth's anxieties over the relationship between *The Prelude* and the *Recluse* project and his efforts to settle on a "theme"
for *The Prelude* exhibit Wordsworth's development of his particularly Romantic strategy of self-representation. At one level,
these strategies can be described in terms of traditional Romantic
criticism that reads in *The Prelude* a narrative of the self-
presence of the unified subject of autobiography, a narrative that
makes its foray into a fragmented past in order to emerge into a
unified present. Wordsworth, however, complicates this autobiographical trajectory when he acknowledges and attempts to master the reader's power to figure in and disrupt that narrative.

Chapter 3 begins with an examination of the aspects of book 4 of *The Prelude* in which Wordsworth explores the specifically linguistic and textual nature of perception and of the relationship between subject and object. This analysis serves to highlight the way in which Wordsworth's autobiographical project is not simply a presentation of his experience, but rather a reading of that experience in and through the process of representing it. Particular attention is given to the compositional history of *The Prelude* in order to establish the way in which Wordsworth highlights and demonstrates the process of reading whereby he constructs his autobiographical narrative. The chapter further argues that this demonstration is directed specifically at the "reading public" that Wordsworth addresses in the preface to *Lyrical Ballads*.

Chapter 4 examines Wordsworth's representation of Coleridge in *The Prelude* and its significance with regard to the overall design of Wordsworth's autobiographical project. I use the analysis of *The Prelude* presented in the previous chapters as a basis for examining Wordsworth's address to Coleridge in the poem. While my discussion of Coleridge's role as a figure in *The Prelude* has some basis in recent theories of literary influence, I am concerned more specifically with Wordsworth's conception of Coleridge as a potential reader of not only *The Prelude*, but also of the entire body of Wordsworth's work. In this sense, Coleridge serves as a figure that motivates Wordsworth's development of strategies of reading and writing the self that can disarm the threat posed by Coleridge's powers of reading, particularly the threat of reading himself into Wordsworth's narrative of the self. Although some of this ground has been covered in recent studies of Wordsworth and Coleridge's literary exchanges, the interest here is not in tracing a pattern of influence or of dialogical exchange, but in examining how such patterns are specifically grounded in autobiographical discourse.[9] The chapter goes on to explore Coleridge's own definition, in *The Friend*, of the very strategies of reading that Wordsworth seeks to counter in *The Prelude*. Finally, I present an analysis of Coleridge's poem "To William Wordsworth" as a demonstration of these strategies in which Coleridge's praise of Wordsworth accomplishes its own sort of self-representation by re-reading Wordsworth's poem into the context of Coleridge's own project of self-representation.

Chapter 5 examines Coleridge's *Biographia Literaria*. The

chapter begins by confronting the problems of defining the genre of the *Biographia*, coming to the conclusion that while the *Biographia* may not fit the strictest formal definitions of autobiography, it perhaps goes one step beyond that in being an exploration of the process and methods of its own composition. This chapter focuses on the strategies of textual appropriation and re-appropriation that Coleridge uses in order to construct his reader within his own text. Rather than offering a general account of the readers' responses to Coleridge's text, this chapter presents an analysis of Coleridge's placement of re-appropriated texts as a means of constructing a reading of those texts. However, one significant and quite public exchange of readings of Coleridge's works is presented, that which is occasioned by Hazlitt's reviews of *The Statesman's Manual* and the *Biographia*. In this exchange we have material evidence of the workings of the strategy of textual appropriation and re-appropriation. Chapter 6 focuses on one of the primary targets of Coleridge's textual strategies: Wordsworth.

Chapter 7 examines Coleridge's famous and infamous definition of the imagination in chapter 13 of the *Biographia Literaria*. This analysis explores the connection between Coleridge's definition of the imagination and his theories of language as developed in the *Logic* and elsewhere. I argue that the linguistic basis of Coleridge's concept of the imagination defines imaginative activity as necessarily both linguistic and autobiographical in nature. By tracing these connections, I develop the argument that Coleridge's concept of the "verb substantive" (to be) serves as the grounding for his efforts to capture what he calls the "indivisible moment" in which "the subject . . . becomes a subject by the act of constructing itself." For Coleridge, this moment is constituted in the act of textual re-appropriation through which he attempts to author the "author-function." The chapter concludes with a discussion of how the distinctive strategies of self-representation used by Romantic autobiographers are designed to meet the force of the author-function that begins to assert itself at the end of the eighteenth century.

1

The Writing of Autobiography in Romanticism

Romantic autobiography emerges during the rise of what has been called eighteenth-century "print culture." The expanding modes of publication and distribution and the constitution of a whole host of "readerships," along with radically altered conceptions of "authorship" and authority, that characterized this culture constituted a challenge to the Romantic autobiographers' most fundamental notions not only of how their accounts of themselves would be received and interpreted but also of how their "lives" would be constituted and defined by the processes of representation and reception themselves. The *Biographia Literaria* clearly testifies to Coleridge's concerns about the reception of his works. *The Prelude* is rather different in that Wordsworth can be said to have considered the work, at least during his lifetime, as a private document, a work that would not have been designed to address a public readership. However, it is clear that *The Prelude* had at least one very materially present reader in Coleridge and that the poem also figured prominently in the very public literary exchanges between Wordsworth and Coleridge. Also, as my reading of *The Prelude* argues, Wordsworth's strategies of self-representation constitute an address to "the reading public" that so concerned Wordsworth in the preface to *Lyrical Ballads*.

Traditional concepts of autobiography are not formulated to account adequately for the complex exchanges between writer and reader that figure in Romantic autobiography. Almost every notion of autobiography that I would call traditional takes as its starting point some conception or paradigm of selfhood.[1] These paradigms are generally drawn from models of spiritual, intellectual, or personal development such as the Christian confession, the conversion experience, Cartesian rational enquiry, historical consciousness, psychology, psychoanalysis, and so forth. Thus traditional accounts of autobiographical writing generally examine the way in which these models serve as the outline for autobiographers' accounts of their lives and provide the means by which the self that is writing makes the past self into an object for representation. Above all else, these models of selfhood serve to stabilize the relationship between the self that is writing and the self that is written. This stability is no doubt important to the autobiographer—it is what allows one to believe that it is possible both to present the truth of one's life and to preserve it in writing—but perhaps this stability is even more important to those who study autobiography. It is precisely that which allows one to define autobiography, to make the claim that it is a distinct genre. However, as the number of different models of "essential" selfhood would indicate, the relationship between the subject and the object of autobiography, the self writing and the self written, is not so easily described or defined in any final terms.

The significance of poststructuralist theory for the study of autobiography is that rather than trying to pin down this relationship and to resolve it into some stable model of selfhood, poststructuralist theory has made the very instability of writing and the process of the production of "meaning" its subject and has highlighted the fact that such production takes place equally in unpublished as well as published climates of reception. Thus, in terms of the study of autobiography, poststructuralist theory takes as its starting point the notion that the self that is writing simply cannot be separated from the self that is written. The relationship between the author of an autobiographical narrative and the life that is presented in that narrative is at best a problematic one in that the autobiographical subject is constituted in the process of its own representation.

However, rather than simply deconstructing the theories of language and of subjectivity that underlie most traditional accounts of autobiographical writing, poststructuralist theory provides an avenue by which we can, in fact, come to a better understanding of the divided subject of autobiography. There are two particular aspects of poststructuralist theories of subjectivity on which I focus here. The first is Lacan's notion of the textual nature of consciousness itself, and the second is Derrida's exploration of the way in which the "signing" of the self takes place in an autobiographical text.

In his account of psychoanalytic practice, Lacan represents it as a reading of the discourse of the unconscious. Such a reading is a useful guide to autobiographical representation in which the subject writes the self in and through a reading of the discourse of the self. In effect, Lacan argues (and this study concurs) that the writing subject *is* the subject as constituted in and through systems of representation.[2]

Although Lacan is concerned primarily with considering how psychoanalytic practice reads the discourse of the unconscious, his notion of reading the subject in and through its process of discovery, or rediscovery, offers an important means of understanding the way in which the autobiographical subject constitutes itself in and through writing:

> The unconscious is that chapter of my history that is marked by a blank or occupied by a falsehood: it is the censored chapter. But the truth can be rediscovered; usually it has already been written down elsewhere. Namely . . .
> —in archival documents; these are my childhood memories, just as impenetrable as are such documents when I do not know their provenance;
> —in semantic evolutions: this corresponds to the stock of words and acceptations of my own particular vocabulary, as it does to my style of life and to my character;
> —in traditions, too, and even in the legends, which, in a heroicised form, bear my history;
> —and, lastly, in the traces that are inevitably preserved by the distortions necessitated by the linking of the adulterated chapter to the chapters surrounding it, and those whose meaning will be reestablished by exegesis.[3]

In these terms, the subject is involved in a continual process of signification, the generation of narratives which at the same time constitute the generation of a history and the interpretation of that history. In this sense, the narration of the self cannot be separated from the interpretation of that narrative. The constitution of the self and of identity is, from its very beginning, a reading of the "documents" that constitute the history of the self. Identity *is* exegesis. Identity *is* reading.[4]

In order to understand the way in which this general notion manifests itself specifically in the strategies of autobiographical writing, we can turn to Derrida's account of the particular difficulties involved in the attempt to record the text of the self in the form of a book. It is in this form that the autobiographer is forced to confront a figure who has the power (indeed is being given the power) to usurp the autobiographer's function as the reader of the text of his own identity. In Derrida's terms, the reading that constitutes the construction of the text of the self is to be understood in the complex and complicated activity of the "signing" of the text.

Derrida characterizes autobiography as text which bears the signature of the author and whose design is specifically to present that signature, the signing of the self. The predicament of writing or signing the self, however, is that this signing takes place only as a text that is read or, as Derrida conceives it, is heard:

> The signature becomes effective—performed and performing—not at the moment that it apparently takes place, but only later, when ears will have managed to receive the message. In some way the signature will take place on the addressee's side, that is on the side of him or her whose ear will be keen enough to hear my name, for example, or to understand my signature, that which I sign. . . . It is the ear of the other that signs. The ear of the other says me to me and constitutes the *autos* of my autobiography. When, much later, the other will have perceived with a keen-enough ear what I will have addressed or destined to him or her, then my signature will have taken place.[5]

While Derrida goes on from here to assert that the signing of the text by the ear of the other is not peculiar to autobiography, but rather is the condition of all texts, my examination of Romantic autobiography will focus more specifically on the way in which historical circumstances combined to make the Romantic autobiographers more acutely aware of the way in which their choosing to enter into autobiographical discourse carried with it the paradoxical predicament of making themselves the subject of their own discourse while at the same time submitting themselves to being subject to the reading of others.[6] This predicament also links Romantic autobiography to certain eighteenth-century theories of history, particularly the historiography of Vico. It is for this reason that I will examine Vico's *Autobiography* as a paradigmatic demonstration both of his theory of history and of the strategies of self-representation that Romantic autobiographers adopt.

However, before proceeding with a discussion of the specific predicament of the Romantic autobiographer, it seems necessary to address the way in which certain theories of autobiography have co-opted the general critique of a notion of unified subjectivity occasioned by developments in linguistic theory and of poststructuralist accounts of textuality. As I have said, the notion of a subject that is constructed in and through language answers very well to the understanding of autobiographical writing as having two subjects—the self that is writing and the self that is written. However, in trying to bring these two notions into productive conjunction, some theories of autobiography have too easily translated the radical notion of a divided subject into a traditional notion of the autobiographical text as the embodiment, the making present of the self.

Avrom Fleishman's work offers perhaps the most direct attempt to use the terms of Derridean deconstruction in the reading of autobiography. However, in using these terms, Fleishman sees himself as proposing an alternative to what he calls deconstruction's tendency "to see representation and other displacements of the self as a kind of death." The alternative to this tendency that Fleishman proposes is one which:

> opens when the tendency of the self to become other in writing is seen neutrally as a process of self-alteration. Altering, becoming other, need not be taken as making strange but may be remaking. From this position, the death of the self in autobiography may be seen as a sloughing off of the dead self, as exorcism of the living yet baleful one, or as the inveterate need or habit of tinkering with oneself in language.[7]

While understanding the process of self-alteration (or alienation?) as a process of "making strange" may not constitute a neutral point of view, neither does understanding it as a process of remaking.[8] The notion of sloughing off a dead self or of remaking the self within the medium of language (tinkering) carries with it a notion of an essential self which is not threatened, which, finally, can be saved from death because representation need not be seen as the dangerous and threatening thing that Fleishman believes deconstruction made it.[9] Indeed this re- demptive reading also has characterized a number of readings of Romantic texts that ground themselves, at least in part, in poststructuralist theory.[10]

Fleishman's need to resolve the problems involved in aligning himself with poststructuralist theories of language while at the same time trying to preserve a certain stability for the subject, a stability that is preserved by "remaking" rather than "making strange," becomes most apparent in his representation of Der- rida's notion of supplementarity. Fleishman suggests that:

> Perhaps the most satisfactory way of taking the writer's alteration is through Derrida's conception of writing as supplement—the mark of an absence which yet supplies something of what is lacking in the life or lost in writing.[11]

As his development of this notion makes clear, Fleishman is reading supplementarity as little more than metaphor or figura- tive language (as defined traditionally). This reading carries within it the desire to retain a guarantee or at least a hope for a full presentation of the subject and to repress the danger of the "dangerous supplement" that is inherent in any possibility for self-presentation that writing provides.[12] Fleishman's notion of a supplementarity through which the self becomes other in some sort of self-redeeming process also preserves the notion that the autobiographer is master of his text. It does so by seeing any "other" that is involved in the text as being simply another ver- sion of the self as constituted before writing. This notion of sup- plementarity, which preserves the concept of a unified self who writes the self, does not allow for that element that serves to render the text of autobiography so radically open, that is, the other who reads or hears the text and who signs that text in place of the autobiographer.

The description of the linguistic features of autobiographical writing does attempt to move away from a concern with the es- sential selfhood of the autobiographer and toward a concern with the specifically discursive nature of the writing that constitutes autobiographical discourse. In this line, the work of Jean Staro- binski and Elizabeth Bruss warrants particular attention.[13] As much as these writers provide useful and appropriate descriptions of some of the features of autobiographical discourse, they do, however, still center their discussion of these features on the subject of a text who is given a privileged status as the author of the unity that is the life and therefore the work. Indeed, Starobinski and Bruss's approaches to autobiography, each in its own way, point toward reading autobiography as a particularly privileged performance of the self in which the critic-reader is brought to "see" and "hear" the self that is present behind the words of the text.

Starobinski's description of the "style" of autobiography attempts to account for the nature of autobiographical writing by drawing upon Benveniste's distinction between narrative and discourse.[14] Autobiography, as Starobinski sees it, involves a crossing of the two modes of linguistic representation: "*historic statement* . . . a narrative of past events" and "*discourse* . . . a statement presupposing a speaker and an auditor."[15] Starobinski thus defines the "style" of autobiography in terms of an author's particular choices in the alignment of these two modes. Among these choice are that of making one mode dominant over the other, the choices of addressee, and the choice of an imagined interlocutor. In this sense, Starobinski does not begin his work with a notion of a unified subject of consciousness, but he nonetheless sees the "style" of autobiographical writing as "organic," a natural function of the subject that constructs a "text [that] will at least present an 'authentic' image of the man that 'held the pen.'"[16] It is in this sense that Starobinski, like traditional theorists of autobiography, examines autobiographical writing so as to try to see through it and to gain a view of the essential subject of the text.

In grounding her approach to autobiography in speech act theory and the notion of performative discourse, Bruss attempts to offer a clearer account of the nature of autobiographical writing itself (rather than its subject). Her effort to work out a definition of autobiography as a genre focuses on its evolution as a literary act, taking into account the interaction of historically specific communities of writers and readers. However, these communities are suspiciously stable ones in that Bruss conceives of the autobiographical act as an achieved communication and of the critic's task as being that of elucidating or recovering the discursive conditions in which that communication is achieved. The

force of Bruss's "rules to be satisfied by the text and the surrounding context of any work which is to 'count as' autobiography" is summed up in her assertion that "what is vital for
creating the illocutionary force of the text is that the author pur-
port to have met these requirements, and that the audience
understand him to be responsible for meeting or failing to meet
them."[17] This model of communication assumes a high degree
of stability in both the autobiographer and the audience and the
prescriptive force of their "tacit knowledge of the role(s) [they]
are assigned."[18] However, while such assignment of roles may
carry a great deal of force in a speech act, in the literary act a
number of de-stabilizing factors enter into the linguistic exchange that Bruss does not fully take into account. The autobiographer, as constituted in his or her text, is subject to a reader
who in taking possession of a text is "responsible" only to the
reading of the text that he or she constructs.[19] By conceiving of
autobiography as an act rather than as text, Bruss does open up
the possibility of giving the lie to the monolithic view of the
autobiographical text, but the resolution of autobiography into
the act of an individual speaker engaged in communicating with
an auditor simply offers another means of viewing the integrity
and harmony of autobiography as the reflection of the integral
unity of the performer. Although this view of the autobiographical text does justice to its discursive quality and the necessary
presence of an auditor, it still does not do justice to the possible role of that auditor as reader, as someone who has the
power to "sign" the text and thereby usurp the "authority" of the
autobiographer.

As I have begun to explore it here, autobiographical writing
involves two separate but related problems or tasks. The first of
these tasks is the performance of a reading of the self in and
through the construction of the autobiographical text. The second task is that of confronting the way in which the production
of the autobiographical text makes the author subject to the reading of others. To a certain extent, Derrida's notion of the "signing" of the autobiographical text by the other offers us a general
understanding of the nature of this task. However, Derrida's discussion of autobiography focuses primarily on describing the
predicament that gives rise to the task, rather than on examining
the way in which the task might be carried out. It is through

Foucault's account of the radical change in the nature of representation that occurs at the end of the eighteenth century and in his notion of the "author-function" that we can begin to arrive at an understanding of the specific nature of this predicament for Romantic autobiographers and the strategies that they use in confronting it.

A whole range of studies have addressed the issue of the historical and material basis of the concept of authorship, and many of these studies have located the emergence of this concept in the latter half of the eighteenth century.[20] Among these studies, Foucault's work is particularly important to my examination of Romantic autobiography because of his notion of an "author-function" which is "characteristic of the mode of existence, circulation, and functioning of certain discourses within a society."[21] While Foucault is most concerned with establishing the general characteristics of the author-function and with tracing the trajectory of its different historical manifestations, I am most interested in a specific moment that he locates in this trajectory. It is the moment at which "a system of ownership for texts came into being, once strict rules concerning author's rights, author-publisher relation, rights of reproduction, and related matters were enacted—at the end of the eighteenth century and the beginning of the nineteenth century."[22] Although Foucault sees the "risks" of authorship being reduced, or transformed, once the act of authorship became "goods caught up in a circuit of ownership," there is another aspect of the author's placement in a system of property that introduces a different sort of risk—that which is generated by the very distancing of the author from his product. Once writing is no longer an act, but an object, the risk of alienation from or appropriation of this property becomes all the more prominent. Certainly the law defines who may and may not profit from the production of these goods, but this monetary gain carries with it a corollary loss. A text that has entered into the system of exchange (been bought and paid for) is no longer subject to the authority of its producer, and in the system of linguistic exchange the author becomes subject to the reader (purchaser).

The situation of "the man of letters" did not always make him/his text subject to appropriation. Indeed, Jerome Christensen has made the case that the Enlightenment man of letters was in a position to make of writing "a symbolic practice, a career, that exploited, facilitated, and epitomized the operations of the commercial society which it persuasively represented."[23] However, as Foucault designates it, there is a limit to such powers of representation that is reached in the latter part of the eighteenth century, and it is within such limits that Romantic authorship constitutes itself.[24] The Romantic construction of authorship is carried out in the face of a developing awareness of the disappearance of the author, as such, and the emergence of an author-function that opens one's textual production to appropriation by the reader/consumer. The strategy with which the Romantic autobiographer meets this predicament is what I would call an attempt to "author" the "author-function." Such authoring takes the form of an attempt to exploit the emerging limitations of representation in such a way as to retain a certain authority over its functioning.[25] Foucault's reversal of the traditional definition of the author affords us a view of the nature of this exploitation:

> the author is not an indefinite source of significations which fills a work; the author does not precede works, he is a certain functional principle by which, in our culture, one limits, excludes, and chooses; in short, by which one impedes the free circulation, the free manipulation, the free composition, decomposition, and recomposition of fiction. In fact, if we are accustomed to presenting the author as a genius, as a perpetual surging of invention, it is because, in reality, we make him function in exactly the opposite fashion. One can say that the author is an ideological product, since we represent him as the opposite of his historically real function. . . . The author is therefore the ideological figure by which one marks the manner in which we fear the proliferation of meaning.[26]

No longer in a position to avail themselves of the powers of representation exploited so successfully by the Enlightenment "man of letters," Romantic authors turn instead to the very limitations of representation, the control, the impediment to meaning that the "author" comes to represent, as the means of establishing their own authority over the author-function which defines them. Specifically, Romantic autobiographers recognize the way in which the free circulation of their texts makes not only their writing, but the identity constituted in and through that writing, subject to the proliferation of meaning produced in the act of reading. They therefore attempt to assert their own authority over the author-function, which makes them subject to this reading, by developing strategies of writing that will figure in their texts the reading process itself.

In my examination of the autobiographical writings of Words-worth and Coleridge, I look at two different ways in which this strategy of authoring the author-function is carried out. The first of these strategies, which I associate primarily with Wordsworth, involves an exploitation of the power of reading by inscribing one's own act of reading in the writing of the text.

Such inscription serves to circumvent (not negate) the power of the other as reader by constructing a narrative of the reading process out of which the autobiographer produces his text and thereby figures in the text the very processes in which the reader of the autobiographical text engages. Texts that write the self in this way seek to ground themselves in the processes of reading and writing that they themselves enact and upon which they depend. In such texts, reading is not simply an act performed on the text, it is an act which may be figured in the text in such a way as to structure the performance into which the reader is drawn in attempting to "read" the text.

The second strategy for authoring the author-function, which I associate primarily with Coleridge, addresses acts of appropria-tion that a reader performs on a published text, and does so by constructing the autobiographical text by re-appropriating texts that have been placed in circulation and have become subject to the reading of others. One takes possession of one's own writing by reproducing it in a literary life that authors a reading of that writing. In the practice of this strategy of self-representation, the production of a literary life becomes a process of reproducing one's writing as that life, and the writer becomes, in effect, his own reader and possessor of his own text.

The distinctiveness of these strategies for Romantic writers can perhaps best be seen by examining how and why traditional models of autobiography cannot account for these strategies. In the course of this examination I also propose and analyze what I believe to be a more appropriate model of eighteenth-century autobiographical discourse. The dominant (founding) model of autobiographical discourse is that of Augustine's *Confessions*, and this model has held particular sway in the examination of Romantic autobiography. This dominance is due in large part to the significance and influence of M. H. Abrams's reading of

Romanticism in general and in particular to his grounding of his reading of Wordsworth's *Prelude* as "crisis-autobiography" in what he calls "the first sustained history of an inner life," Augustine's *Confessions*.[27] Even among the more serious challenges to Abrams's reading of *The Prelude* and of Romantic autobiography, the tendency has been to retain the Augustinian model, albeit in an altered form, rather than to recognize and examine the very different discursive conditions that govern autobiographical writing from the eighteenth century on.[28]

The primary problem with an Augustinian model of autobiography for Romanticism is the way in which Augustine grounds his textual production of identity in scripture, the Word of God. Abrams makes a relatively easy translation of the spiritual grounding of Augustine's text ("the three points of reference which serve as the premises and prime functional terms throughout the *Confessions*: God, the natural creation, and man"[29]) into Wordsworth's grounding of his self-representation in a secular system of reference. The problem with this translation is that Abrams simply proceeds as though the revised system of reference does nothing more than serve the same set of "spiritual" ends with Nature subsuming the function of God. However, the system of reference is revised much more radically than Abrams imagines, and this revision involves a direct recognition of the contemporary conditions of textual production.

Interestingly enough, another application of the Augustinian model of autobiographical discourse in discussing Romantic autobiography, that of Paul Jay, has taken the very opposite of Abrams's approach. Jay sees in the *Confessions* "an allegory of the self-reflexive writer's problematic efforts to bridge the distance between past and present—between himself and his own textual representation of himself."[30] However, the application of this model once again errs by collapsing the historical coordinates of the discourse of self-representation. While Jay does concern himself quite directly with the way in which certain historical differences in conceptions of subjectivity give rise to very different forms of self-reflexive discourse, the problematic nature of self-representation remains the same. The autobiographical subject is always already divided against itself, and the differences in autobiographical discourse reflect the degree to which the autobiographer may assert a hope for self-renewal in the face of this division or perhaps, as in the case of the post-

structuralist autobiographer, embrace and celebrate this difference as the endless play of signification.

It is not, however, Jay's attention to the divided status of the
subject of autobiography with which I take issue.[31] Clearly that
status plays a large role in my own account of Romantic autobiography. Rather, what concerns me, and what is not taken into
account in Jay's study, is the way in which the textual production
of identity in autobiography is, in any given historical period,
linked to and conditioned by very specific textual practices, both
on the part of the author and the reader.

The textual practices of Wordsworth and Coleridge serve here
as cogent illustrations of the historical pressures on Romantic
ideas about the nature and possibility of autobiography. Rather
than present an exhaustive survey of examples of Romantic autobiography, the aim here is to analyze the complex textual exchanges between Wordsworth, Coleridge, and their readers in
such a way as to present a model for reading the whole range of
Romantic autobiographical discourse.

In order to offer what I think is a more appropriate model
of Romantic autobiographical discourse than that provided by
traditional readings of Romanticism and also to set up some of
the terms in which I will examine the autobiographical writing
of Wordsworth and Coleridge, I turn to the writings of an eighteenth-century figure that are very much caught up in the change
in the status of the author that occurs in that century. The writings of Giambattista Vico may seem a peculiar choice as a model
by which to begin to read Romantic autobiography. However,
Vico's *Autobiography* is in many ways quite typical of the age
that produced the creature known as the "man of letters," the
age in which authority and authorship go beyond being matters
of authenticity and become matters of property. Vico's *Autobiography* is especially typical of this age's prominent form of self-
representation in which authors represent themselves not so
much through the events of their lives, but through accounts of
their writings. In effect, their textual productions, their books,
are presented *as* the events of their lives.

Although Vico and the Romantics are at different ends of the
Enlightenment and of the emergence of the author as a legal
construct, among the differences in their historical circumstances, there are significant similarities as well. Vico's publica-

tions are produced in a world of commissions and patronage, and his primary concerns with regard to publication are divided between the desire to contribute and give form to the philosophical discourse of his time and the very immediate and material desire of attaining an academic position. Unlike Vico's writings, the writings of Wordsworth, Coleridge, and other Romantic writers contend in the full-blown literary marketplace that is the product of eighteenth-century commercial society. As Jerome Christensen expresses it, the Romantic era was one in which "the man of letters had come to regard himself as a wage slave to anonymous capitalists."[32] However, when Vico and the Romantics narrate the events of their lives, they focus on their lives in print and particularly on the way in which autobiographical discourse can provide the means of authenticating their textual productions. Whereas spiritual autobiography in the Augustinian tradition may be seen as a means by which its author takes possession of his life by interpreting its events, the autobiography as a literary life, the form that develops its currency in the eighteenth century, offers the means by which the writer seeks to take possession of his textual productions. And herein lies the specific significance of Vico's *Autobiography* to a discussion of Romantic autobiography. In autobiographical writing, Vico and the Romantics narrate a tale of their texts that seeks to establish their authority over their own alienated writings by reproducing them in an autobiographical narrative.

In 1725 Count Gian Artico di Porcia asked Vico to write his autobiography in order to contribute it to a project in which "creative scholars" would present their personal histories for the sake of "the advancement of learning."[33] This request gives Vico the general focus for his narrative, but what Vico produces is not simply an intellectual autobiography. The narrative of Vico's life and his intellectual development is a narrative of the composition and production of the *New Science*.[34]

The means by which Vico attempts to establish his authority over the *New Science* is his apparent revision of the dates of composition of the three different parts of the *Autobiography* that were written at different times. Available evidence tells us that part A of the *Autobiography* was written in the spring of 1725 in response to Porcia's initial request, which is just after Vico had completed what he later referred to as the *New Science* in "negative form"—a version which was never published. Part

B of the *Autobiography* was written in December 1725 just after the first publication of the *New Science*. These two parts were published in March 1728 along with Porcia's proposal. The third part of Vico's *Autobiography*, what is called the continuation, was written in 1731, shortly after the publication of the "second" *New Science*. Thus, taken separately, each of these parts narrates one stage in the history of the writing of the *New Science*. However, when read as a continuous narrative, it is apparent that the continuation engages in some strategic revision of the other two parts.

In the continuation, Vico states that Porcia's request was made not in 1725 as the known history of the *Autobiography's* composition tells us, but at "about the same time" in 1727 that Vico was writing his oration on the death of Donna Angiola Cimino (*Autobiography* 180–82). Vico does not seem to be trying to set a specific date of composition, and the ambiguous phrasing ("*about* the same time") may allow room for the two years' difference between the date of Porcia's proposal and the funeral oration. However, if we accept this collapsing of dates, the frames of reference for parts A and B of the *Autobiography* are significantly revised. If written in 1727, part A does not refer to Vico's intellectual development that leads up to the composition of the unpublished *New Science* in its "negative form," but to the first published edition of the *New Science*. This misrepresentative dating accomplishes in temporal terms what Vico seeks to accomplish in narrative terms at the outset of part B. Part A had narrated Vico's life and intellectual development up to the point of the devastating blow of his unsuccessful competition for a chair in civil law. Part B picks up the narrative at this point, but passes so quickly over what we know to be the composition of the *New Science* in its negative form and the circumstances surrounding its failure to be published, that it seems as though this early version of the *New Science* hardly existed. However, we know that part A was composed just after Vico had completed the *New Science* in a "negative form," and preceded Vico's decision in July 1725 to recast his work in a "positive form" and to assume the cost of its publication himself. This decision was necessitated by the withdrawal of the original sponsorship of the work and because of its excessive length and the expense to publish it. The revision of the dates of composition that is accomplished by the continuation of the *Autobiography* not only erases the existence of the *New Science* in a negative form, thus making the first edition an original and "authoritative" text, but it also negates the power of the conditions of textual production that prevented him from publishing the "negative" *New Science*.

The continuation further reads and revises parts A and B by giving Vico the opportunity to correct Porcia's representation of the *Autobiography*, upon its first publication, as a model for others to follow. Vico believed that doing so would and did cause him, "through no fault of his own . . . to suffer from the envy of others" (*Autobiography* 186). This false representation of him was in need of further correction in that, according to Vico, when his original protestations against Porcia's manner of presenting the *Autobiography* were published, Vico suffered further due to the "unkindness of the printer, who bungled the typesetting and made numerous errors, even in important passages" (*Autobiography* 187). Similarly, the continuation also allowed Vico to give an account of the "lies" that he said the reviewers of the "first" *New Science* had told about him and to reply to these lies.[35] Thus in the continuation, Vico attempts to circumvent two of the most material embodiments of the problem of reading: the work of the printer who shapes the self in the book by producing the book itself, and the "reading" of the reviewers who shape the self in their "reading" of the text. Through Vico's narrative, all of these seeming obstacles to authority are transformed into an opportunity to establish that authority.

In and of itself, Vico's duplicitous account of the dates of composition might be said to represent little more than a mildly willful misrepresentation of the facts of his life and writings—the sort of interestingly gratifying misrepresentations that it always delights us to discover in an autobiography. However, when we consider this misrepresentation in light of one of the grounding principles of the *New Science*—the principle of verum *factum*—this reconstruction of the facts of Vico's life takes on the status of a demonstration of the theory of the *New Science*.[36] In keeping with the principle that the true and the made are convertible (verum *factum*) and that we can know for certain only that which we ourselves have made or created, Vico makes a life that conforms to the narrative of his composition of the *New Science* and thereby authenticates not only that life but the book that constitutes it. The truth of Vico's life and his authority over it, according to the principles of the *New Science*, are not to be found in the lived facts of the life, but in its writing and particularly in the publication of the writing. Vico both constitutes and takes possession of his life in the publication of the *Autobiography,* but more importantly he also takes possession of the *New Science* in the act of making his life an account of its composition.

The principle of *verum factum* provides the starting point for understanding how Vico's enactment, in the *Autobiography,* of the figurative history constructed by the *New Science* serves to establish Vico's authority over his life and the texts that constitute it. In accord with this principle, Vico asserts that one can have certain knowledge only of that which one makes or does. This principle serves as the basis for Vico's analysis of human institutions in the *New Science,* but it also may be said to be the basis for the figurative history that he constructs in his autobiography.[37] In one sense Vico may be said to have knowledge of himself, to be able to profess with authority on his subject as having lived (made) his own life. However, according to Vico's theory, authority that is gained by *making as living* is subject to question in much the same way that knowledge of natural phenomenon may be questioned in that the individual, as a physical being, cannot be said to be his own maker. Just as Vico asserts that one cannot have knowledge of physical nature because only God who has made that nature can have such knowledge (*New Science* 85 [331]), the individual does not, in the same sense, have knowledge of himself. However, the making of a life that is constituted in the textual representation of that life can, according to Vico's terms, be a source of "certain" knowledge. Vico gains an authority over himself as written subject that, according to his theory of knowledge, he cannot have over himself as an individual in and of himself.

Vico's strategic representations of the composition of his *Autobiography* and the *New Science* function as do the strategies of Romantic autobiography; they attempt to author the author-function, as I have outlined it above. In accordance with the first strategy, Vico exploits the power of reading by inscribing his own act of reading in the writing of his text. This reading is constructed in the continuation of the *Autobiography* that reads parts A and B so as to revise the earlier misrepresentation of the work that occurs because of Porcia's suggestion that it serve as a model for other writers, and to correct the errors of "unkind printers" that occurred when he himself tried to protest against Porcia's representation of the *Autobiography*. In this sense, the continuation inscribes within the text a model by which the reader's activity is to be governed.

In the process of inscribing this act of reading within the text, Vico also engages in the second strategy of autobiographical representation that I described above. Through the revision of the dates of composition that the continuation accomplishes, Vico shifts the frame of reference of parts A and B, erasing the existence of the *New Science* in "negative form" and re-appropriating the theory of the *New Science* by grounding his representation of himself in the principle of *verum factum*. He narrates his textual productions as the events of his life, taking possession of and establishing authority over both those productions and his life as things which he has "made."

Having suggested that Vico and the Romantics' strategic appropriation and reappropriation of their writings in autobiography is a historically specific phenomenon that arises with the construction of the notion of authorship in the eighteenth century, there are at least two significant questions that arise and will be addressed in the chapters that follow. I believe that the examinations of Wordsworth and Coleridge's writings that I present will serve as a means of exploring these questions. First, there is the question of what, if anything, makes Wordsworth and Coleridge's strategies for constructing their lives in and through writing specifically Romantic. Clearly Wordsworth and Coleridge are writing their lives at a time when "lettered" persons are becoming acutely aware of their being made subject to their writings rather than their being the masters of them. In part I want to suggest that this situation may account for the central place of autobiography in Romantic writing, and for the fact that the word *autobiography* is not used in the English language until the very beginning of the nineteenth century.[38] In this regard Romantic autobiography may be considered simply an example of the way in which the pressures of the publishing world exert themselves on general notions about authorship and authority. But autobiography does not simply respond to these pressures. It comes into existence as a genre and defines itself as a means of making claim to an authority that is not available in other genres and is no longer available as it was, according to Jerome Christensen, to the eighteenth-century "man of letters."[39]

The second question has to do with whether the literary life in the Romantic period succeeds in attaining a privileged status that protects it from appropriation by the reader, the degree to which the author-function may be authored successfully. Can the autobiographer ever have done with writing the literary life—or can "authority" only be claimed through a perpetual process of re-inscription and re-appropriation? Wordsworth's strategy in this regard is significant in that he repeatedly submits *The Prelude* to being read, both literally and figuratively, by Coleridge, but he finally can make his best effort to master the reader by not submitting it to publication. Private circulation, however, does not forestall the hazards of publication in that Coleridge makes his readings of the poem quite public, both through allusion and direct quotation. Coleridge, on the other hand, by direct confrontation with the self that has been figured in the reading of his published works, tries to turn the mechanism of publication into the means of taking possession of his textual productions.

2

The Subsidiary to Preparation

THE status of *The Prelude* as an autobiographical poem and as a central example of Romantic self-representation is one of the mainstays of Romantic criticism. It is, however, a different matter to place *The Prelude* alongside other examples of this emerging genre precisely because the poem is one that Wordsworth did not intend to publish as an autobiography, at least in his own lifetime. Although Wordsworth was the present and living author of the text, it was for him a private document with a very limited circulation and circle of readers. For this reason, it may seem somewhat illogical to talk about the 1805 *Prelude* as an autobiographical work that uses strategies that confront the threat to authority posed by the commodification of writing. It is the 1850 *Prelude* that Wordsworth prepares for publication as an autobiographical narrative that will be subject to the reading public. The 1805 *Prelude* was never conceived of as standing on its own as an autobiography. During the time while completing *The Recluse* still seemed to be possible, *The Prelude* was to function as an element in that project and its status as autobiographical discourse was secondary.

The 1805 *Prelude* is nonetheless the apt choice to illustrate certain strategies of Romantic autobiography because, even more so than 1850, it confronts the power which the reader exerts over the subject of autobiography, and it does so because Wordsworth's most powerful (though not always accurate or accommodating) reader, Coleridge, is most materially present. Many of the revisions that go into 1850 are indeed made during Coleridge's lifetime when his powers as a reader might still have to be guarded against. However, it is in 1805 that Coleridge's construction of Wordsworth's poetic powers and identity holds its greatest sway. The 1805 *Prelude* is not, however, simply an element in a private exchange between Wordsworth and "the friend" to whom the poem is addressed. The figure of the reader, or rather Wordsworth's effort to figure the performance of reading in the text, pervades the poem, particularly in the effort to structure the reading of The Recluse.

Within the traditional terms of autobiographical writing, there is little about The Prelude, at least in its opening lines, that surprises. In the moment that marks the beginning of Book 1, Wordsworth is the epitome of the autobiographical subject—he is fully present to himself. This self-immediacy is most apparent in Wordsworth's declaration of his freedom to "locate" himself where he will:

> Now I am free, enfranchised and at large,
> May fix my habitation where I will.
> What dwelling shall receive me, in what vale
> Shall be my harbour, underneath what grove
> Shall I take up my home, and what sweet stream
> Shall with its murmurs lull me to rest?
> The earth is all before me—[1]

Wordsworth's sense of his "freedom" to "locate" himself wherever he will is the perfect beginning for an autobiographical narrative.[2] It represents precisely the sort of self-presence that is at once the motive and the goal of autobiography—to make oneself fully and immediately present both to oneself and to others. However, the opening of the poem also inscribes the doubling of the subject that is inherent in autobiographical writing, the doubling that is marked by the difference between the self that is writing and the self that is written, and necessarily conditions the strategies by which the poem proceeds. These strategies attempt to write this doubling and difference as immediacy. Even in the poem's initial moments of ecstatic self-assertion, Wordsworth is reminded of this difference:

> It is shaken off,
> As by a miraculous gift 'tis shaken off,
> That burthen of my own unnatural self,
> The heavy weight of many a weary day
> Not mine, and such as were not made for me.

(1.21–5)

Here we see the way in which the autobiographical subject's "freedom" to make himself present in and through writing (to locate himself where he will) necessarily carries with it that which self-presentation seeks to deny, the conception of the self as divided and in need of shaking off the "unnatural self." Even as Wordsworth represents himself as being free to fix his habitation where he will, he carries with him the consciousness of a self that is "different" from that which he would "locate" in and through his narrative. The opening lines of the poem thus present us with the typical situation of autobiographical writing. The aim of the autobiographical project is to present a narrative of the self that makes it fully present, but the very process of writing that narrative necessarily divides the subject into the self that is writing and the self that is written. In this case, Wordsworth's effort to present a unified narrative that will heal this division in the self takes the form of his assertion of his freedom to locate himself where he will. However, these lines also introduce a further complication of the typical situation of autobiography in that the only way in which this unified narrative can be produced is through a continual mediation of past and present, the representation of a "unified" self in and through its own self-dividedness. These opening lines express the desire to transcend this process of mediation and to ascend into a narrative of full self-presence, leaving behind the "burthen of [the] unnatural self," but as the poem proceeds it becomes apparent that the only way which the writing of the self can proceed is by working within this structure of mediation rather than attempting to transcend it.[3]

The opening lines of The Prelude attempt to represent an immediate moment of origin, a moment when there is only the unmediated presence of the "natural" self. What becomes apparent as the poem proceeds, however, is that this origin can only be represented in terms of a series of beginnings, an origin whose representation is continually deferred.[4] There are two particularly important and related contexts in which this deferral needs to be viewed. First and foremost it must be understood in terms of the compositional history of the 1805 Prelude, specifically that of the material added to the 1799 two-book Prelude in the process of composing what becomes book 1 of 1805. Second, this history must be understood in terms of the relationship between The Prelude and the Recluse project. Wordsworth himself raises these two issues in concert after he has made his declaration of freedom.

The context of this declaration is Wordsworth's desire to dedicate himself to "chosen tasks," and the most prominent of these tasks is The Recluse.[5] But even as Wordsworth recognizes the opportunity that he has gained to dedicate himself to this work, he also must recognize the way in which the very power that marks this opportunity troubles itself:

> . . . if I may trust myself, this hour
> Hath brought a gift that consecrates my joy;
> For I, methought, while the sweet breath of heaven
> Was blowing on my body, felt within
> A corresponding mild creative breeze,
> A vital breeze which travelled gently on
> O'er things which it had made, and is become
> A tempest, a redundant energy,
> Vexing its own creation. 'Tis a power
> That does not come unrecognised, a storm
> Which, breaking upon a long-continued frost,
> Brings with it vernal promises, the hope
> Of active days, of dignity and thought,
> Of prowess in an honorable field,
> Pure passions, virtue, knowledge, and delight,
> The holy life of music and of verse.
>
> (1.39–54)

In this moment of "present joy," as Wordsworth will refer to it in subsequent lines, he looks toward "vernal promises." The "hope . . . of prowess in an honorable field" is a projection of his future poetic career in general, but it is specifically a hope for success in proceeding with his plans for The Recluse. Wordsworth's desire to be able to trust himself that "this hour / hath brought a gift" is the desire to establish an untroubled moment of origin for the Recluse project. But it also is clear that the gift in which the poet would like to be able to trust exists only in hope, for the "mild creative breeze" becomes a "redundant energy" that vexes "its own creation." The active days of "dignity and thought" are not present, rather they are yet to come; they exist only as "vernal promises."

Not only is this promised activity deferred, but according to the language of the passage itself it is already at another remove.

The passage begins with the poet's present tense assertion "I am free" (1.36), but shifts to the past tense when Wordsworth represents the gift that this present hour has brought. The feeling that a gift has been bestowed upon him occurs "while the sweet breath of heaven / *was* blowing on [his] body." This hour does not bring the gift, but *"hath brought"* it; the "mild creative breeze" is not what the poet *feels*, but rather what he *felt*. Although the passage is supposed to be one in which the poet is making a "present joy" the "matter of [his] song," in writing it Wordsworth nonetheless represents himself as being removed from the experience of that "present" joy; it is already in the past. This account of the poet's hope for active days cannot sort out the narrative of origins into a linear sequence of events; it expresses a desire to do so, but cannot. Rather, the glad preamble represents the vexing of origins that "originates" the writing of the self.

The shift in tense in the "glad preamble" marks a strategic moment in Wordsworth's composition of *The Prelude*. It marks the point when the narrative of the origin of his poetic powers in childhood experience, which had been the focus of the 1799 two-part *Prelude*, becomes a narrative of the process of poetic composition itself. The 1799 *Prelude* had begun with the vexingly non-referential question, "Was it for this," a beginning which in the 1805 *Prelude* will be deferred for 270 lines. When Wordsworth begins the poem anew, he opens with his glad preamble.[6] If we also consider that the glad preamble was written at about the same time that Wordsworth was completing the 1799 *Prelude*, it would appear that once these lines are placed at the beginning of the 1805 *Prelude*, the mark of the past which intrudes upon the present is a double one. The glad preamble of 1799, when Wordsworth begins work on the poem again in 1804, is a "present" moment long past, and the "present" moment of the poem's joyous beginning is already a moment that comes rather far along in the poem's own history. The shift in tense signifies a division between past and present that is already "present" in the narrative of full presence. While the 1799 *Prelude* concerns itself with the relation between past and present, its interest is in what joins them. The 1805 *Prelude* accomplishes a radical shift by making the very problem of the division between past and present its subject, and this shift is one that is, for Wordsworth, at once both necessary and designed.

The necessity is apparent at the very beginning of the poem

when Wordsworth seeks to represent the presence of the natural self and can do so only in and through an account of his shaking off his "unnatural self." Wordsworth incorporates this necessity into a strategy by representing "present joy" as that which from its beginning is already in the past. In place of the impossible narrative of full self-presence, we are given the narrative of the necessary difference between the present and the past. The 1805 *Prelude* takes as the subject of its narrative the failure to achieve what the 1799 *Prelude* sought to accomplish, a unified narrative of the relationship between past and present.[7] To characterize the 1799 *Prelude* in this way is by no means to consider the poem itself as being incomplete or being a "failed" poem. As a poem it exhibits both a thematic and a formal unity that has been well demonstrated.[8] My point rather is that even while we may call the 1799 *Prelude* a "complete" poem, it is not "finished" as the enabling narrative that Wordsworth sought to make it. It was meant to fill the space that is left when for various reasons Wordsworth is unable to proceed with *The Recluse*, and it does for a time fill that space, but once it is completed, Wordsworth has still not solved the problem of writing *The Recluse* and has in fact compounded it.

If we follow Johnston's account of *The Recluse*, Wordsworth's next step in producing that work, after completing the two-book *Prelude*, is his work in 1800 on "Home at Grasmere." But this poem is only an attempt at a beginning, and it very tellingly closes with the "Prospectus" to *The Recluse*.[9] Wordsworth's narrative in the 1799 *Prelude* fills a space, but it does not enable him to produce the work whose absence the "poem to Coleridge" had been designed to fill. In fact his success in completing the unified work that is the 1799 *Prelude*, once it is complete and *The Recluse* still not substantially underway, is in its very unity an even stronger sign of Wordsworth's inability to knit past to present, to fulfill in the present the promise that all of his past gifts have heralded. This disjunction of the past and the present is inherent in the textual production of the self, and in the 1805 *Prelude* Wordsworth chooses to engage in a confrontation with this disjunction, rather than evading it in a quest for unmediated poetic presence. The question then is, how is it that this disjunction may enter the language of the poem as a means by which the process of the self-representation may proceed rather than stand as a mark of its continual deferral?

In the poem's opening lines, Wordsworth signals a shift from expressing a desire for self-presence in the immediacy of the moment to a focus on the motivation for and the problems inherent in this desire. The change of tense in the glad preamble signals this shift, and the strategy of self-representation involved in it becomes apparent in Wordsworth's initial address to Coleridge:

> Thus far, O friend, did I, not used to make
> A present joy the matter of my song,
> Pour out that day my soul in measured strains,
> Even in the very words which I have here
> Recorded. To the open fields I told
> A prophesy; poetic numbers came
> Spontaneously, and clothed in priestly robe
> My spirit, thus singled out, as it might seem,
> For holy service. Great hopes were mine:
> My own voice cheared me, and far more, the mind's
> Internal echo of the imperfect sound—
> To both I listened, drawing from them both
> A chearful confidence in things to come.
>
> (1.55–67)

This passage marks the beginning of what Johnston calls the "post-preamble" or "topical introduction," and the point at which Wordsworth took up the main composition, first of the five-book *Prelude* and subsequently of the thirteen-book *Prelude* of 1805.[10] The disjunction between past and present, before implicit in the tense shift, now manifests itself in this passage as a disjunction between the poet and the friend whom he addresses.[11] In one sense this address to another helps to repress the dividedness of the subject by turning the poet's utterance into the unified voice of one subject addressing another, giving the impression of the immediacy of speech. On the other hand, though, the address to the other is presented specifically to mark a disjunction within the subject himself, a disjunction which the poet still desires to see as opening up the possibility of establishing an origin. The poet asserts that his own voice, the seemingly unmediated self-presentation of the opening lines of the poem, does cheer him; however, he is more cheered by "the mind's / internal echo" of that voice, which is in and of itself "imperfect." As Mary Jacobus has noted, this reversal of the usual figuration of echo in which it is represented as the imperfect repetition of the original voice is an important moment in Wordsworth's accounting for and constituting his own poetic voice.[12] Jacobus is quite right in her notion that this surprising account of speech as secondary and the echoing internal voice as a perfecting of that voice represents Wordsworth's effort to achieve a transcendental poetic voice that is safe from the threatening realization that voice is not the guarantee of the existence of unified consciousness. What I wish to do is to take Jacobus's account of voice in Wordsworth's poem yet a step further to assert that this play upon the self-dividedness of voice constitutes Wordsworth's initial gesture in the project of exploiting the divided nature of the autobiographical subject.[13] Here, Wordsworth begins to represent the dividedness, which he had previously hoped to leave behind, as opening up the possibility of fulfilling his desire to "locate" himself. This doubling of voice and mind, of self and other, allows Wordsworth to construct a narrative that will figure his self-dividedness as a strategy of self-presentation. While this strategy is a central component in the process of composing The Prelude itself, it also plays an important part in Wordsworth's conception of The Prelude in relation to the Recluse project. In order to begin to comprehend more fully the strategies of self-representation that operate in The Prelude, we must examine these strategies in this context as well.

When Wordsworth published The Excursion in 1814, he prefaced it with an account of the Recluse project in which The Prelude figures rather prominently. Among other things, the preface provides an opportunity to present an important justification for his composition of The Prelude. This account of The Prelude can be understood simply in terms of Wordsworth's efforts to present his design for The Recluse and the various works that it will contain, which is the motive for the famous Gothic cathedral analogy. And while it is not unusual for an author to use a preface to project the course of future publications, it is curious to see an author, in effect, deferring the publication of a work that is said not only to be completed, but also one which provides the grounding and preparation for the work that is being prefaced. Although we know of Wordsworth's belief that The Prelude should be published only in its proper setting as a part of the Recluse project, the significance which he attaches to it in the preface is all the more striking for its being a work that cannot be read, or at least will not, for the time being, be read by anyone other than Wordsworth himself.[14] With the advantage of a retrospective gaze that was not available to the readers of Wordsworth's preface to *The Excursion*, we can see the ways in which the 1814 representation of *The Prelude* offers an account of that poem that turns us back upon the opening book of the *The Prelude* with a fairly striking sense of contrast.

Wordsworth's account of the origin of the *Recluse* project takes us back to the initial motivation and design of *The Prelude*:

> Several years ago, when the Author retired to his native mountains, with the hope of being enabled to construct a literary work that might live, it was a reasonable thing that he should take a review of his own mind, and examine how far Nature and Education had qualified him for such employment. As subsidiary to this preparation, he undertook to record, in verse, the origin and progress of his own powers, as far as he was acquainted with them. That Work, addressed to a dear Friend, most distinguished for his knowledge and genius, and to whom the Author's Intellect is deeply indebted, has been long finished; and the result of the investigation which gave rise to it was a determination to compose a philosophical poem containing views of Man, Nature, and Society; and to be entitled, 'The Recluse'; as having for its principle subject the sensations and opinions of a poet living in retirement.[15]

This account offers a fairly straightforward narrative sequence for both the composition of *The Prelude* and the initiation of the *Recluse* project. There are four distinct moments in this narrative, all of which are represented as following easily one upon the other. The first of these moments is "the hope of being able to construct a literary work that might live," and it is followed by a "reasonable thing": a "review of [the poet's] own mind" as a preparation for constructing the "work that might live." Third, as part of the "preparation," comes the "subsidiary to this preparation," which is the record of "the origin and progress of [the poet's] powers" in a work that "has long been finished": *The Prelude*. And finally the "result of the investigation which gave rise to it" [*The Prelude*] is the "determination to compose a philosophical poem": *The Recluse*. The moments set out in this narrative sequence proceed from hope, to preparation, to the subsidiary to preparation, and ultimately to the final determination to write. This account is designed to give the series of deflections and substitutions that are The Prelude the shape of a relatively simple narrative. In this narrative, The Prelude is the "subsidiary" to the preparation for writing The Recluse. As such it is work that necessarily precedes that writing. However, the problematic nature of The Prelude as a "subsidiary" is apparent in that it is not simply a necessary precedent to Wordsworth's determination to write The Recluse. As book 1 of The Prelude makes quite clear, it is also a substitute for The Recluse.

Whereas the preface to The Excursion tries to present a coherent narrative account of the origin of both The Prelude and the Recluse project, in The Prelude itself Wordsworth is only able to make and read a series of beginnings.[16] Of specific interest here are the ways in which these fitful beginnings are tangled in Wordsworth's account of the origins of the Recluse project as The Prelude seeks to serve both as the preparation and a substitute for The Recluse. The preface to The Excursion seems to erase the poem's double status, but in doing so it uses the very strategies of writing that drive The Prelude itself. An examination of this parallel will provide us with a basic outline of the structure of supplementarity that I have identified above as being basic to the autobiographical predicament of writing.

Although I have asserted that there are parallels between the narrative of the preface to The Excursion and that presented in The Prelude, it is quite clear that the account of Wordsworth's composition of The Prelude is very different from the one that is presented in book 1.[17] One way of accounting for the differences between the "narrative" in the preface and that presented in book 1 of The Prelude is simply to note that book 1 is not the whole story; the "determination" of which Wordsworth speaks in the preface is something that is arrived at only after he has "finished" The Prelude. Nonetheless, this perspective still does not fully account for the way in which the preface represents the movement from The Prelude to the determination to write The Recluse as a simple line in a straightforward narrative. Not only does that narrative condense the entire course of The Prelude, eliding the complications that are presented in such detail in book 1, but it also erases the moment at which Wordsworth fails in his attempts to proceed with The Recluse and attempts to offer The Prelude as a necessary, even if momentary, substitute

2: The Subsidiary to Preparation

for the former. At the very least we must note that Wordsworth's "reasonable . . . review of his own mind" consisted of three different versions, the two-book, the five-book, and finally, although not ultimately, the thirteen-book *Prelude* of 1805. However, Wordsworth's "reading" of the composition of these poems, while seeming to turn us away from the complications involved, also offers us an understanding of how and why the strategies of self-representation operate as they do in *The Prelude*. The narrative in the preface to *The Excursion* reads *The Prelude* in precisely the same way in which *The Prelude* itself constitutes a reading of Wordsworth's own history. In writing the preface, Wordsworth reads *The Prelude* and all of its complicated beginnings into the uncomplicated tale of origins that he cannot write in the poem itself; he can read that origin, but he cannot write it.[18] This is precisely the problem with which Wordsworth is faced in writing *The Prelude*. In undertaking "to record, in verse, the origin and progress of his own powers," Wordsworth must arrive at a strategy for representing that origin. As I have demonstrated by reading the complications of that narrative record, the strategy at which he arrives is precisely that used in the preface, reading the narrative of the self in and through writing, the autobiographical project of the Romantic poet.

This strategy is most clearly at work in *The Prelude* when Wordsworth turns from the glad preamble and the various moments at which his efforts to make a present joy the matter of his song have failed and he admits that with each new beginning his "harp / Was soon defrauded." It is at this point that the effort to proceed with *The Recluse* project becomes the specific focus of the narrative. Here the "determination" of which the preface to *The Excursion* speaks can be presented only as a desire for such determination:

> But speedily a longing in me rose
> To brace myself to some determined aim,
> Reading or thinking, either to lay up
> New stores, or rescue from decay the old
> By timely interference. . . .

(1.123–27)

By substituting the narrative of a desire for a determined aim for the actual fulfillment of that aim, Wordsworth achieves precisely such a "timely interference." What had been a very untimely interference in his poetic production is now read and thereby figured in that production as a timely opportunity, and the interference of forces beyond the poet's control is transformed into the poet's own interference with those forces through the power of figuration. This is the same strategy of timely interference that "rescues" The Prelude in the preface to The Excursion and reads its complicated beginnings into the uncomplicated narrative of the origins of The Recluse. The strategic performance that we witness in the preface figures doubly in The Prelude in that performance is enacted as well as examined as a construct that constitutes Wordsworth himself as a poetic figure.

In narrating the failure to proceed with the Recluse project, Wordsworth establishes the strategic move that will allow him to proceed with the production of the self in writing. He finds the means of performing this writing in the "interference" that is constituted in the divided subject of autobiography. While returning once again to meditate on the possibility of proceeding with the great work that he hopes to produce, Wordsworth enumerates a series of themes that he believes he might pursue (1.169–224).[19] However, Wordsworth sees these themes as turning "shadowy and insubstantial" (1.228) and focuses finally on his "last and favorite aspiration ... some philosophic song" (1.229, 230). As always, though, he finds this project a burden, and finds his refuge from it in the very thing that prevents him from bearing that burden:

> But from this awful burthen I full soon
> Take refuge, and beguile myself with trust
> That mellower years will bring a riper mind
> And clearer insight. Thus from day to day
> I live a mockery of brotherhood
> Of vice and virtue, with no skill to part
> Vague longing that is bred by want of power,
> From paramount impulse not to be withstood;
> A timorous capacity, from prudence;
> From circumspection, infinite delay.
> Humility and modest awe themselves
> Betray me, serving often for a cloak
> To a more subtle selfishness, that now
> Doth lock my functions up in blank reserve,

Now dupes me by an over-anxious eye
That with false activity beats off
Simplicity and self-presented truth.

(1.235–51)

This passage marks the "crisis," poetic, personal, and perhaps even political, that has become the hallmark of Wordsworth criticism. Whether we follow the line of criticism, led by M. H. Abrams, that reads *The Prelude* as a classical crisis autobiography, or if we take the approach of Geoffrey Hartman that leads us to an account of the apocalyptic dimensions of the Romantic imagination, or even if we pursue more recent attempts to understand more fully the political dimensions of this crisis, we nonetheless end up taking the crisis for granted and move quickly on to construct our various accounts of its resolution.[20] What we too often fail to note here is that while Wordsworth feels the full weight of the crisis, it is not just Wordsworth's loss of poetic and moral direction that is the problem; resolution itself is called into question.

In part, Wordsworth is setting the scene that will initiate his visionary triumph over loss, writing the antecedent of the previously nonreferential question "was it for this?" (1.271). But this setup for "future restoration" also carries with it a questioning of certain modes of restoration and resolution, leading us to consider that Wordsworth's point in *The Prelude* is something more and other than the achievement of that resolution. Wordsworth sums up his sense of the crisis by asserting that the "false activity" of an "over-anxious eye . . . beats off / Simplicity and self-presented truth." Overcoming this false activity and the despotic power of the "over-anxious eye" certainly is the goal of Wordsworth's narrative, but the question that must be answered is whether "simplicity and self-presented truth" are indeed what Wordsworth is seeking, or is this truth just another version of the self-beguilement in which Wordsworth represents himself as taking refuge.

Especially important to note here is that a certain kind of trust in resolution is what gives rise to the crisis of judgment. Wordsworth doesn't just describe this crisis; he designates it as a product of a self-beguiling trust that time will bring a resolution, describing the consequences of this self-delusive trust: "*Thus from day to day / I live a mockery of brotherhood / of vice and* virtue" [my emphasis]. While we might be led to believe that the problem here is for Wordsworth to figure out how to escape from this false activity and find the path to "simplicity and self-presented truth" (as I would assert we have been led to do by the critical accounts of *The Prelude* as a "crisis" poem that I have cited above), the initial rejection of a trust in the clear insight of a riper mind indicates that as much as the "mockery of brotherhood / Of vice and virtue" must be called into question and confronted, so must the simplicity of self-presented truth itself.

The problematic nature of such self-presented truth in *The Prelude* is highlighted by the way that it figures in the preface to *The Excursion*. There Wordsworth asserts that in *The Recluse* it was not his "intention formally to announce a system: it was more animating to him to proceed in a different course; and if he should succeed in conveying to the mind clear thoughts, lively images, and strong feelings, the Reader will have no difficulty extracting the system for himself" (*Poetical Works* 589). Here we clearly have the simplicity of self-presented truth, not a system, but rather "clear thoughts, lively images, and strong feelings." In *The Prelude*, however, Wordsworth takes a different course. What Wordsworth's poem concerns itself with is not finding the means to self-presented truth, but with struggling within those oppositions that cannot be separated; they are the very signs of his own self-dividedness that become the subject of the poem. The "subtle selfishness," which locks his functions up in "blank reserve" as long as he continues in a quest for simple self-presentation, becomes the very means by which the writing of the self proceeds.

Wordsworth closes this reflection on his self-dividedness with a representation of his retreat from it:

> I recoil and droop, and seek repose
> In indolence from vain perplexity,
> Unprofitably travelling towards the grave,
> Like a false steward who hath much received
> And renders nothing back.

(1.267–71)

As despairing as these lines sound, they nonetheless perform a figurative function that drives the poem forward. This moment of defeat, a self-defeat by self-dividedness, constitutes, in two specific ways, the means by which Wordsworth generates the production of the self in writing. First, Wordsworth's representation of his desire for repose places him, if not in the grave itself, then at least on the way to it. In this image of the grave, Wordsworth finds the means of representing the death of the desire for the simple self-presentation that would constitute the great philosophical work that he seeks to write. Such simplicity of self-presented truth is the death-like stasis of a beguiling trust in the insight to be brought by mellower years. Here we have the beginning of Wordsworth's "discourse of self-restoration."[21] With this movement toward the grave Wordsworth opens up the possibility for a mode of self-representation that will operate within the structure of conflicts and divisions that confront the autobiographer rather than attempting to find a means by which to retreat from them. The allusion to the parable of the false steward from Matthew 25:14–30 is the demonstration of this strategy and its recuperative powers in that Wordsworth "renders" himself present in the text in the representation of his rendering nothing back.

The possibility that is opened up by the death of the project of simple self-presentation provides the means by which Wordsworth's retreat generates the production of the self in writing. After representing his defeat in the face of his own self-dividedness, Wordsworth uses the rhetorical structure of the question and the referential function of language itself both to produce the writing of the self and to "locate" the opening of the poem within his discourse of self-restoration:

Was it for this
That one, the fairest of all rivers, loved
To blend his murmurs with my nurse's song,
And from his alder shades and rocky falls,
And from his fords and shallows, sent a voice
That flowed along my dreams? For this didst thou,
O Derwent, travelling over the green plains
Near my 'sweet birthplace' didst thou, beauteous stream
Make ceaseless music through the night and day,
Which with its steady cadence tempering
Our human waywardness, composed my thoughts
To more than infant softness.

(1.271–82)

These crucial lines have figured prominently in critical accounts
of Wordsworth's efforts to construct a self-constituting discourse
in The Prelude.[22] These accounts focus primarily on the way in
which the move embodied in the rhetorical question and the
subsequent address to the river Derwent constitute a turning
point in Wordsworth's narrative that leaves behind the division
between past and present self along with the "graveward" journey. However, the position of these lines at the beginning of the
1799 two-book Prelude, and the subsequent shift in the referent
of "this" once the preceding lines of 1805 are added, offer the
guidance that we need in order to understand the way in which
this passage serves to make of the self-dividedness of the autobiographical subject a strategy of production of the self in writing.[23]
In the context of the 1799 Prelude the reference is vague, but the
ambiguous field of reference is nonetheless a single and unified
one—Wordsworth's present state and the apparent confusion in
which he finds himself with regard to his poetic career. He
asks, was the present [this] what was being prepared for by the
past [it].[24] Once these lines are preceded by the narrative stops
and starts of the 1805 Prelude, the reference still is ambiguous,
but the referential possibilities have been doubled. With this
double reference Wordsworth embarks on the project of self-
representation that will proceed now that the project of simple
self-presented truth has met its necessary death. In its context
in the 1805 Prelude, the relative pronoun "this" serves as a link
between the present discourse of the self and the narrative of the
past self as it did in the 1799 Prelude, but here it is more than
a device that initiates the discourse of self-presentation. In its
linking function, "this" does refer to the "present" confusion
that Wordsworth experiences in his doubt about his poetic powers, the "vexing" of the desire to achieve a simple self-presented
truth. But it also refers to the narrative itself, the halting and
problematic course that the poem has taken up to this point.
(This is the reference that is obviously unavailable in the 1799
Prelude.) One could take the position that there is little difference between these two referents: one is Wordsworth's experience of doubt and confusion, and the other is his narrative of
that experience that tells the tale of the death of the project of
simple, self-presented truth. But it is precisely this difference-
in-sameness that Wordsworth plays upon and exploits in constructing the narrative that precedes the question. The first field

of reference (Wordsworth's experience of doubt and confusion) represents Wordsworth's past self, the autobiographical subject that is being written, while the second (Wordsworth's narrative of that experience) represents the "present" self, the autobiographical subject that is writing. In giving the vague reference of 1799 a narrative context in which to operate in the 1805 *Prelude*, Wordsworth turns from a narrative that is designed to heal the break between past and present to one that figures that break as a strategy of writing. It is the death of the project of self-presented truth that generates this strategy of writing, embracing the dividedness of the autobiographical subject instead of attempting to repress it. The double reference both to the "present" state of his poetic career and the narrative of the death of the project of self-presented truth figures that divisiveness of language and the self in a structure that will accommodate self-representation.

Much of the remainder of Book 1 is taken up with Wordsworth's narratives of childhood experiences and his subsequent reflections upon them, which are the rhetorical extensions of the question "Was it for this?" The narratives focus on the gifts bestowed upon Wordsworth by Nature, and as such they represent what has brought Wordsworth to "this." The several episodes, the stories of robbing others' snares, plundering a nest, and stealing the shepherd's boat are instances either explicitly or implicitly of what Wordsworth calls "the severer interventions" of Nature as it serves to form him as a "favored being" (1.370, 365). These narratives and Wordsworth's presentation of them are instances of "timely interference" both at the level of Wordsworth's experience as a child and at the level of the narrative itself.[25]

In the episodes there is something of a progression in the intervention/interruption. In the first two instances it is sound or imagined sound that impresses upon the boy an image of his own activity. When he robs another's snares, the boy hears "low breathings" coming after him, and the "sounds / Of indistinguishable motion, steps / Almost silent as the turf they trod" (1.330–32). When plundering the birds' nest, the boy hangs upon a perilous ridge, but he also hangs upon an utterance: "With what strange utterance did the loud dry wind / Blow through my ears; and the sky seemed not a sky / Of earth, and with what motion moved the clouds" (1.348–50).[26] Geoffrey Hartman has pointed out the way in which Wordsworth projects Nature as something that speaks "rememberable things" in order to achieve a textualization of the voice of nature.[27] This notion of the textualizing of voice seems quite appropriate here, but in considering the autobiographical nature of Wordsworth's narrative it is instructive to carry this notion of textualization a step further, and to note the attention to and preference for a seemingly secondary quality, as in the echo that cheers Wordsworth more than the immediate sound of his voice.[28] But here it is not an echo that attracts Wordsworth. Rather, it is the images that represent these sounds that attract him: the "sounds of indistinguishable motion" that are heard/read as "almost silent" steps, the "loud dry wind" that is heard/read as a "strange utterance." These sounds fascinate him precisely because they are texts whose "secondary" status, their distance from a determinate origin, makes them available for "reading." The boy experiences the "sounds" of nature's intervention, but Wordsworth represents those sounds not as a voice that is heard, but as something which is read in the images of the experience, and this reading is what is at issue in Wordsworth's attempts to interpret nature's "severer interventions" in his childhood.[29]

The series of narratives of childhood experiences in book 1 climaxes in the story of the stolen boat, but here the scene is a silent one, one of looming images rather than haunting voices. In his description of his boyhood "act of stealth / And troubled pleasure" Wordsworth tells how he rows the stolen boat guided by fixing his view upon a ridge which is "the bound of the horizon," but this boundary proves to be an illusory one:

> And as I rose upon the stroke my boat
> Went heaving through the water like a swan—
> When from behind the craggy steep, till then
> The bound of the horizon, a huge cliff,
> As if with voluntary power instinct
> Upreared its head. I struck, and struck again,
> And, growing still in stature, the huge cliff
> Rose up between me and the stars, and still
> With measured motion, like a living thing
> Strode after me.

(1.403–12)

Rather than the imagined sound of pursuit or the voice of the wind, this experience leaves the boy with an image, the remnant of a visual message that he attempts to read, but cannot:

> There, in her mooring-place, I left my bark
> And through the meadows homeward went with grave
> And serious thoughts; and after I had seen
> That spectacle, for many days my brain
> Worked with a dim and undetermined sense
> Of unknown modes of being. In my thoughts
> There was a darkness—call it solitude
> Or blank desertion—no familiar shapes
> Of hourly object, images of trees,
> Of sea or sky, no colours of green fields,
> But huge and mighty forms that do not live
> Like living men moved slowly through my mind
> By day, and were the trouble of my dreams.
>
> (1.415–26)

Here there is no sound or utterance to be heard, but neither is there anything to be seen in any sense of immediate or familiar perception. With no familiar shapes or objects to be seen, Wordsworth is left with the "huge and mighty forms that do not live / Like living men." Or is Wordsworth even asserting that these forms are alive? Is it that they are *not* alive, but nonetheless move like living men? On one level it may seem important to determine whether or not these highly significant forms are living or dead, but the attempt to choose between the seemingly contradictory readings misses the point. The apparent contradiction is beside the point if the "location" of the meaning of these lines is shifted. The contradiction can be said to dissolve because, as Timothy Bahti has asserted, "both readings yield an equivalent rhetorical representation."[30] What is significant here, what the lines "mean," is not to be found in either or both of the contradictory readings, but rather in the movement of the rhetorical forms themselves.

The troubling nature of this passage is not in its "meaning," but rather in the trouble that is produced in trying to read the passage into Wordsworth's narrative of his childhood. The tendency has been to read Wordsworth's representation of his own troubling experience as being resolved through the process of purification which Wordsworth outlines in the lines that follow his narration of the boat stealing episode[31]:

Wisdom and spirit of the universe,
Thou soul that art the eternity of thought,
That giv'st to forms and images a breath
And everlasting motion—not in vain,
By day or star-light, thus from my first dawn
Of childhood didst thou intertwine for me
The passions that build up our human soul,
Not with the mean and vulgar works of man,
But with high objects, with enduring things,
With life and Nature, purifying thus
The elements of feeling and of thought,
And sanctifying by such discipline
Both pain and fear, until we recognize
A grandeur in the beatings of the heart.

(1.428–41)

In examining this apostrophe to the "wisdom and spirit of the universe" one must remember both its complicated rhetorical status, with the apostrophe functioning as a strategy of self-presentation, and the place that Wordsworth assigned to this "spirit" in his narrative. Although he would seem to be asserting that its influence on him was "not in vain" because it has brought him to a present ability to "recognize / A grandeur in the beatings of the heart," he immediately turns to mark this influence not on the "present," but once again on his youthful activity. The apostrophe attempts to undo the deadness of the troubling forms that populate his dreams by representing them as being resolved in the "Wisdom and spirit of the universe . . . / That giv'st to forms and images a breath and everlasting motion." If we try to read this moment in the narrative as an achievement of the integration of past and present, we miss the possibility that Wordsworth may be representing the way in which the troubling forms of his experience were once resolved in an apparently "present" moment of apostrophe. But this resolution is not yet the "reading" of that experience that will constitute Wordsworth's writing of the self.

The reading/writing of the self constituted through the childhood narratives is not presented in the apostrophe. And if we see it as an aspect of that childhood experience rather than as a commentary on that experience, its own dream-like quality is apparent. Rather than trying to negate the troubling quality of the images that haunt him as he does in the dream-like apostrophe to the wisdom and spirit of the universe, Wordsworth generates a reading out of the troubling dead forms themselves that populate his dreams. When Wordsworth turns again to the "presences of Nature," rather than seeing them as breathing life into the dead forms and thereby undoing their troubling aspect, he sees Nature as impressing on those forms the sign of a threat:

> Ye presence of Nature, in the sky
> Or on earth, ye visions of the hills
> And souls of lonely places, can I think
> A vulgar hope was yours when ye employed
> Such ministry—when ye through many a year
> Haunting me thus among my boyish sports,
> On caves and trees, upon woods and hills,
> Impressed upon all forms the characters
> Of danger or desire, and thus did make
> The surface of the universal earth
> With triumph, and delight, and hope, and fear,
> Work like a sea?
>
> (1.490–501)

Although Wordsworth specifies the character that is imprinted upon things as being that of "danger or desire," and these are the emotions of high adventure that we understand would be naturally attractive to a young boy, it is clear that he sees the most significant action of Nature as being that of *impressing* these forms with characters, placing upon them signs and marks that are to be read. Also, these are signs of danger and of threat, the threat that cannot be separated from the desire for self-representation. Here we have Wordsworth producing the self in writing by reading these signs and marks, rather than, as in the previous passage, trying to undo the danger of those dead forms by seeing nature as endowing them with a life that serves to make him recognize "a grandeur in the beatings of the heart." Thus the significance of the narratives of childhood experience is first and foremost in Wordsworth's having learned to read the signs of his own self-dividedness in the fear and the sense of threat that are produced by acts that generate guilt.[32] And just as the childhood experience is significant for the way in which this self-dividedness constitutes a powerful insight, so, too, is

the writing of the self in *The Prelude* made powerful by its figuring of the dividedness of the autobiographical subject.

At the close of book 1, Wordsworth is attempting to find a
way to draw together all of the varied reflective and apostrophic
moments which were to mark a path through his narrative, and
he does so by explaining how he has indeed found his way.
Wordsworth still has the *Recluse* project on his mind and speaks
of his hope that he might be spurred on to "honorable toil."
However, as he has done earlier in the book, he uses the form of
the question, and a very complex question, as the means of turning from the hoped-for writing to the writing that is at hand:

> Yet should these hopes
> Be vain, and thus should neither I be taught
> To understand myself, nor thou to know
> With better knowledge how the heart was framed
> Of him thou lovest, need I dread from thee
> Harsh judgments if I am so loth to quit
> Those recollected hours that have the charm
> Of visionary things, and lovely forms
> And sweet sensations, that throw back out life
> And almost make our infancy itself
> A visible scene on which the sun is shining?
>
> (1.653–63)

Clearly this question, a question that carries the weight of an
assertion, is intended to deflect Coleridge from his desire to see
Wordsworth get on with *The Recluse* and to remove the sting
of not proceeding with a work for which Coleridge has such
tremendous expectations.[33] However, the question is meant just
as much to deflect Wordsworth's own writing as it is to deflect
Coleridge's criticism. The question provides Wordsworth with
the means by which he can turn from the hoped-for work at
which he had aimed, the great philosophical poem, to the end
that he has found in writing the narrative of his childhood experiences. Thus the substitution of *The Prelude* for *The Recluse* is
accomplished:

> One end at least hath been attained—
> My mind hath been revived—and if this mood

Desert me not, I will forthwith bring down
Through later years the story of my life.
The road lies plain before me. 'Tis a theme
Single and of determined bounds, and hence
I chuse it rather at this time than work
Of ampler or more varied argument,
Where I might be discomfitted and lost
And certain hopes are with me that to thee
This labour will be welcomed, honoured friend.

(1.664–74)

Wordsworth is leaving a project into which he cannot yet find his way and taking up one into which he already has written his way. It is clear at the end of book 1 that *The Prelude* is seen as an end in itself, not merely as a way of preparing to write *The Recluse*.[34] In representing this end as a theme of "determined bounds," however, Wordsworth does more than simply find a project that is manageable. This notion of the boundaries of his theme has a close connection to the scenes of childhood adventures through which Wordsworth has tried to represent the visitations of Nature. These adventures most often involved operating within bounds, either seeking to reach the edges of them or breaching them, and it is precisely because Wordsworth is testing these boundaries that he is able to discern the shapes and forms that become the "signs" of his narrative. It is in the effort to delineate these bounds that Wordsworth has found shapes and forms looming up before him, and they will not allow him a simple visionary resolution to the problem of self-representation. Rather, he finds his way precisely because these signs haunt him and insistently demand to be read, thus generating the production of the self in writing.

The writing of the self to which Wordsworth commits himself in turning away from the project of the great philosophical poem both defines and offers the means of resolving the problems that seem to trouble Wordsworth in his efforts to proceed with *The Recluse*. In his confrontation with writing as an inherently autobiographical endeavor, Wordsworth takes as a given element of the structure of this writing the very self-dividedness that prevents him from writing a simple and self-presented truth:

A tranquilizing spirit presses now
On my corporeal frame, so wide appears

> The vacancy between me and those days,
> Which yet have self-presence in my mind
> That sometimes when I think of them I seem
> Two consciousnesses—conscious of myself,
> And of some other being.
>
> (2.27–33)

This doubling of consciousness is no longer a division of the mind that will not allow Wordsworth to settle on a theme for his great work. Rather it is a division which opens up a space, a vacancy, within which he may position himself in the act of writing, the act of writing the self in the space between the past and the present, thus marking the self-dividedness of the subject of autobiography.

Book 1 of *The Prelude* represents Wordsworth's struggle to proceed with *The Recluse* project. In making that struggle itself the subject of book 1, Wordsworth constructs a reading of *The Prelude* that allows him to proceed with that poem without turning away from *The Recluse*. According to the reading that Wordsworth constructs, *The Recluse* project is to be the ultimate embodiment of his poetic power, and essential to that work and power is the construction of a history of the growth of the poet's mind. However, what becomes apparent in the process of constructing this history is that it is not only a necessary "subsidiary to preparation," but with equal necessity it stands in place of that project, figuring the power that cannot be made present as "simple self-presented truth."

This reading of *The Prelude* into the context of *The Recluse* project provides the model for Wordsworth's turn in *The Prelude* from an effort to construct a narrative that heals the division between past and present selves to one that makes that division its focus and seeks to figure it in that narrative. This shift is an enabling one for Wordsworth in that it offers him a means of producing the self in writing by the power of the very forces that necessarily divide the subject of autobiography. But even as an enabling move, it has its consequences, and Wordsworth must continually develop strategies to deal with these consequences while trying to maintain the efficacy of his strategy of figuring the self in its own self-dividedness. These consequences are most apparent in the problem that one confronts when the writing of the self turns from the effort to get itself started, to the effort to construct the self in relation to others. In book 1 Wordsworth arrives at a sense of how it is that he can read the narrative of his life for himself, but as *The Prelude* proceeds these strategies are tested in Wordsworth's effort to come to terms with the reading that others may construct out of his text. Once Wordsworth has established his own sense of authority over the text of *The Prelude* by reading it into the context of *The Recluse* project and has taken possession of a text that had seemed initially to possess him, he must shift his attention to the threat that the reading of others poses to this authority. Just as Wordsworth uses his reading of *The Prelude* into the context of *The Recluse* project as a model for his own reading of the divided subject of autobiography, he will, as he proceeds with *The Prelude*, construct a narrative of the reading process out of which he produces his own text, thereby attempting to impose a model of reading on the processes in which the readers of his text will engage.

3

The Surface of Past Time

By Wordsworth's own account *The Prelude* is a narrative of the growth of the poet's mind, and one of the ways in which Romantic criticism often has analyzed this narrative is as a conflict between sense perception and imagination that is ultimately resolved in the ascendancy of the poetic imagination.[1] I do not dispute this general account of the narrative, but it does need to be taken further in order to establish the link between the Romantic poetic project, its conceptualization of the power of poetic imagination, and the pervasiveness of autobiographical writing in Romanticism. Wordsworth's autobiographical poem is typically read as the paradigm of Romantic self-representation. Nonetheless, the representations of imaginative achievement in Wordsworth's various tales of the collision between sense perception and imagination are not sufficient in themselves to accomplish the ends of Wordsworth's autobiographical project. It is only when the tales become explications of the process of reading whereby the autobiographical subject writes itself that the tale of imagination is complete.

Wordsworth's strategies for representing himself to others become prominent in *The Prelude* when he presents his account of his first extended encounter with the life of a community other than his native and rural one in the lakes, and chronicles the turmoil of his time at Cambridge. Wordsworth represents his experience of the displacement as that of being a figure in another's reading, and it is appropriate to begin our examination with Wordsworth's narrative of his return home after this dislocating encounter has occurred. Here we can begin to see most clearly the strategies of writing that will take hold in the face of Wordsworth's repeated experiences of displacement and dislocation, these experiences themselves being versions of the process of writing the self.

Most prominent in Wordsworth's account of his summer vacation from Cambridge in book 4 is the sense of a disjunction that is marked by a double frame of remembrance. In book 4 Wordsworth presents his memories of his vacation, but many of the incidents related are themselves instances of remembering. Wordsworth's narrative expresses his surprising sense of how things had changed and represents this experience as a process of remembering how things once had been. Wordsworth describes the new sight afforded by this sense of change as an alternative form of vision. This alternative vision not only describes the new way in which he sees his childhood home, but also seems to describe the "vision" of himself as constituted in the process of self-representation:

> Yes, I had something of another eye,
> And often looking round was moved to smiles
> Such as a delicate work of humour breeds.
> I read, without design, the opinions, thoughts,
> Of those plain-living people, in a sense
> Of love and knowledge: with another eye
> I saw the quiet woodman in the woods,
> The shepherd on the hills. With new delight,
> This chiefly, did I view my grey-haired dame. . . .
> (4.200–208)

Through the image of altered vision, Wordsworth is trying to represent the new and renewed sense of delight and joy that he feels in re-establishing contact with the community that nurtured him as a child, and he chooses to identify this feeling as the "freshness" that he now finds in "human life" (4.181–82). However, this renewal is found within the context of another return, that which is represented by the writing of the poem. Thus we come upon a parallel between the altered vision that Wordsworth has of his childhood surroundings and his account of the process and structure whereby he represents himself in and through writing. Just as Wordsworth viewed the scene of his childhood with "another eye," and with that eye "read . . . the opinions, thoughts, / Of those plain-living people," so too does he read his own history, the reading that produces the self in writing.

Most critical accounts of book 4 focus on the narrative of the discharged soldier and how Wordsworth uses that encounter as a way of resolving the "inner falling off" (270) that follows fast upon his efforts in the first half of the book to describe the "dawning" in him of a new sense of "human-heartedness."[2] Dissatisfaction with Wordsworth's efforts to re-assert his human-heartedness through his concern for the discharged soldier is understandable and may account for the fact that most criticism of book 4 has taken the Dawn Dedication (330–45) as its point of departure. But this sort of critical emphasis follows, in effect, Wordsworth's own impulses in trying to overcome the sense of falling off rather than examining the strategies of his self-representation. These accounts do not consider fully enough Wordsworth's description of the course of the narrative itself, and thus read the latter half of book 4 in the context of Wordsworth's experience rather than in the context of his own "reading" of that experience in constructing his narrative. Wordsworth describes the course of his narrative in this way:

> As one who hangs down-bending from the side
> Of a slow-moving boat upon the breast
> Of a still water, solacing himself
> With such discoveries as his eye can make
> Beneath him in the bottom of the deeps,
> Sees many beauteous sights—weeds, fishes, flowers,
> Grots, pebbles, roots of trees—and fancies more,
> Yet often is perplexed, and cannot part
> The shadow from the substance, rocks and sky,
> Mountains and clouds, from that which is indeed
> The region, and the things which there abide
> In their true dwelling; now is crossed by gleam
> Of his own image, by a sunbeam now,
> And motions that are sent he knows not whence,
> Impediments that make his task more sweet;
> Such pleasant office have we long pursued
> Incumbent over the surface of past time—
> With like success.

(4.247–64)

Although the passage does seem to present an image of someone trying to get a look at an objective world, "things which . . . abide in their true dwelling," in spite of the interference of the reflections that he tries to exclude from his perception, Wordsworth does not conclude, at least in simple terms, that such objectivity would mark the "success" of the effort.[3] His implicitly ironic jest about the lack of success in parting "shadow from substance" allows us to read that success in two different ways. There is the success that is not achieved, that of sorting out one "region, and the things which there abide" from another. But there also is the success of the task made more sweet by impediments, "the pleasant office . . . long pursued." In combining the effort to perceive objectively and the impossibility of doing so in one image, Wordsworth gives us a most appropriate image of the process of representing the "full presence" of the self in and through the necessary self-division of the autobiographical subject. While Wordsworth winks ironically at the success of the project of objective perception, he also, nonetheless, points to the success of the narrative, "incumbent over the surface of past time."

It is especially important to note that the image of the narrative's success is far from being an image of a unified vision of the self in its surroundings. Rather it is an image that is fraught with division, uncertainty, and "impediments." Wordsworth expresses a seemingly calm delight in the mixing of subject and object and in the inability to part shadow from substance in which "impediments" make the "task more sweet." The sense of the division between what is beneath the water and what is reflected on its surface (including the reflected image of the self), along with the desire to keep the two distinct from one another, is coupled with a sense of delight both in the mixing of the two regions and the "unsuccessful" effort to sort them out. Thus the scene not only represents the situation of the subject of autobiography in which it is impossible to separate the perceiving subject from the object of perception, it also represents the way in which the perceiving subject can find a means of self-representation in the struggle to sort out the play of objects upon the surface of perception.

In this metaphoric description of Wordsworth's narrative, we have the equivalent of his account of the experience that he describes in book 1 when he considers the effect that his glad preamble has upon him. There he asserts that he is more cheered by the mind's internal echo of his own "imperfect" voice than by the immediately present sound of that voice. In both instances Wordsworth chooses from the two available alternatives just the opposite of what we would expect. In book 1 the seemingly secondary echo, not the immediacy of voice with its "imperfect sound," is the source of the greater "chear." And here in book 4, Wordsworth asserts that somehow the inability to establish a clear perception is the proper image of the "success" of his narrative. The processes that might normally be considered problematic and open to question—echo and in this case impeded perception—become the very means by which a successful representation of the self may be achieved. But here Wordsworth is not simply representing his experience of a given moment, his momentary sense that self-dividedness may be its own resolution, as he did in book 1. Rather, Wordsworth's narrative itself is being represented as the means whereby self-dividedness is the enabling structure for the production of successful self-presentation. This passage does not simply represent a moment in Wordsworth's narrative; it also is a moment in the Romantic account of the power of the imagination.

Our general understanding of the Romantic imagination has taught us that the Romantics conceived of the imagination as a faculty that through the mechanism of memory could serve to resolve "the divorce between subject and object by making perception an act of self-knowledge."[4] Thus the process that Wordsworth is analogizing in the passage from book 4 can be seen as a "reflection" of this conception of the imagination. However, this moment in Wordsworth's narrative also carries within it a complication that requires us to examine this representation of perception in terms of its status as a linguistic construct.[5] The linguistic nature of this moment can be located in Wordsworth's highlighting of this image as a construct that is constituted by a series of signs, none of which has distinct meaning in and of itself, but all of which together constitute the "meaning" of his narrative. Furthermore, this series of signs is not an isolated image; it too exists within a relational construct as a sign of Wordsworth's narrative and its relationship to the "surface of past time." The analogy that Wordsworth draws between the surface of the water and the "surface of past time" establishes a relationship between the perceptual process and historical representation. The analogy is built up in the image of the boat moving across the water and the reflections that move with it. In this representation the perceptual moment also is a movement, one that requires a continual adjustment between the perception of reflections that move across the surface of the water and of objects in the "bottom of the deeps," along with the perception of the relationship between the collected moments of this movement. The gleam of one's own image and the movement of the sunbeam across the surface of the water are coupled with the movement of the boat, and all must be accommodated in the perceptual field, a field which cannot be encompassed in a single act of perception. This accommodation is more than a matter of locating objects in their proper regions; it also is a matter of confronting a historical process, a series of perceptual moments. Rather than representing the integrating and visionary power of the imagination, this passage represents the perceptual situation as the equivalent of constructing and reading the past. The complexities of the perceptual situation, the perplexity of the succession of objects that are textualized on a reflecting surface and those objects in the deeps that one attempts to see through these reflections, represent the complexities of constructing and reading history, in this case the history that is read in the process of textual production.

In this image of Wordsworth's narrative imagination, mind, narrative, and history all come together as counterparts in an essentially textual scheme of perception and representation, in which to produce an autobiographical text is to read the surface of past time. This reading does not result in a unified narrative that resolves the perplexity, rather that very perplexity is a sign of the "success" of the narrative's process of reading. On an immediate level, we recognize here Wordsworth's "solution" to the autobiographical predicament, his construction of a "successful" narrative in the face of the perplexing task of the autobiographer. But this "success" is more than just a local one, at least in the terms in which Wordsworth seeks to represent it. *The Prelude* is not simply a narrative that seeks to account in strict biographical terms for the sources of Wordsworth's poetic genius and his faculty of imagination.

If we turn now to the Dawn Dedication and the Discharged Soldier, we can begin to see some of the limitations involved in focusing on these passages as momentary resolutions of a crisis that will return again and again until the final resolution of the poem is achieved. Adopting such a focus results in attempting to read Wordsworth's experience itself rather than examining his own reading of that experience in the process of representing it.

Wordsworth's description of the successful course of his narrative in encountering "impediments that make his task more sweet" points us not so much to the resolution itself, but to the alternation and tension between "falling off" and resolution. In accounting for this falling off, Johnston points us in the right direction when he cites the threat that is raised by Wordsworth's approach to the theme of *The Recluse* and his effort "to extend his private visions to Human Life." But in emphasizing the repeated pattern of *The Prelude*—"unexpected revelation leading to revised interpretation of the mind's power"—Johnston focuses on the integrative aspect of the latter half of book 4 without considering the way in which the overall pattern of the narrative works to highlight disjunction.[6] The image of the narrative as a perceptual situation in which one continually struggles to read a perplexing movement of images and moments points us to the alternations themselves and directs our attention toward reading *all* of the images that arise while we pursue our "pleasant office . . . incumbent over the surface of past time." Rather than obsessively searching only for those discoveries in "the bottoms of the deeps" that can be integrated into a unified account of Wordsworth's "vision," we should look for our "success" in the very inability to part shadow from substance.

In his encounter with the discharged soldier Wordsworth is confronting his own desire to be read by others, and the status of this encounter as an exchange of reading is pointed up in several ways in this incident.[7] At the level of Wordsworth's experience we see the juxtaposition of Wordsworth's own failed reading that gets caught up in the surface gaiety of "public revelry." This failed reading is set off against the exchange with the discharged soldier in which Wordsworth carefully delineates the old man as a figure against the landscape and probes his history. Wordsworth represents himself as moving from a slipshod reading that focuses only on the surface play of images, "a swarm / Of heady thoughts jostling one another" (273–74), to one that seeks to combine image and history. But the account does not stop here. As Charles Rzepka has pointed out, Wordsworth is insistent, even to the point of insensitivity, about gaining from the old man some evidence of his sensibility of Wordsworth's presence.[8] Although the old soldier's reply is at best minimal, it does provide Wordsworth with the acknowledgment he seeks and serves to locate him within a community of readers, albeit

3: The Surface of Past Time

one which he patronizes and perhaps even manipulates, much as his charity to the old man seems self-serving. In response to Wordsworth's "reproof" for lingering in the public ways, the old man responds: "'My trust is in the God of Heaven / And in the eye of him that passes me'" (4.494–95). Upon receiving this reply, Wordsworth notes in the old man's words of thanks "a voice that seemed / to speak with reviving interest, / Til then unfelt" and parts from him with a "quiet heart" (498–500, 504). This quietness of heart is achieved once the old man has taken an interest in Wordsworth's presence and, in effect, provided him with a confirmation of his own presence within the structure of a linguistic exchange. Because the old man's voice speaks with "reviving interest" it then has for Wordsworth the status of a sign of his own presence, and by producing this sign of interest, the old man, in effect, becomes a reader. Wordsworth's act of "charity" in turning the old man over to the cottager and the old man's "mild reproof" may not be satisfying proofs to us of Wordsworth's human-heartedness, but they are certainly satisfying to Wordsworth. The satisfaction does not result so much from Wordsworth's having done the right thing, but from the fact that the encounter validates his presence to himself in the sign of interest that is constituted in the reading of another.

The importance of the presence of a reader who takes an interest in Wordsworth's own "presence" is impressed upon us at the level of Wordsworth's account of his own narrative as well. Just as Wordsworth works to have the old man produce a reading of his presence, so, too, does he work to produce the reading of his presence that is to be constituted in the reading of *The Prelude*. This process parallels that of the reading which Wordsworth performs in turning away from reading only the surface of the "promiscuous rout." He chooses instead to read the perplexing and unresolvable commingling of the play of images on the surface and objects in the deeps (the old man's perplexing presence and the intermingling of his history with Wordsworth's own), recognizing the impediments to "reading" as the sign of his own success in reading his history. And our own uneasiness with Wordsworth's concluding re-assertion of human-heartedness at the end of the book is not something that we need pass over in order to read a coherent account of the history of a poet's mind. The perplexity that this reading evokes is not a flaw in the narrative but a sign of its "success"; that is, if we follow the example of Wordsworth's own performance of reading and, as the discharged soldier does, give him the reading that he has structured into the encounter.

The reading that Wordsworth structures into his encounter with the discharged soldier is more than an effort to use an exchange with the other as a means of constructing identity. It also is a model for Wordsworth's confrontation with, as he conceived it, the "reading public." Wordsworth's own failed reading under the influence of the "promiscuous rout" is a version of the malady that he hopes to counter or correct in *Lyrical Ballads*:

> A multitude of causes unknown to former times are now acting with a combined force to blunt the discriminating powers of the mind, and unfitting it for all voluntary exertion to reduce it to a state of almost savage torpor. The most effective of these causes are the great national events which are daily taking place, and the encreasing accumulation of men in cities, where the uniformity of their occupations produces a craving for extraordinary incident which the rapid communication of intelligence hourly gratifies.[9]

This derogatory characterization of "the public," which also applies to Wordsworth's own "vague heartless chace / Of trivial pleasures" (4.304–5), leads to the distinction that he makes in the 1815 "Essay, Supplementary to the Preface" of his collected poems between "the Public" and "the People."[10] Here Wordsworth circumvents the misreading of the Public by addressing himself only to the People, an ideal audience that Charles Rzepka asserts Wordsworth had by 1815 "apparently managed to internalize, and in the presence of which, gradually, he had come to establish a sense of his identity independent of what 'the Public' made of it."[11] In the 1805 *Prelude* the Public's making of Wordsworth's identity must be confronted directly precisely because he represents himself as having been subject to the very forces that blunt the discriminating powers of their minds.

The relationship between Wordsworth's process of reading his own experience and the course of his narrative is very much in evidence in the "history" of books 7 and 8. The compositional history of these books is notable for the fact that they are written after books 9 and 10, which is accurate in terms of the chronology of Wordsworth's life; his time at Cambridge is followed by his residence in France and then by his "sojourn" in the city. But when Wordsworth organizes the 1805 *Prelude*, he chooses to violate this chronology and instead places the two different accounts of London in books 7 and 8 before his account of his residence in France. There is much to be said of this particular realignment or reading of that experience.[12] But I focus primarily on the realignment that takes place within this adjustment, when Wordsworth composes book 8 concluding with one account of his experience in London, then goes on to compose book 7, presenting a very different account of the city, and finally chooses to place the latter before the former in the overall structure of *The Prelude*.

Given what we have seen of Wordsworth's procedures in making beginnings, it should not be a surprise to see the process of rearrangement that goes on with the beginnings of books 7 and 8. The lines that open book 7 (1–50) were originally composed to begin book 8, and the lines originally composed to begin book 7 eventually were placed in book 8 (711–51).[13] Additionally, the simile of the cave presented in book 8 (711–51) starts out as a passage that Wordsworth composed in the spring of 1804, just after composing his account of crossing the Alps and before the apostrophe to Imagination of book 6. When Wordsworth places the simile in book 8, he makes an important addition that adapts it especially to its context, and it is in that form that I now consider the passage.

Although I examine books 7 and 8 in the order in which they are arranged in the 1805 *Prelude*, I begin by first considering on a general level what goes on in the change from the original arrangement to the final one. That book 8 was written first would seem to offer grounds for speculation that at the time of its writing Wordsworth had not intended to give the extended treatment of an entire book to his experiences in London, dating approximately from his return from France to his taking up residence at Racedown.[14] Before the extended treatment of London is constructed in book 7, book 8 stands primarily as a stopping point at which Wordsworth sums up the course of his narrative and points it in the ultimate direction that he sees it as taking, thus the title "Retrospect: Love of Nature Leading to Love of Mankind." After he establishes this turning point, Wordsworth seems to have wanted to move on. However, the powerful evocation of London with which he concluded the book turned him in another direction, back to London, rather than onward in his history. Thus when he first composed book 7, Wordsworth began it with the powerful passage that later serves to sum up his experience of London at the end of book 8 in the 1805 *Prelude* and also marks a distinct difference in the two treatments of London: the passage that compares his view of London to the experience of entering a cave and going through three different stages of perception to finally arrive at a 'second look' that produces "A Spectacle to which there is no end" (8.741).[15] When he does arrange these books in their final order, he takes the passage that had begun book 8, describing his return to work on *The Prelude* in the fall of 1804, and places it at the beginning of book 7. The act of repositioning the original beginnings provides us with a clue as to what Wordsworth was doing in constructing book 7 after he had seemingly finished with his London experience in book 8. Book 8 is a profound reading of that experience and carries with it innumerable marks of the reading process, but without book 7 there is little sense of what has been read, or of the power of the reader who could extract from the "spectacle" of London the powerful reading that Wordsworth produces. Also missing is the very important element that book 7 adds: the representation of the population of London as a horrifying gathering of corrupted readers who have been possessed by the textual productions of urban life. Wordsworth constructs book 7 to make this problem and the process of reading it as explicit as possible and thus to ensure a "proper" reading of his own reading/writing of the self in book 8.

The key word in Wordsworth's accounts of London, and indeed in any number of his attempts to read the "hubbub" of the world, is the word *spectacle*.[16] The spectacle was, in effect, a genre of the theater and of the visual arts. Wordsworth refers to the goings on in the theater as "spectacles / Within doors" (7.245–46) and by implication represents his initial description of London that precedes this as an account of spectacles out of doors. What Wordsworth describes in this account are the panoramas and dioramas that were presented in theaters with incredibly elaborate "special effects," and he also draws significantly on the theatrical metaphors that abound in the political rhetoric of the times.[17] As impressive as these scenes are, there is for Wordsworth a severe problem at the heart of them in that they are "mimic sights that ape / The absolute presence of reality" (7.249–50). David Simpson has pointed out the threatening exercise of power and aggrandizement of self that such aping implies for Wordsworth, a threat that is embodied at two levels.[18] First there is the threat of a powerful reading that passes off a mimic version of reality as "the absolute presence of reality," thus negating the power of that presence and substituting for it a mere facsimile. Second, the threatening power of this reality is apparent in the inability of those who are subject to it to step back from it and get that 'second look' that Wordsworth believes to be so necessary. In what follows this initial account of the "spectacles within doors," Wordsworth demonstrates the effects of this power upon himself and others.

When Wordsworth presents his accounts of the pantomimes and melodramas at Sadler's Wells, he gives us a demonstration of the sort of powerful effect that these structures of representation, which he associates with urban life, can have on him, particularly when they read something of Wordsworth's own rural history: the Maid of Buttermere.[19] Wordsworth contrasts what he speculates to have been the irreverent treatment of "too holy a theme for such a place" (7.318) with his own "direct" knowledge of the facts of Mary Robinson's life and her surroundings. It is important to note that Wordsworth's insertion of the Maid of Buttermere at this point in the narrative marks the production of his own spectacle in that the actual production of the Maid's story was not one that he saw during his residence in London, but one that had been performed in the spring of 1803. Wordsworth makes no attempt to assert that he actually saw a performance of this melodrama during his residence in London, identifying it as one that was "of late / Set forth," and he marks his speculative account of the production by referring to what it "doubtless" was like (7.317–19). The significance of this staging of Wordsworth's reflections on the Maid's history has been examined, but some of its implications with regard to the subsequent reflection on the "rosy babe" have not.[20] While Wordsworth's account of the "rosy babe" does constitute a nominal return to the narrative of London spectacles, it also comments upon Wordsworth's narrative itself. The account of the rosy babe represents the way in which the child occupies a privileged position in the midst of the corrupt and potentially corrupting scene around him, but the very forces that protect him also threaten him, and this is a threat in which Wordsworth's own "memorial verse" for the Maid is implicated as well.

Wordsworth represents the rosy babe as "eternally nature's"[21]; however, the privilege bestowed upon the child by nature seems to be a mixed blessing. For one thing, the impression that the boy is "eternally nature's" highlights the fact that the boy cannot always remain a child. He is, in effect, blessed by contrast with what he will no doubt become as he grows up. Also the child is blessed primarily by contrast with his surroundings; he seems in "this [place] / A sort of alien scattered from the clouds" (7.377–78). The boy is "saved" from this corruption by Wordsworth's remembrance of him, but the nature of this remembrance throws a shadow over the apparent gift of Nature that the boy has been given in that Wordsworth says that the boy appears in his memory "as if embalmed / By Nature" (7.400–401).[22] Just as the boy is preserved from the corruption of his surroundings in his own environment on the "board" that is "his little stage in the vast theatre," so too are Wordsworth and Nature working to preserve him in memory.[23] However, all three are implicated in an "embalming" process, thus indicating that such preservation may give the appearance of life, but it does so by hiding the reality of death. This status also can be transferred to Wordsworth's "memorial verse" for the Maid in that it, too, is a spectacle, one that is produced upon the stage of Wordsworth's narrative. Thus Wordsworth shows himself to be under the influence of the powerful reading of reality that constitutes the spectacle of urban life. At the very moment when he would produce a counter to its mimicry, he himself can only offer an aping of the "absolute presence of reality."

Wordsworth is implicated in the degenerative effects of these urban spectacles not only in that he is represented as feeling their effects during his residence in London, but also in that his own narrative of that experience exhibits these effects. This double implication is apparent in his account of the pleasure that he feels in being made conscious of the artificiality of the theater. Wordsworth establishes what would seem to be the continuing influence of this attraction to artificiality when he tries to account for the pleasures he experienced during his residence in London by citing a pleasure that was handed down to him from earlier times:

                        For then,
    Though surely no mean progress had been made
    In meditations holy and sublime,
    Yet something of a girlish childlike gloss
    Of novelty survived for scenes like these—
    Pleasure that had been handed down from times
    When at a country playhouse, having caught
    In summer through the fractured wall a glimpse
    Of daylight, at the thought of where I was
    I gladdened more than if I had beheld
    Before me some bright cavern of romance,
    Or than we do when on our beds we lie
    At night, in warmth, when rains are beating hard.
                                        (7.476–88)

The security that Wordsworth feels in being made conscious of artifice is quite disturbing and certainly offers an unflattering view of his enthrallment with the theater as he represents his past failure to live up to the apparent progress that he had made "in meditations holy and sublime."[24] What is even more striking, however, is that the "girlish childlike gloss of novelty" survives even into the present moment of the narrative. After describing this sense of pleasure, Wordsworth steps back from the narrative to offer a justification for his pursuit of a matter which is "neither dignified enough / Nor arduous, and is doubtless in itself / Humble and low" (7.490–92). In doing so he exhibits the manner in which the past influence of the spectacle has been brought down into the "present" narrative:

                    More lofty themes,
    Such as at least do wear a prouder face,
    Might here be spoken of; but when I think
    Of these I feel the imaginative power
    Languish within me. Even then it slept,
    When wrought upon by tragic sufferings,
    The heart was full—amid my sobs and tears
    It slept, even in the season of my youth.
                                        (7.496–503)

The "now" of his narrative and the "then" of his residence in London are linked in the experience of a languishing of imaginative power. This diminishment of imaginative power is that whose negative influence is apparent in the account of the Maid of Buttermere and the "rosy babe," the power of mind that can preserve only by embalming.

The means by which Wordsworth attempts to remedy the corrupting influence of the powerful reading that constitutes the spectacle of London is through the spectacle itself—this time a spectacle that reveals itself for what it is and which Wordsworth is able to read rather than being dominated by the reading that it projects: the blind beggar. This famous passage does not need to be examined in detail once again here, except to point out that its function in Wordsworth's narrative is to turn him from a sort of reading that only reproduces spectacle to one that can at least distance itself enough from the spectacle in order to expose its limitations and dangers, thus achieving a comment upon the spectacular nature of all human experience.[25] It is a spectacle which has for its subject the inability to read and the consequences of that inability—a projection of Wordsworth's experience into a reflection on what it would be like to become like the blind beggar: an object dependent upon the power of someone else to write his history and also dependent upon the force of that history to provide him with sustenance. Through this projection Wordsworth momentarily distances himself from the unreadable "characters" of London, but the most that this distancing can accomplish for him is to make an emblem of this inability. For the moment, Wordsworth is caught in the predicament of the autobiographer and suggests that the most one may be able to do in this predicament is little more than what the blind beggar does—hold out to the world a written placard that tells a tale which he cannot read.[26]

It is this predicament that Wordsworth presents in his hellish account of St. Bartholomew's Fair. At the outset of this scene he represents the degree to which his own powers of reading are impaired by imploring a conventional muse for aid.[27] Wordsworth is making a judgment on the activity of the fair and those who participate in it, the "blank confusion" of it all, but he also is making a judgment on his own narrative at a point where the story that he tells is no different to him than is the blind beggar's. This is apparent in the way in which Wordsworth characterizes the help that he seeks from the muse. He asks to be "wafted on her wings," and placed "above the press and danger of the crowd— / Upon some showman's platform" (7.657–59). Here is a stage on which Wordsworth produces the spectacle of his own poem, not as a challenge to the deadening powers of the fair's spectacle, but as an acquiescence to the powerful reading of reality that it can impose upon him. The best that Wordsworth can do under the influence of this reading is to preserve himself "above the press and danger of the crowd," much as he has preserved the Maid of Buttermere and the "rosy babe" by embalming them in his narrative.

But as book 7 concludes, we begin to see the place of this "failure" of reading in Wordsworth's narrative, as he moves back toward the vision of London that will be presented in book 8 and which motivated this demonstration of the oppressive powers of the urban spectacle. Having demonstrated the dominating power of the first look at London, a reading so powerful that even Wordsworth's own narrative cannot escape its influence, Wordsworth can then effectively and properly represent his 'second look' in the context of his retrospect. That is what he points toward at the end of book 7 when he posits the possibility that "a straggler here and there" (698) may escape the oppression of the blank confusion that is the city and be one:

> who looks
> In steadiness, who hath among least things
> An under-sense of greatest, sees the parts
> As parts, but with a feeling of the whole.
>
> (7.710–13)

The attention, comprehensiveness, and memory that are necessary to attain such a steady look come from the "early converse with the works of God" (7.719) that Wordsworth will attempt to sum up in book 8.

It is admittedly a bit difficult in book 8 to follow Wordsworth with conviction from the account of his "love of nature" to his "love of mankind." This difficulty stems in part from the weakness of Wordsworth's argument concerning his sense of the power that "Nature" had over him, but I think it also has a great deal to do with the fact that the book is not so much a demonstration of how love of nature leads to love of mankind as it is a demonstration of how the reading of the self in textual production may overcome the oppression of the powerful reading of the other that dominates Wordsworth in his encounter with specta-

cle.[28] The description of Grasmere Fair at the opening of book 8
clearly serves as the rural remedy to the hellishness of the urban
St. Bartholomew's Fair. Here, rather than Wordsworth raising
himself above the press of the crowd by getting a foot up from
the muse, he represents the scene as it may be seen by the summit
Helvellyn itself, looking down upon the fair. Wordsworth has
substituted the "eminence" of nature for the imagined showman's platform that he himself had occupied in his account of
the urban fair. His narrative of the way in which love of nature
leads to love of mankind is, in effect, made subordinate to his
account of how he will master the oppressive reading of others.
And this is apparent in the sudden shift from his account of the
privileged status of the inhabitants of this vale to his own sense
of how this scene had served him in his experience of London.
While Nature serves as mediator, Wordsworth moves abruptly
from the image of "old Helvellyn, conscious of the stir, / And
the blue sky that roofs their calm abode"(8.60–61) to London:

> With deep devotion, Nature, did I feel
> In that great city what I owed to thee:
> High thoughts of God and man, and love of man,
> Triumphant over all those loathsome sights
> Of wretchedness and vice, a watchful eye,
> Which, with the outside of our human life
> Not satisfied, must read the inner mind.
>
> (8.62–68)

Here is the reading that Wordsworth describes himself as being
nearly incapable of in book 7, not only while he is actually in
London, but also even as he attempts in book 7 to narrate that
experience. The image of the "watchful eye" that "must read the
inner mind" not only represents the way in which Wordsworth
can now prevent himself from succumbing to the oppressive
spectacles of London, but it also represents the process of reading whereby he can structure his narrative as precisely the sort
of "spectacle" that results from turning to 'look again.' And this
process itself is represented in the analogy he draws between his
experience in London and the series of perceptions that people
experience upon entering a cave (8.111–51).

In this passage Wordsworth literally returns to book 7 in that
lines 711–51 of book 8 were the original beginning of book 7. In

the context of book 7, this passage had been an anticipatory reading of an experience not yet related. In the context of book 8, however, it not only performs that reading, but it also stands as a demonstration of the very act of turning to 'look again' that Wordsworth is trying to describe. He begins with the description of the chaotic commingling of "substance and shadow, light and darkness" (8.719) that one experiences on first entering a cave, reminding us of the effort to part substance from shadow in book 4 (247–64), and this analogy clearly parallels the chaotic perceptions of London with which Wordsworth struggles in book 7. The second stage in this process of perception is one in which "The scene before him lies in perfect view / Exposed, and lifeless as a written book" (727–28). This is just the sort of "perfect view" of the Maid of Buttermere and the "rosy babe" that Wordsworth produces under the influential reading of the theatrical reality of London. The status of this passage as a reading of the narrative that precedes it also is apparent in the way in which the simile is extended when Wordsworth removes it from its "original" place in book 6, between the crossing of the Alps and the apostrophe to imagination. There he had closed with the image of lifelessness of a written book in order to evoke the way in which the textualizing power of the mind can indeed dull the power of experience. When Wordsworth places this passage in book 8, we see a double re-reading—the reading/revision of the perceptual scene evoked by the image of the cave in its original context and the reading of Wordsworth's experience of London that this second account of that experience presents.

It is in 'looking again' as Wordsworth does here in returning to read once again his experience of London, that one then can "read" a "spectacle to which there is no end." It is this lack of an end that is significant in distinguishing this sort of spectacle from that of London in book 7. For all its chaos and formlessness, the London spectacle is static and resists any effort to read it, at least while one is in its immediate vicinity. Although there is a sense of "mastery" afforded in being presented with the panoramas that seem to "plant us upon some lofty pinnacle," all evident power is in the "greedy pencil" (7.261, 258). If the spectator observing this vista has any sense of activity then it can be little more than illusory.[29]

If we attend once again to the process of Wordsworth's composition of books 7 and 8, it is clear that this reading of his London experience is one that he was capable of producing before he had described and demonstrated so fully the oppressive influence of the spectacle of London.[30] Indeed, the simile of the cave is possible as a reading of his experience even before Wordsworth begins to compose his representation of London. However, what was not possible and what would seem, at least in part, to have prompted the composition of book 7 after 8 was completed was the demonstration of how that reading might be achieved. The straightforward narrative sequence of love of nature leading to love of mankind is not enough in and of itself to constitute the double activity of writing and reading. Such a narrative does not provide an adequate representation of the forces that threaten to disrupt that sequence and thereby play a constitutive role in the narrative. Writing the narrative that finally takes its place in book 8, Wordsworth recognizes not only the threatening power of the spectacle that could master his perception and deaden his imagination, but he also recognizes the even greater power constituted by his own writing that would allow him to turn upon that spectacle and read it. By demonstrating its oppressive power in composing the account of London that is eventually placed in book 7, Wordsworth is able to demonstrate his own power, in the face of this threat, to produce in his reading of his own representations a "spectacle without end," and thereby to demonstrate his ability to take possession of the text that would possess him.

Wordsworth's tale of his poetic development, the paradigm of the construction of Romantic subjectivity, explicates the process of reading by which the autobiographical subject writes itself. The primary motives of this strategy of self-representation are to demonstrate a model of reading that attests to Wordsworth's power to read/write the text of his life and to set up that model as the guide to be followed by any reader of the poem. In one sense this guidance is one of the means by which Wordsworth sought to counter the blunted "discriminating powers" of the reading Public. However, this strategy also is directed at a whole other sort of reader, one whose powers may be all too discriminating—Coleridge. Coleridge is an especially powerful reader of the poem not only because he has access to the essential private document, but also because he avails himself of his position as private reader to represent the poem publicly.

4
To Thee the Work Shall Justify Itself

When thou dost to that summer turn thy thoughts,
And hast before thee all that which then we were,
To thee, in memory of that happiness,
It will be known—by thee at least, my friend,
Felt—that the history of a poet's mind
Is labour not unworthy of regard:
To thee the work shall justify itself.

(13.404–11)

In *The Prelude* the "friend" serves as a figure against which Wordsworth can define his own strengths as a poet and through which he can disarm the threat that Coleridge, as a reader, poses to his writing. But the figure of the friend also provides Wordsworth with the means by which he can mask his own revisionary reading of Coleridge. Thus the effort to disarm Coleridge's power as reader serves both to counter a threat to Wordsworth's self-presentation and to strengthen that presence in establishing Wordsworth's own power as reader. The interplay of sympathy, anxiety, and aggression in Wordsworth's representation of Coleridge issues in a series of defensive and aggressive strategies designed to counter Coleridge's influence over Wordsworth, while still maintaining the sense of the vital link between them.[1] Rather than being a simple case of the "anxiety of influence," the representation of Coleridge in *The Prelude* must grapple with the complexities of Wordsworth's tie to an intimate contemporary. As an all-too-enthusiastic conceptual force behind *The Recluse*, Coleridge may be said to take on the role of Wordsworth's "precursor." But it is not just Coleridge's poetic influence with which Wordsworth must deal. He also must confront the power that Coleridge has, both actual and potential, as a *reader* of *The Prelude*. In such a case, rather than examining the process

81

of reading and writing involved in the poet's aggressive and defensive strategies only from the point of view of the poet who is attempting to work out his relationship to a precursor, it is necessary to examine how reading itself, as performed by a contemporary, may act as an influence against which the poet must defend himself.[2] In this respect, the relationship between Wordsworth and Coleridge and their writings involves more than just a question of influence, or how one author writes the texts of another into his own. In the relationship between contemporaries, the intimate tie between reading and writing is foregrounded—it is the very tie that Wordsworth seeks both to establish and to disarm in his representation of the friend. The poem must establish a discourse in which it can speak its justification, but the finality of justification requires that the goal of this discourse be to close itself off.[3]

The anxiety over the relationship between The Prelude and The Recluse project that Wordsworth expresses in the preface to The Excursion leads him to characterize The Prelude as "subsidiary" to his preparation for constructing The Recluse. However, because The Recluse is so intimately linked to Coleridge's projections of Wordsworth's poetic powers, Wordsworth's anxieties in beginning The Prelude cannot be separated from his concerns about Coleridge's place in this project. Thomas McFarland ably traces these anxieties in Wordsworth's "Prospectus" to The Recluse by analyzing how the "Prospectus" serves to revise the nature and scope of the philosophical poem that Coleridge wanted Wordsworth to write.[4] On one level, in writing The Prelude and addressing it to Coleridge, Wordsworth seems to be putting aside, at least temporarily, the issue of the philosophical poem along with any expression of his divergence from Coleridge on the matter. Toward the end of book 1, Wordsworth expresses his hope that it will not seem "to thee, my friend, so prompt / In sympathy, that I have lengthened out / With fond and feeble tongue a tedious tale" (1.645–47). This address to Coleridge, along with most of such passages in the first two books of the 1805 Prelude, were originally part of the 1799 two-book Prelude. It is in that context that we can read much of the genuine sympathy and admiration for Coleridge that these lines express. However, in the context of 1805, this address and those I will proceed to examine have other implications as well. The expression of the hope for a sympathetic reception in this ad-

dress to Coleridge at the end of book 1 also is an expression of
the anxiety that this reception will not be forthcoming. An even
greater concern is that in the face of a tedious tale, the friend
may begin to fill in and re-direct the narrative for himself. Wordsworth counts on Coleridge's sympathy to induce him to listen
rather than take the narrative as an occasion to read into it the
philosophical design of *The Recluse* project. Thus, this desire
for a sympathetically induced silence has an added aspect in
which sympathy becomes the means by which Wordsworth can
try to master Coleridge's necessary but nonetheless threatening
presence.

Consider, for example, Wordsworth's account of Coleridge's
habits of mind and their history. The often repeated theme in
this account is Coleridge's isolation and his solitary habits of
mind; much as Wordsworth sympathizes with his friend's solitary sufferings, he also sees in them a dangerous tendency toward solipsism, and not just in his friend, but in himself as well.
By quoting Coleridge's "Frost at Midnight" in speaking of the
"far other scenes" of the "great city" in which Coleridge was
raised, Wordsworth recognizes the difficulty of that different
road by which Coleridge has reached with him the "self-same
bourne" (2.467–68).[5] But even while Wordsworth identifies Coleridge as a brother in his devotion to Nature, he still dwells upon
critical distinctions. Wordsworth's efforts to express his confidence in Coleridge as a sympathetic listener also carry the impression of his threatening, even if silent, presence. Wordsworth
states his confidence in the friend:

> And for this cause to thee
> I speak unapprehensive of contempt
> The insinuated scoff of coward tongues,
> And all that silent language which so oft
> In conversation betwixt man and man
> Blots from the human countenance all trace
> Of beauty and of love.
>
> (2.469–75)

The cause for this confidence is their having reached the "self-
same goal," and Wordsworth's lack of apprehension has its
source in his sense of Coleridge's sympathy and in his expression of his own sympathy and well wishes in the lines that follow

these. But Wordsworth's statement that he is not apprehensive also functions as an admission the he *is*, and "that silent language" asserts itself in Wordsworth's insistence on the distinctions between himself and Coleridge. The differences of Coleridge's city-breeding are reasserted in the lines that follow immediately upon these when Wordsworth distinguishes Coleridge as someone who had "sought / The truth in solitude" (2.475–76). The book ends with the image of Coleridge "seeking oft the haunts of men— / And yet more often living with thyself, / And for thyself" (2.481–83). In its original context in the 1799 *Prelude*, this is an image of Coleridge, in effect, being able to preserve himself from the corrupting influence of the "haunts of men" as he goes on to pursue a living as a journalist in London. Thus his living with and for himself does not carry a strong sense of admonishment for his solitariness; it is a tendency with which Wordsworth identifies.[6] The hopeful projection of Coleridge's future with which Wordsworth ends the two-part *Prelude* reflects this identification and sympathy as Wordsworth expresses his hope for Coleridge "—so haply shall thy days / Be many, and a blessing to mankind" (2.483–84). However, in the context of the 1805 *Prelude*, Wordsworth's sympathetic representation of Coleridge that had drawn them together against the power of the "silent language" (2.472) of others begins to draw distinctions between them which write that silent language. The sympathy that Wordsworth expresses becomes the basis for his critical point about the distinctions to be made between his history of a poet's mind and the form that such a history might take in a Coleridgean narrative. The "two consciousnesses," which at the outset of book 2 define Wordsworth's autobiographical predicament and his strategy for taking possession of himself in the production of an autobiographical text are, in effect, doubled here. There are the two consciousnesses of the 1798–99 narrative, Wordsworth writing and written. But now there also is the Wordsworth who wishes Coleridge well in embarking on his new work as a journalist in London, and the Wordsworth who in 1804 has since experienced the "silent language" of Coleridge's reading. The power of that reading leads Wordsworth to read/ write distinctions where he had earlier represented sympathy.

The grounds of these distinctions are established earlier in book 2 when Wordsworth pauses in his narrative of his youthful associations with Nature to express his sense of how a history such as his might take a false turn:

> But who shall parcel out
> His intellect by geometric rules,
> Split like a province into round and square?
> Who knows the individual hour in which
> His habits were first sown even as a seed,
> Who that shall point as with a wand, and say
> 'This portion of the river of my mind
> Came from yon fountain'?
>
> (2.208–15)

For Wordsworth such a narrative seems false in that it makes distinctions that have no meaning. The reference here to the science of geometry also places Wordsworth's account of this falsifying narrative method within the framework of his own intellectual history. Wordsworth's attitude toward science, particularly mathematics and geometry, figures prominently not only in his own narrative but in critical accounts of *The Prelude*.[7] In terms of that history, we have a moment at which Wordsworth is highly suspicious of the abstract and rigid forms of geometric science, just as he will later express his suspicions of the abstractions of an apparently Godwinian rationalism. Nonetheless, Wordsworth goes on to suggest that "science" need not be the purveyor of false and abstract distinctions and that for Coleridge it may in fact be possible to delineate the sources of the faculties of the mind:

> Thou, my Friend, art one
> More deeply read in thy own thoughts; to thee
> Science appears but what in truth she is,
> Not as our glory and our absolute boast,
> But as a succedaneum, and a prop
> To our infirmity. Thou art no slave
> Of that false secondary power by which
> In weakness we create distinctions, then
> Deem that our puny boundaries are things
> Which we perceive, and not which we have made.
>
> (2.215–24)

The power attributed here to Coleridge does not escape the implications of the preceding lines, and in part, the ambivalent representation of science, first in the guise of the potential falsification of geometric rules and then as "what in truth she is . . . a prop to our infirmity," has its source in Wordsworth's own developing sense of the significance of geometry and science in relation to the poetic imagination. Wordsworth's different attitudes toward geometry and mathematics, his suspicion of them (book 2) and his praise for the pleasure and insight that they afford him (book 6), can provide an index of his ambivalent representations of Coleridge.[8] Coleridge knows the truth of "science," but he also is very much subject to its potential falsifications. Although Wordsworth believes that Coleridge may have the skill to construct a narrative that "parcels out" his intellect because he is "more deeply read" in his own thoughts, it is clear that Wordsworth's own narrative, by design, is not to be of that sort.

Wordsworth seems to want to keep a distance between himself and his "science," and this distancing is apparent in his representation of Coleridge. In asserting that Coleridge is "more deeply read" in his own thoughts, Wordsworth implies that he will not and perhaps cannot conduct the sort of self-examination that Coleridge might. At the same time he acknowledges that Coleridge's power to read his own thoughts is something with which to reckon. But even while praising Coleridge's power to read, Wordsworth counsels against the danger of assuming that the exercise of this power is creative rather than merely responsive. In fact, the reference to things created rather than perceived might even be taken as a possible source of Coleridge's later corrective of Wordsworth in "To William Wordsworth." In that poem Coleridge recounts Wordsworth's narrative in The Prelude with the statement that Wordsworth's "soul received / The light reflected, as a light bestowed."[9] The larger context for this apparent disagreement over a creative versus a reflective power of mind are to be found in Wordsworth and Coleridge's debate over the relationship between poetic power and the power of Nature and in their dispute over the definitions of imagination and fancy. This debate also can be linked to Wordsworth's confrontation with the problematic relationship between sense perception and creative imagination in The Prelude.[10] But the more immediate grounds for Wordsworth's critique are evident in his praise for Coleridge which cites two of Coleridge's habits of mind that, at a very basic level, Wordsworth cannot help but see as flaws. Although he allows that Coleridge might be equal to the "hard task" of analyzing the soul, Wordsworth still holds to his sense of the impossibility of that task by stating that "each most obvious and particular thought / Not in a mystical and idle sense / But in the words of reason deeply weighed— / Hath no beginning" (2.234–36).

Wordsworth implies that Coleridge's efforts to read his own thoughts may lead him into the solipsistic belief that he can parcel out the intellect by "geometric rules." While Wordsworth posits Coleridge as a guide whose more highly developed skills in reading the human mind can keep Wordsworth from composing a narrative of such vain distinctions, Wordsworth also recognizes in Coleridge the same tendency toward a quasi-scientific solipsism that he sees as a threat to his own poetic development.[11] Coleridge is the embodiment of the threat that Wordsworth feels within himself. The power of this threat comes from its being a perversion of the very powers and habits of mind that Wordsworth believes to constitute the truth of his own poetic insight: his connection through nature with his fellow human beings. This threat is given added force because the aspect of *The Recluse* (and by implication *The Prelude*) that gives Wordsworth the greatest difficulty is that which depends upon his establishing poetically and philosophically this sense of connection.[12]

Once again we need to understand the double reading that is constituted in this representation of Coleridge in book 2. In its original context in the 1799 *Prelude*, the representation of Coleridge as a model and guide has the immediate precedent of the guidance that Coleridge gave Wordsworth in his rejection of and emergence from Godwin's influence.[13] In this context, the praise of Coleridge's ability to read his own thoughts and his ability to be equal to the hard task of analyzing the soul would ring quite true. But in the context of the 1805 *Prelude* this language of praise takes on other echoes as well, many of which can be heard in Wordsworth's representation of the friend in book 10, thus lending a great deal of emphasis to the implied critique of Coleridge in book 2 of the 1805 *Prelude*.

In book 10 when Wordsworth details his own errors and false turns that lead to his ultimate crisis of imagination, the echoes of his "praise" of Coleridge are still heard. Giving an account of

his apparent rejection of Godwinian rationalism, Wordsworth
expresses his sense that his reasonings were misguided precisely
because they are of the sort that he called vain, when in book 2
he was trying to direct his narrative to a more productive pursuit.
Wordsworth describes the false path taken in his own efforts to
analyze the soul:

> Thus I fared,
> Dragging all passions, notions, shapes of faith,
> Like culprits to the bar, suspiciously
> Calling the mind to establish in plain day
> Her titles and her honours; now believing,
> Now disbelieving, endlessly perplexed
> With impulse, motive, right and wrong, the ground
> Of moral obligation—what the rule,
> And what the sanction—till, demanding proof,
> And seeking it in everything, I lost
> All feeling of conviction, and, in fine,
> Sick, wearied out with contrarieties,
> Yielded up moral questions in despair.
>
> (10.888–900)

Wordsworth and Coleridge were very much in sympathy in their
disaffection with Godwinian rationalism, but the complexity of
Wordsworth's reaction against the processes of abstract reasoning
needs to be taken more fully into account here.[14] The language
of this passage describes a process of making distinctions where
there apparently are none to be made, and of destroying that
which one examines by "abstracting" out of it all life and meaning. In one sense we have here a destructive version of the "perplexity" that Wordsworth uses to image his narrative in book 4.
But in this instance the perplexity is unending precisely because
Wordsworth makes the error of doing that which he rejects as
error in his narrative—defining his task as being that of parting
substance from shadow, rather than accepting his inability to do
so and finding success in this necessity. Even more significantly,
the endless perplexity of his erroneous effort to find proof for
all things operates by the very processes which Wordsworth at-
tributes to the "false secondary power" named in his account of
Coleridge.[15] Wordsworth had asserted that Coleridge was not a
slave to this false power, but Wordsworth's own enslavement to

it takes a form that cannot help but call to mind his account of the formation of Coleridge's mind.

These echoes of Wordsworth's earlier "praise" of Coleridge are made more distinct by the lines that introduce Wordsworth's account of his own errors both in following and turning away from the abstract methodology represented by Godwin:

> Time may come
> When some dramatic story may afford
> Shapes livelier to convey to thee, my friend,
> What then I learned—or think I learned—of truth,
> And the errors into which I was betrayed
> By present objects, and by reasonings false
> From the beginning, inasmuch as drawn
> Out of a heart which had been turned aside
> From Nature by external accidents,
> And which was confounded more and more,
> Misguiding and misguided.
>
> (10.878–88)

Wordsworth's errors are the result of his having been turned aside from "Nature's way" by "outward accidents," not dissimilar to the "accidents" of Coleridge's city breeding that divert him, too, from Nature's way. The implications of these connections are multiplied by their being made in the context of a reference to *The Recluse*, the "dramatic story" yet to come. In effect, Wordsworth attempts to erase whatever mark Coleridge might make on that project by first giving the impression that Coleridge doesn't already know the truth that Wordsworth will present in it, and second, and perhaps most powerfully, by suggesting that Coleridge is inherently prone to the very errors that Wordsworth had to overcome in order to find that truth.

At first it does seem rather contradictory that Coleridge is implicated in Wordsworth's errors by being aligned with Godwinian rationalism. After all Coleridge is among those influences cited as the sources of Wordsworth's recovery. But given Wordsworth's alternating attitude toward mathematics and abstract "science" in general, Coleridge's "living help" in regulating Wordsworth's soul (10.906–7) is positioned in a striking sequence. The first element in Wordsworth's recovery after having "yielded up moral questions in despair" is his turn "towards mathematics, and their clear / And solid evidence" (10.903–4), and from that follows Coleridge's "living help" along with that of Dorothy whom Wordsworth says "Maintained for me a saving intercourse / With my true self" (10.914–15). The final element in the sequence is "Nature's self" which "revived the feelings of [his] earlier life" (10.921, 924). In the 1850 *Prelude* Wordsworth expands upon the nature of his turn toward mathematics, calling it "abstract science . . . where the disturbances of space and time . . . find no admission" (6.327, 330, 333), and he eliminates what was a somewhat anachronistic reference to Coleridge's influence, which during the "crisis" of 1796 was not as direct as the 1805 *Prelude* appeared to make it. Wordsworth's initial sequencing of saving influences, in which Coleridge's presence follows immediately upon Wordsworth's account of his mathematical pursuits, combines with Wordsworth's subsequent elision of Coleridge in the 1850 *Prelude* and his expansion upon "abstract science" to provide important evidence that Wordsworth clearly associates Coleridge with the habits of mind that drive this abstraction. Coleridge and mathematics represent saving influences, but they also represent the potential for dangerous errors.[16]

The problem that Wordsworth confronts with regard to Godwinian rationalism is that its abstractions provide "solid evidence" only as long as one remains "enthroned where the disturbances of space and time . . . find no admission." He finds comfort and recovery in mathematics precisely because it allows him to operate in a realm in which no demand is made upon him to suffer those disturbances. This realm may feel safe, but as Wordsworth makes clear, it also has significant dangers, particularly for the poet. While Coleridge also repudiated Godwin's philosophical system, Wordsworth repeatedly points out the ways in which Coleridge is equally, if not more, subject to the attractions of "abstract science," but without being grounded in Nature in the way in which Wordsworth is. Thus Coleridge is all the more subject to an erroneous belief in his power to parcel out the intellect and to the dangers of "abstract science."

Wordsworth's effort to establish distinctions between himself and Coleridge and to counter the threat that he represents operates as well when Wordsworth takes up the theme of his "brotherhood" with Coleridge in book 6. Wordsworth gave the first five books of *The Prelude* to Coleridge to have with him when he sailed for the Mediterranean, and the result is that when

Wordsworth proceeds with book 6, he is addressing a Coleridge who figures most explicitly as a reader of the poem.[17] The starting point of the address to the friend is once again a sense of shared experience and a joyful desire for Coleridge's happiness, particularly for the recovery of his health. Here the sense of identification with Coleridge is strong. Wordsworth speaks of the two of them as fellow wanderers and "twins almost in genius and in mind" (6.263). He speaks of himself and Coleridge as beings "predestined ... / To seek the same delights, and have one health, / One happiness" (6.267–69). However, in this context Wordsworth again feels compelled to focus on differences between Coleridge and himself, imagining Coleridge as a schoolboy "liveried ... in the depths / Of the huge city" and living a "cloistered" existence (6.276–77, 289). This distinction repeats the earlier one that sought to play upon the tensions of difference between the two. After presenting this image of Coleridge's life before he went to Cambridge, Wordsworth enters into an even more speculative account of Coleridge's youth. This discussion of Coleridge's education is especially significant in marking a difference between Coleridge and Wordsworth. Wordsworth highlights this difference by strategically placing his speculations about Coleridge at a point in the narrative where Wordsworth is asserting that he has left behind his own childhood.[18]

Wordsworth projects Coleridge into a regressed state, his youth, while imagining himself as advancing in his own journey, and he speculates how Coleridge's time at Cambridge might have been different had Wordsworth still been there when Coleridge arrived. Wordsworth characterizes this imagined circumstance as the product of "impotent fancy," but the terms in which he expresses his revised version of Coleridge's youth indicate the need to negate Coleridge's presence in the poem, or more specifically, they indicate the way in which Wordsworth effects Coleridge's presence precisely in order to negate it:

> I have thought
> Of thee, thy learning, gorgeous eloquence,
> And all the strength and plumage of thy youth,
> Thy subtle speculations, toils abstruse
> Among the schoolmen, and Platonic forms
> Of wild ideal pageantry, shaped out
> From things well-matched or ill, and words for things—

> The self-created sustenance of a mind
> Debarred from Nature's living images,
> Compelled to be a life unto itself
>
> .   .   .   .
> .   .   .   . If we had met,
> Even at that early time: I needs must hope,
> Must feel, must trust, that my maturer age
> And temperature less willing to be moved,
> My calmer habits, and more steady voice,
> Would with an influence benign have soothed
> Or chased away the airy wretchedness
> That battened on thy youth.

(6.305–14, 319–26)

Wordsworth presents his imagined version of the wretchedness of Coleridge's youth precisely in the terms that are used to characterize the error that results from enslavement to that false "secondary power." In this context, the enslavement is called the consequence of the mind being "debarred from Nature's living images," and of the compensatory "toils abstruse" that are the "self-created sustenance" of such a mind. Here Wordsworth's reference in book 2 to Coleridge's habit of living with himself and for himself and of having "sought the truth in solitude" (2.482–83, 475–76) strikes home, and the reference to subtle speculations shaped out from words for things brings to mind the differences between Wordsworth and Coleridge over the nature of poetic language. When the figure of Coleridge as reader looms most powerfully before Wordsworth, he counters this threat with a representation of that threat as an error, a sign of Coleridge's wretchedness that Wordsworth's own presence might have corrected.

After imagining how his influence might have reshaped Coleridge's wretched youth, Wordsworth concedes that "these vain regrets" are "put to shame" by the "march of glory" that Coleridge has trod (6.328–29). This concession raises the possibility that these seemingly ambivalent feelings about Coleridge may be resolved by drawing a line, as Wordsworth does, between the vain speculations of Coleridge's youth and the "truth of Nature" that he comes to understand in maturity. But Wordsworth tempers his own mild criticism of himself by suggesting that Coleridge's ill health should be cause enough to feel grief for him.

And indeed, Coleridge's ill health is made readily available to be read in correlation to the wretchedness of his youth, thus calling into question his present powers as a reader as well. Through the expression of a "natural" sympathy, which provides an excuse for Wordsworth's imagined revision of Coleridge's past, Wordsworth can mask his efforts to negate Coleridge's influence.

It also is important to note the specific context of the address to Coleridge in book 6. The subject matter of the first part of book 6, Wordsworth's time at Cambridge, may account in biographical terms for Wordsworth's confrontation with Coleridge as reader at this point in the narrative. However, biographical coincidence is perhaps just the occasion for more compelling grounds for the placement of this account of Coleridge, in that it immediately precedes the Mont Blanc-Simplon Pass sequence. Given the significance of this sequence in Wordsworth's narrative, it would seem that Wordsworth is, in effect, compelled to address Coleridge and call into question his powers as a reader in order to clear the ground for Wordsworth's own performance and demonstration of reading. A similar strategy is apparent in Wordsworth's final address to the friend in book 13, and it occurs under a similar sign of compulsion.

When Wordsworth takes up the theme of intellectual love in book 13, he addresses himself to the "friends" who have helped him to "complete" himself by guiding him along the path of "intellectual love." This address is meant to mark Wordsworth's attainment, through the ministry of his friends, of this intellectual love and his passage into poetic maturity. However, Wordsworth's representation of Coleridge as his "teacher" in this respect points to a complicated effort to subvert the friend's power over him. After expressing his debt and thankfulness to Dorothy, Wordsworth turns to address Coleridge as the unavoidable object of the line of thought with which he has been proceeding. But rather than expressing his sense of influence unbidden, Wordsworth writes as though under a compulsion:

> With such a theme
> Coleridge—with this my argument—of thee
> Shall I be silent? O most loving soul,
> Placed on this earth to love and understand,
> And from thy presence shed the light of love,

Shall I be mute ere thou be spoken of?
Thy gentle spirit to my heart of hearts
Did also find its way; and thus the life
Of all things and the mighty unity
In all which we behold, and feel, and are,
Admitted more habitually a mild
Interposition, closelier gathering thoughts
Of man and his concerns, such as become
A human creature, be he who he may,
Poet, or destined for a humbler name.

(13.246–60)

It is not a coincidence that this sense of compulsion comes at a moment when Wordsworth is describing an influence that serves to define *The Recluse* project. He is indebted to Coleridge, but the sense of this debt stands as a threat. The expressed compulsion serves to question the value of what Wordsworth owes to Coleridge. Wordsworth's feeling that he owes to Coleridge the development of his sense of community with other human beings, his sense of his own basic humanity, is apparent in this account of Coleridge's influence. But it is this very understanding that generates the uneasiness of Wordsworth's address to the friend, marking it with a sign of compulsion.

The language of teaching in Wordsworth's address to Coleridge, as well as to Dorothy, is meant to account for the way in which "these figures have educated him through the unconscious doctrine of love."[19] It is this love and the memory of shared happiness that Wordsworth suggests will help his friend to know "that the history of a poet's mind / Is labour not unworthy of regard" (13.408–9). Thus Wordsworth states that "the work shall justify itself" to the friend. But Wordsworth's account of the friend's influence is not designed only to represent a fostering and educative process; it also is designed to mark the end of this process, an end that makes Wordsworth distinct from, rather than continuous with, the forces that have influenced him. The language of teaching serves a strategic purpose similar to Wordsworth's re-imagining of Coleridge's youth in book 6. But here, rather than serving to clear the ground for a Wordsworthian scene of reading, it comes after Wordsworth's fullest realization of these powers to produce a text in which to read himself—the Mount Snowdon sequence.

The necessity of marking a difference between himself and Coleridge rather than asserting an equivalent, if not shared, experience is made apparent by Wordsworth's concluding address to Coleridge, which also supplies the concluding lines of the poem as a whole. The difference that Wordsworth marks could be no more distinct; it is the difference between life and death:

> Oh, yet a few short years of useful life,
> And all will be complete—thy race be run,
> Thy monument of glory will be raised.
> Then, though too weak to tread the ways of truth
> This age fall back to old idolatry,
> Though men return to servitude as fast
> As the tide ebbs, to ignominy and shame
> By nations sink together, we shall still
> Find solace in the knowledge which we have,
> Blessed with true happiness if we may be
> United helpers forward of a day
> Of firmer trust, joint labourers in the work—
> Should Providence such grace to us vouchsafe—
> Of their redemption, surely yet to come.
> Prophets of Nature, we to them will speak
> A lasting inspiration, sanctified
> By reason and by truth; what we have loved
> Others will love, and we may teach them how:
> Instruct them how the mind of man becomes
> A thousand times more beautiful than the earth
> On which he dwells, above this frame of things
> (Which, 'mid all revolutions in the hopes
> And fears of men, doth still remain unchanged)
> In beauty exalted, as it is itself
> Of substance and fabric more divine.
>
> (13.428–52)

The monument of glory may indeed be the monument that Coleridge and Wordsworth believe themselves to be erecting through their joint labors as prophets of nature, but Wordsworth's designation of "thy race" and "thy monument" also is quite ominous.[20] The shift from the second person possessive (thy) to the first-person plural (we) unites Coleridge with him in sharing the solace that they, as prophets of nature, find in the knowledge they possess. While the monument may be read as that which

Coleridge himself will raise by the power of his own work, it may be also considered as a monument to Coleridge, and that is why it is designated as his alone. The monument may speak of his glory, but it exists because Coleridge is buried under it, marking the division implicit in Wordsworth's use of the collective "we" to name both Coleridge and himself as "Prophets of Nature." If the monument speaks of Coleridge's glory, it speaks with Wordsworth's voice.[21] In the monumental gesture of this address to Coleridge, Wordsworth is able to accomplish what the ambivalent representations throughout the poem have sought to achieve, a representation of his kinship with Coleridge as difference, a kinship that does not require Coleridge's presence, and in fact requires his absence. In this manner, Wordsworth assures himself that the friend does not have a place either in or outside of the poem from which to speak in his own words. By asserting that they will teach others about the mind of man, Wordsworth is indeed returning to the theme of the philosophical section of *The Recluse*, the work on which Coleridge was to exert so much influence. However, Wordsworth is doing so by projecting a prophecy that, in the terms of the poem, can be "spoken" by Coleridge only from beyond the grave, whereas Wordsworth himself is present not only as the voice of his poem but also as the living poet that, in 1805, Coleridge is not. The 1805 *Prelude* is indeed prophetic, not of the redemption of mankind, but of Coleridge's death both as a poet and a man.[22]

While Wordsworth sees Coleridge as returning from the dead, as it were, he does so with a voice and a power that exist only in being absorbed into the Wordsworthian "we." The monument that Wordsworth raises to Coleridge ensures that he will be present only in the voice that Wordsworth gives him. Yet this is not just a matter of Wordsworth asserting poetic priority; Wordsworth also is attempting to deny Coleridge another role in relation to the poem, the role of the reader who would project his own philosophical concerns into Wordsworth's poetic project. Wordsworth thus disarms any role that Coleridge might play in the poem by having him speak Wordsworth's own prophecy of Nature from beyond the grave, and by making Coleridge, as auditor, one who listens rather than reads.

Coleridge's most immediate response to *The Prelude* comes in his poem "To William Wordsworth," written in 1807 after hearing Wordsworth read his poem. Coleridge offers important evidence that Wordsworth has good reasons to be concerned about whether or not *The Prelude* will justify itself to Coleridge. But "To William Wordsworth" deals primarily with Coleridge's representation of Wordsworth and his work, not with Coleridge's account of himself as "the friend." Rather it is in the appropriately named periodical, *The Friend*, that this account takes form. Coleridge's general conception for the periodical can be traced as far back as a notebook entry in 1804, but his actual work to realize this project begins in 1808.[23] The broad coincidence of Coleridge's production of *The Friend* and Wordsworth's representation of Coleridge as the friend in *The Prelude* is given added force by several other connections between the two works. *The Friend* is clearly not addressed specifically to Wordsworth as is *The Prelude* to Coleridge; nonetheless, Coleridge's general notion of his periodical as a work that will offer sympathetic support and guidance to its readers significantly parallels Wordsworth's expressions of sympathy and support for Coleridge in *The Prelude*. At one level, *The Friend* offers a more general fulfillment of the wish that Wordsworth expresses to Coleridge: a wish for Coleridge to experience "health and the quiet of a healthful mind" accompanied by a desire on Wordsworth's part to have his poem serve as the inspiration for that health (*Prelude* 2.480). But in addition to this general wish, Coleridge's earliest title for his projected work concerns precisely those "subtle speculations" and "toils abstruse" of his that so alarmed Wordsworth (*Prelude* 6.308). This descriptive title of the periodical appears in a letter to Thomas Poole:

Consolations and Comforts from the exercise and right application of the Reason, the Imagination, and the Moral Feelings, addressed especially to those in Sickness, Adversity, or Distress of Mind, *from Speculative Gloom*, etc.[24]

Thus in *The Prelude* and *The Friend*, Wordsworth and Coleridge each assign a significant role in their projects to the sympathetic bond between writer and reader and characterize this bond as one of "friendship." Coleridge's conception of this bond is apparent in his very careful efforts to define the audience to and for whom he writes:

I do not write this Work for the *Multitude* but for those, who by
Rank, or Fortune, or official Situation, or Talents and Habits of
Reflection, are to *influence* the Multitude. I write to found true
PRINCIPLES to oppose false PRINCIPLES, in Criticism, Legislation, Phi-
losophy, Morals, and International Law.[25]

Here Coleridge defines a task that is rather similar to that which
was set out in Wordsworth's image of himself and Coleridge as
prophets of Nature, nothing short of the revitalization of the consciousness of mankind. But there also obviously are certain crucial differences, the first being the shift from the concrete reality
of Nature to the abstract ideals of reason and imagination. But
Coleridge's understanding of his relationship to his readers also
is important here along with the very different sort of audience
that he decides to befriend. While Coleridge writes to guide and
support those who are in positions of influence, Wordsworth
writes to assert himself in the face of a reader whose influence
seems to have reached threatening proportions.

Moreover, Coleridge's means of obtaining his readership for
The Friend was intimately linked to the most concrete workings
of friendship in that he actually called upon his friends in dis-
tributing the prospectus to the periodical and in gathering the
names of the subscribers. The complications of these intimate
connections are quite apparent. There are the more or less pre-
dictable instances of the duplicitousness of friends who express
support and encouragement to Coleridge himself, while expressing doubt about Coleridge and his project to one another. But
these intimate connections become even more complex and
problematic in Wordsworth's case. The reason that Wordsworth
is most prominent among those who profess support while
wholly doubting that Coleridge will succeed is that he is the one
who seems to stand to lose the most by *The Friend's* success
inasmuch as its intellectual project revises and runs counter to
Wordsworth's own designs in representing the growth of his
mind as a poet in *The Prelude*.

Although Southey and Stuart are perhaps no less duplicitous
in their dealings with Coleridge over *The Friend*, it is Wordsworth's sense of the hopelessness of Coleridge's endeavor that
stands out, ringing loudly with the echoes of his account of Coleridge in *The Prelude*. It is not simply that Wordsworth shares
with Coleridge's other friends a doubt in his ability to follow

through on this or any other plan, a weakness that Coleridge himself confesses.[26] Rather, Wordsworth's conviction that Coleridge will fail is so strong that his greatest hope is that the periodical will never begin:

> I am sorry to say that nothing appears to me more desirable than that this periodical should never commence. It is in fact *impossible*—utterly impossible—that he should carry it on; and, therefore, better never begin it; far better, and if begun, the sooner it stops, also the better—the less will be the loss, and not greater the disgrace . . . I give it to you as my deliberate opinion, formed upon proofs that have been strengthening for years, that he neither will nor can execute anything of important benefit either to himself his family or mankind.[27]

So much for Coleridge as a prophet of nature. Certainly there had been any number of strains on their friendship that might account for Wordsworth's utter despair of Coleridge's success in contrast to his expressions of sympathy, debt, and friendship in *The Prelude*.[28] At the same time, there can be no more clear example of what Wordsworth calls in *The Prelude* "the insinuated scoff of coward tongues / And all that silent language which so oft / In conversation between man and man / Blots from the human countenance all trace / Of beauty and of love" (2.471–75). Although Wordsworth asserts in *The Prelude* that he is not apprehensive of any contempt from the friend, the grounds for his apprehension that such silent language might be the friend's response to the poem become all the more apparent in light of his own contempt for *The Friend*.

How do these personal and biographical issues figure in *The Prelude* and in the project of *The Friend* itself? Wordsworth's disdain for and apparent anxiety over *The Friend* would seem not to be simply the result of his having lost patience with Coleridge's failures, or even of the overwhelming sense of the toll that these failures had taken on Coleridge and those who loved him. Wordsworth's response has at least a partial source in the fact that Coleridge's design for *The Friend* embodies the "insinuated scoff" and "silent language" which cause Wordsworth such anxiety in *The Prelude*. In this respect, *The Friend* and Coleridge's plans for it run parallel to those he made for Wordsworth's projected work, *The Recluse*. It is, in effect, Coleridge's rendering of many of the issues, if not ideas, that would have found a place in the "philosophical section" of *The Recluse* never written by Wordsworth.

The epigraph to the first number of *The Friend* identifies it as a project that has a strong bearing on Wordsworth's "history of a poet's mind" and the question as to whether or not the writing of such a history is "worthwhile labour." Coleridge presents a quotation from Petrarch as a definition of his own aim in publishing *The Friend*:

> I . . . aim not so much to prescribe a Law for others, as to set forth the Law of my own mind; which let the man, who shall approve of it abide by; and let him, to whom it shall appear not reasonable, reject it. It is my earnest wish, I confess, to employ my understanding and acquirements in the mode and direction, in which I may be enabled to benefit the largest number possible of my fellow creatures. (Friend 2:5)[29]

This epigraph indicates that Coleridge is writing his own version of *The Prelude*, but with important distinctions. Rather than presenting the history of a poet's mind, the worth of which is initially defined by Wordsworth in terms of its value as a "subsidiary" to the preparation for writing another work and subsequently in terms of its value in itself, Coleridge's work is to offer laws and precepts as a guide to his fellow men. Coleridge's work then also is the sort of project for which *The Prelude* served as Wordsworth's preparation. In effect, it would seem that Coleridge did not see his designs fulfilled in Wordsworth's poetry and proceeded in *The Friend* to realize that design in his own philosophical terms. Were Coleridge's plan to succeed, it would therefore imply Wordsworth's own failure to achieve the poetic realization of Coleridge's design.

While *The Friend* represents the completion of an unrealized endeavor of Wordsworth's, it also represents many qualities and habits of mind that Wordsworth rejected in *The Prelude* as being inimical to his own growth and development as a poet, the very qualities with which he associates Coleridge. The first number of *The Friend* consists of Coleridge's justification of his own endeavor, and this justification centers on just these qualities:

> It is my object to refer men to PRINCIPLES in all things; in Literature, in the Fine Arts, in Morals, in Legislation, in Religion. Whatever

therefore of a political nature may be reduced to general Principles, necessarily indeed dependent on the circumstances of a Nation internal and external, yet not especially connected with this year or the preceeding—this I do not exclude from my scheme. (*Friend* 2:13)

In great part, this justification is a defense against what Coleridge represented as the erroneous judgments of the radical nature of his politics.[30] While this focus on "whatever . . . of a political nature may be reduced to general principles" is pointed in a very different direction than the Godwinian rationalism that both Wordsworth and Coleridge had repudiated, it still carries with it the echoes of the project that led Wordsworth to despair in his efforts to determine abstract rules of reason and to apply them to all matters of judgment (*Prelude* 10.890–901). Coleridge's justification also defines the work of *The Friend* in terms that closely parallel the "hard task" of analyzing the soul which Wordsworth, in *The Prelude*, had suggested might be within the range of Coleridge's power, but had nonetheless deemed an impossibility. Coleridge's elucidation of principles in setting forth the law of his own mind is exactly the parcelling out of intellect by geometric rules and the dragging of "all passions, notions, shapes of faith, / Like culprits to the bar" that Wordsworth is at the very least suspicious of in Coleridge and rejects as error in himself. I am not suggesting that Coleridge is embracing the Godwinian rationalism that Wordsworth (as well as Coleridge) represented himself as rejecting. Rather, I am focusing on a procedure of inquiry that in itself, regardless of the political motives or philosophical position informing it, was seen by Wordsworth as threatening.

In the second number of *The Friend*, one can almost hear the direct address to Wordsworth when Coleridge attempts to anticipate his readers' apprehension:

May I not hope for a candid interpretation of my motive, if I again recur to the possible apprehension, on the part of my readers that The Friend
"O'erlaid with Black, staid Wisdom's Hue"
with an eye fixed in abstruse research and brow of perpetual Wrinkle is to frown away the light-hearted Graces, and "unreproved Pleasures"; or invite his Guests to a dinner of herbs in a Hermits Cell? if I affirm, that my Plan does not in itself exclude either impassioned

style or interesting Narrative, Tale, or Allegory, or Anecdote. (Friend 2:30)

Although Wordsworth may project onto Coleridge a need for an "influence benign" to chase away "the airy wretchedness" induced by "toils abstruse" (Prelude 6.309, 329–30), it is clear that Coleridge would not choose to submit to the remedy, which indeed he asserts is unnecessary.

Finally, as a model and guide setting forth the law of its own mind, The Friend embodies the very threat to Wordsworth's history of his own mind that leads him to reject that law in The Prelude. For one of the important elements of the law of The Friend's own mind is the law of reading. In setting forth his plan for The Friend, Coleridge is continually concerned with its relationship with and reception by its readers. He feels that The Friend will obtain its best reception not because its readers accept its presentation unquestioningly, but because they are in fact highly critical and refined readers, and indeed are themselves "friends." In his effort to "win the more on" his "learned and critical Readers" Coleridge presents this law for readers that he identifies as a quotation from Erasmus:

> A reader should sit down to a book, especially of a miscellaneous kind, as a well-behaved visitor does to a banquet. The master of the feast exerts himself to satisfy all his guests; but if after all his care and pains there should be still something or other that does not suit this or that person's taste, they politely pass it over without noticing the circumstance, and commend other dishes, that they may not distress their kind host, or throw any damp on his spirits. For who could tolerate a guest that accepted an invitation to your table with no other purpose but that of finding fault with everything put before him, neither eating himself or suffering others to eat in comfort. And yet you may fall in with a still worse set than even these, with churls that in all companies and without stop or stay, will condemn and pull to pieces a work which they have never read. But this sinks below the baseness of an Informer yea, though he were a false witness to boot![31]

Coleridge is, as usual, grinding his axe against anonymous reviewers and his sense of their deplorable practices, and they are the object of his invective against "churls," but the characterization of the proper guest points both toward The Friend and its readers. Coleridge imagines that *The Friend* exists as a dialogue of readers. *The Friend* reads the law of his own mind in the biography of his sentiments (2:9), and the subscribers are the polite guests who in their own reading of *The Friend* savor and reflect upon or pass by that which displeases them in anticipation of the next "dish" that will be presented (with the assurance that they will not have to endure "a dry dinner of herbs in a Hermit's Cell"). It is in this exchange of reading that Coleridge believes he will "win on" his readers:

> I perceived . . . in a periodical Essay the most likely Means of winning, instead of forcing my Way. Supposing Truth on my Side, the Shock of the first Day might be so far lessened by Reflections of the succeeding days, as to procure for my next Week's Essay a less hostile Reception, than it would have met with, had it only been the next Chapter of a present volume. (*Friend* 2.17)

It is in this sense that Coleridge, in *The Friend*, envisions himself as engaging in the very sort of dialogue that Wordsworth seems anxious to close off in *The Prelude*.

In his poem, Wordsworth requires and constructs "the friend" to be a listener who sits silently and submits, and who must do so because the poem offers no opening for any sort of critical exchange. And in effect, Wordsworth's anxiety over Coleridge as a reader is that he will or has become the very sort of fault-finding guest, described by Coleridge in *The Friend*, who destroys all comfort.[32] Indeed, Wordsworth's efforts to block Coleridge's activities as a reader are motivated by an anxiety that Coleridge, in reading his own designs into Wordsworth's poetry and thereby failing to read what Wordsworth has indeed written, can very easily take on the role of the churl who pulls apart what he has never "read." But primarily Wordsworth sees Coleridge as a bad guest because of his insistence on responding to Wordsworth's writings in precisely the way that Coleridge imagines that the readers of *The Friend* should respond to it: seeing the work as an ongoing process in which the reader is himself engaged. It is not, however, that Coleridge is not equally committed to disarming the objections of his readers as is Wordsworth; both seek with equal force to "win" their way. Each wants his audience to be silent, but Wordsworth designs that silence as the negation of a threatening reader's presence, while Coleridge designs it as a space for reading and reflection. Certainly Coleridge's empowering of the readers of *The Friend* gives him much the same authority over the reader that Wordsworth seeks to gain by silencing the reader in *The Prelude*.[33] But it is because Coleridge will not accept Wordsworth's account of reading as silence that Coleridge is able to construct a place for himself (other than the monument to him that Wordsworth erects) in his "reading" of *The Prelude*.

The role of friend and reader that Coleridge assumes in his poem "To William Wordsworth" fulfills the aim of Coleridge's project as "reader" that *The Friend* represents. In his poem's response to *The Prelude*, Coleridge does recognize, and almost seems to embrace, the dissolution that Wordsworth figures for him. In calling Wordsworth a "teacher" and Wordsworth's poems a "prophetic lay," Coleridge does accept, to a degree, the language that Wordsworth's poem gives to him. Coleridge even adopts Wordsworth's imagery of the grave and applies it to himself, speaking of his own genius and knowledge as flowers "Strewed on [his] corse, and borne upon [his] bier" (74). However, in embracing this language, Coleridge does something more and other than acknowledge Wordsworth's achievement. He may see himself in the grave, but he also manages to raise something of a monument over Wordsworth, whom Coleridge envisions in a perhaps all-too-angelic "choir / Of ever-enduring men" (49–50). Despite his expression of humility, Coleridge refuses to remain in the passive role of auditor. Rather than conversing in the "silent language" of which Wordsworth was apprehensive, Coleridge seems to adopt the very language that Wordsworth has worked so hard to disarm, thus accomplishing a subtle re-reading of Wordsworth's doctrine, and of *The Prelude* itself.[34] Coleridge's reading in his own poem of *The Prelude* and of his relationship to Wordsworth points out why Wordsworth's self-representation requires the negation of Coleridge's presence. Coleridge will only go so far with the words that Wordsworth gives him, and the break is readily apparent in the poem's revision of Wordsworth's phrase from the "Intimations" ode that refers to "thoughts . . . too deep for tears." Coleridge's allusive revision reads: "thoughts . . . too deep for words." In this subtle but explicit revision Coleridge asserts that words rather than tears, be they adequate to the task or not, are the proper measure of the depth of thought. Considering the importance of Wordsworth's ode in his own aesthetic project, this revision is all the more strategic. In the ode Wordsworth represents a problematic aesthetic negotiation in a world of thoughts represented as deeply felt and seemingly inexpressible emotions. But in Coleridge's rendering this negotiation takes place not in the realm of emotions, but in words, which Wordsworth would see as pushing dangerously close to mistaking "words for things."[35] Also, as William Galperin has pointed out, Coleridge suggests that the authentication of Wordsworth's greatness may finally be beyond utterance, beyond the powers of even the greatest poet—"too deep for words"—thus only to be realized by the one in whom these thoughts are inspired, the reader.[36]

In the very process of praising Wordsworth's poem and his poetic power, Coleridge continues to project his own philosophical concerns onto and into the language of Wordsworth's poetry. An even more marked re-reading is apparent in Coleridge's recounting of a time in Wordsworth's narrative "when power streamed from thee, and thy soul received / The light reflected as a light bestowed" (18–19). Wordsworth's account of the poetic imagination does recognize the necessary and important distinctions between the powers of imagination and of Nature, and one point of Wordsworth's narrative is to delineate his own movement away from being subject to the power of "a light bestowed." But Wordsworth also deliberately chooses not to designate the "light" of his poetic power as being exclusively either reflected or bestowed. Thus, if Coleridge is not going so far as to correct Wordsworth's account of the nature of the poetic imagination, he is at least using a terminology that Wordsworth himself chose not to use. Despite Wordsworth's efforts to deny him an active role in *The Prelude*, Coleridge will not relinquish his role as "friend," a role that he interprets specifically as that of an active reader who brings his own language to bear on the text that he reads.

In addition to engaging in an active reading of Wordsworth's poem, Coleridge also subverts the silence that Wordsworth attempts to impose on him. Although Coleridge writes that as Wordsworth reads his poem, he is a silent listener, "like a devout child" (95), this passivity is not his final stance. At the end of Wordsworth's reading of his poem, as Coleridge represents it, Coleridge suddenly turns from his passive stance:

> I sate, my being blended in one thought
> (Thought was it? or aspiration? or resolve?)
> Absorbed, yet hanging still upon the sound—
> And when I rose, I found myself in prayer.
>
> (109–12)

At the very least one may suggest, as does Walter Jackson Bate, that "the prayer probably includes a prayer to rival the friend."[37] Although Coleridge asserts that he is "absorbed" and his prayer might be considered a prayer of praise inspired by Wordsworth's poem, Coleridge deliberately leaves that question open with his own parenthetical set of questions and opens up the possibility that the posture of prayer can serve to shift the power of Wordsworth's poetry into Coleridge's poem. In this sense, Wordsworth's language may become the vehicle of Coleridge's own philosophical project. In this posture of prayer, Coleridge assumes the stance that the end of *The Prelude* insists upon taking away from him; rather than coming from beyond the grave and through the voice of another, his "voice" is that of a contemporary reader who generates the text of his own poem out of his reading of Wordsworth's poem.

By assuming the posture of just such an active reader, we are able to read more accurately the implications of Wordsworth's "justification." Wordsworth's poem can justify itself and present itself as justification only to the figure of Coleridge that Wordsworth buries under the monument that he erects as a sign of Coleridge's absence. Wordsworth's need to construct a monument that negates Coleridge's presence in the poem marks Wordsworth's justification as a vindication necessary to establish his own power and presence in the poem. And it also marks the significant difference in Coleridge and Wordsworth's parallel, but different, projects of producing the self in writing. Each are focused on the power of reading and its role in confronting the autobiographical predicament of writing. However, the differing accounts of the writer's relationship to the reader offer us an insight into the two different sorts of imaginative projects that Wordsworth and Coleridge pursue.

At this point it is possible to offer a brief summary of the nature of these projects. Confronted with the autobiographical predicament of writing, Wordsworth chooses to make that very predicament the center of his strategy of producing the self in writing, to inscribe the differential character of writing into a performance of reading in and through writing. The necessary element in this performance of reading is that Wordsworth stands as master-reader while all others occupy the role of auditor. Indeed, the power of Wordsworth's poetry derives from his ability to confront the threat to the self that *is* writing, without repressing or denying the reality of that threat and even making that threat the very center of his strategy of writing the self. As I have suggested above, Coleridge confronts the same predicament, but from an entirely different angle. Whereas Wordsworth sought to harness the power of the differential text in becoming the master-reader of his own text, Coleridge, in his fascination with the seemingly unmasterable character of the text, tried to align himself with that very power of textuality, in effect, figuring himself as textuality itself. Wordsworth sought to construct an unassailable reading of the self, the power of which was made available to his readers in their assent to that reading. Coleridge's goal, on the other hand, was that of teaching others to read actively and properly, and thus of writing himself as the master-teacher of reading.

5

The Sense of Before and After

Based on the majority of critical estimations, *The Prelude* stands as the model of Romantic autobiography. However, there is a certain irony, if not appropriateness, to the fact that Wordsworth's concerns in composing *The Prelude* were not primarily autobiographical. He begins the poem as a preliminary to or substitute for another work, showing much more concern for proceeding with the *Recluse* project than with constructing an autobiographical record.[1] On the other hand, Coleridge's explicit efforts to write an autobiography in the *Biographia Literaria* are most often met with embarrassment, apology, or rejection when it comes to making the claim that this work is an autobiography or even, in some sense of the word, a book. Indeed, in analyzing the *Biographia* as an autobiography one has to confront and engage in the debate that swirls around that text with regard to its unity, or lack thereof, its plagiarisms, and all of its numerous "errancies," be they literary, compositional, or even ethical.[2]

Perhaps the most productive approach to this problem has been given to us by Jerome Christensen in his account of Coleridge's "marginal method" in the *Biographia*.[3] This notion of a marginal method, whereby Coleridge "annexes [a text] into his manuscript to supply a sustaining text that he can cover with marginalia,"[4] is especially useful in helping us to recognize the strategies that produce the de-centered text of the divided subject of autobiography. By bringing to bear the implications of post-structuralist theories of subjectivity and textuality on Coleridge's effort to represent himself in the *Biographia*, Christensen points us toward the way in which the traditional paradigms used in analyzing autobiographical writing must be re-thought in light of these theories. But Christensen's work can be frustrating to someone who wishes to grapple with the status of the *Biographia* as an autobiography. Christensen's exploration of the "literary life of a man of letters" lays out all of the terms for examining the *Biographia* as an autobiography, but continually chooses to deal with the question of genre by answering it in the negative. Christensen then proceeds to offer a formulation for the status of Coleridge's literary life that takes us into a textual territory where questions of genre and unity and of authenticity are themselves the "subject" of the text rather than Coleridge's own life. This territory is certainly the proper site for examining Coleridge's self-construction of his "literary life," but I would argue that this territory is, in spite of Christensen's assertion to the negative, most properly called autobiographical. And it is Christensen's own negation of the *Biographia's* status as an autobiography, which is based upon traditional definitions of the unitary status of autobiographical narrative, that can be used to establish its propriety as such.[5] Christensen states that, for Coleridge, the *Biographia* is:

> not an autobiography, the literary life is a propadeutic toward one. . . . Coleridge's text is poised over the question of whether he can be the author of a life or must remain the writer in a biographia literaria, existing to himself and his reader only by records in himself not found.[6]

It would seem that in the terms in which I have begun to define it, autobiography necessarily is, always, just that, a propadeutic toward itself: a preliminary to and a lesson in, for both the writer and the reader, the art or method of producing itself.

In this light, it seems that the most productive procedure with which to begin reading Coleridge's autobiographical lesson is to center on those disruptions and displacements that occur in Coleridge's narrative and which have proven so worrisome to critics who address the status of the *Biographia* as an autobiography. Many of these worries center around the seemingly haphazard compositional history of the work: its beginnings as a preface to *Sibylline Leaves*, its subsequent expansion into a "book," its misfortunes with publishers, and its final "padding out" with previously published material in order to make it into a neatly proportioned set of volumes.[7] These matters most often lead to a seemingly endless critical debate over the integrity of the *Biographia* as a coherent and complete work, yet the desire to prove or disprove the coherence of the work as an autobiography prompts critics to overlook many aspects of the work that are integral components of its status as autobiography. The question of coherence leads us in the wrong direction because it is the disruptions and discontinuities of the narrative that constitute its most prominent autobiographical features.

One of the important insights that the apparently haphazard manner of the *Biographia's* composition can offer us is an understanding of how the work, as an autobiography, is always about the process of its own composition. But unlike an autobiography such as Wordsworth's *Prelude*, in which the process of the poem's composition takes its guide from the narrative trajectory of Wordsworth's poetic development, Coleridge's "life of letters" seeks to read the text of his life rather than simply constructing it in a retrospective narrative. In this regard, the beginnings of the *Biographia* as a preface could not be more appropriate. The preface is that which precedes a work when published, but which, in terms of its function, can be written only after the work is completed. Thus, that which precedes must almost always come after.[8] Just as the preface must always maintain the illusion of coming before, the autobiography must maintain the illusion of being a closed form, although the necessary dramatization of the act of its own composition belies its formal gesture toward completion. By its very nature, autobiography must attempt to give an account of a life that is not yet completed and for which the author cannot, therefore, be fully accountable.[9] The composition of an autobiography, then, involves a double gesture: that made toward completion, and that which must belie the possibility of completion, and thus the most proper and "complete" story that an autobiography tells is the story of its own composition.[10] It is in much the same sense that a preface tells the story of the composition of the text which follows it, and thus Coleridge's commencement of the *Biographia* as a preface could not offer a more appropriate beginning for an autobiography.

Making so much of these complications of composition and publication does involve us in trying to make a virtue of Coleridge's failings, but that itself is what Coleridge's autobiographical narrative seeks to do, particularly with regard to his accounts of his own publishing career. In the many pages that Coleridge devotes to accounts of his own publications, he most often does so under the guise of advice to those who would become authors.[11] These accounts are very much a part of a process of self-justification. The double gesture of composing an autobiography operates in that Coleridge offers himself as a negative example—what those who would becomes authors should not become—while at the same time presenting the "authentic" history of his publishing career. In authoring this history, Coleridge establishes himself as the author who had not been fully "present" because of the complications and misrepresentations inherent in the process of publication. Even so, these efforts to make himself present in the *Biographia* are being formed by the demands of publishers and by the demands of "the book." In the *Biographia* these conflicting demands and pressures are complexly articulated. Coleridge's self-produced pressure to make himself present in his work in the manner in which he desires to be read is equally bound up and at odds with the publishers' pressures to produce the sort of work they are demanding. The work is one that is shaped by conflicting drives, and the conflicts involved in this process of self-representation offer an emblem for all of Coleridge's autobiographical writings and perhaps for the genre of autobiography itself.

It is Coleridge who offers us the clues as to where to begin grappling with the status of the *Biographia* in that Coleridge himself struggles to define and re-define just what it is that he is writing. There is little doubt that in some sense we must recognize an element of autobiographical narrative in the work, but the *Biographia* also is a work of practical literary criticism (particularly in its account of Wordsworth's poetry) as well as being a theoretical/philosophical work about the nature of poetry and poetic experience in general. All of these different definitions of the *Biographia* can be resolved under the label that has been used to construct some widely varied critical accounts of the work by critics who adopt Coleridge's term, a "literary life."[12] But Coleridge's understanding of this term does not simply place the *Biographia* in some hybrid subcategory of autobiography, literary criticism, and theory. A critical focus on such a hybrid category most often leads not to a consideration of how all of these genres are brought into productive conjunction, but rather to the setting up of a hierarchical order which places the critical, the theoretical, or the autobiographical in the premier place in the hierarchy. Rather than choosing one of these modes of writing as the key to reading the *Biographia*, I focus on their intersection and examine Coleridge's autobiography as an example of the way in which all autobiographical writing is necessarily a "literary life." In Christensen's terms, the autobiographer always is someone who exists "to himself and to his reader only by records in himself not found."[13]

Coleridge's own references to the generic status of the *Biographia* offer us an insight into the nature of the literary life that is autobiography. In his subtitle, Coleridge designates the *Biographia* as "biographical sketches of my literary life and opinions." Here it would seem that neither the biographical nor the literary life nor opinions takes precedence, and the implication is that the biographical sketch, with its preliminary and "sketchy" character, is a form which can bring into an illustrative conjunction the elements of a literary life and literary opinions. In a notebook entry of 1803 (one of the first references to the project that would become the *Biographia*), Coleridge announced the intention to write "my metaphysical life as *my Life* & *in* my life."[14] Thus for Coleridge, the writing of what he calls an "autobiographia" is not a matter of writing down the records that are to be found in himself. It is a matter of composing a work that exists *as* his life and exists *in* his life. The life and the work do not exist as separate entities. Coleridge clearly seeks to write a "life," but the question still remains as to what kind of life that might be.

This question echoes all the more loudly in that Coleridge himself distinguishes between the life he has written and what he has not written. In his concluding chapter, Coleridge makes a point (clearly disingenuous) of his having left out matters of personal justification, complaint, or explanation, particularly with regard to what he sees as the causes for the delay in publishing the *Biographia*. Coleridge attests to the "eventful" nature of his personal history by noting that he does so in spite of a warning example of the author of an "Auto-biography" who calls "eventful" a life that Coleridge finds "as meagre in incident as it is well possible for the Life and Individual to be." As to the possibility of writing his own autobiography, Coleridge says:

> Yet when, not withstanding this warning example of Self-importance before me, I review my own life, I cannot refrain from applying the same epithet [eventful] to it, and with more than ordinary emphasis—and no private feeling, that affected myself only, should prevent

me from *publishing* the same (for to *write* it I assuredly shall, should life and leisure be granted me). (*Biographia*, 2:237)

This expression of the intention to write an account of his personal life would apparently indicate that Coleridge did not consider the *Biographia* an autobiography, at least in the sense of an autobiography being a narration of the events of a life.[15] But his subtitle indicates that while he may not be narrating the events of his personal life, he is presenting "biographical sketches" of his literary life and opinions, giving biographical form to the "literary" life, and presenting his opinions as events: his metaphysical work *as* his life and *in* his life. Although there is an autobiography that Coleridge doesn't write (the narration of the events of his personal life), his not having written this work does not make the *Biographia*, as a narration of the events of his literary life, any less, in its own terms, an autobiography. Indeed, the decision to construct his literary life and opinions in a biographical form indicates that this form is of specific import in accounting for that life and conveying those opinions.

At one level, Coleridge's choice of the biographical form can be attributed to a very straightforward desire to take advantage of the ordering principles of narrative. Coleridge can locate and give eventful substance to abstract opinions and principles by assigning to them a "sense of Before and After," a developmental narrative. In the first paragraphs of the *Biographia*, Coleridge explains his use of the biographical sketch as a narrative form to represent his "literary life and opinions" by saying that:

I have used the narration chiefly for the purpose of giving continuity to the work, in part for the sake of the miscellaneous reflections suggested to me by the particular events, but still more as introductory to the statement of my principles in Politics, Religion, and Philosophy, and the application of the rules, deduced from philosophical principles, to poetry and criticism. (1:5)

According to these terms, it seems that Coleridge's choice of a biographical form and its narrative frame is simply that: a formal choice that gives continuity to that which is of primary concern, the presentation and application of principles. The narrative is the pretext for this primary text; the literary life is the pretext of the text of literary opinions. However, as Coleridge concludes his narrative, it becomes apparent (as indeed it does throughout the work) that the continuity that the narrative gives to the statement and application of principles is equally a demonstration of those principles.

In his final chapter and in his typically convoluted style, Coleridge offers an explanation of the function of explanations, even while he says that there are certain explanations from which he refrains. In justifying the explanations of his own behavior and opinions that he has offered in the course of the narrative, he speaks of the consolation that is to be had from an understanding and expression of the relation between the causation of faults and the punishment for them. Such comfort is something that, in his case, he believes has been denied him in being punished by incidents that his own faults had no part in causing.

> It sometimes happens that we are punished for our faults by incidents, in the causation of which these faults had no share: and this I have always felt the severest punishment. The wound indeed is of the same dimensions; but the edges are jagged, and there is a dull underpain that survives the smart which it had aggravated. For there is always a consolatory feeling that accompanies the sense of a proportion between antecedents and consequents. The sense of Before and After becomes both intelligible and intellectual when, and *only* when, we contemplate the succession in the relations of Cause and Effect, which like the poles of the magnet manifest the being and unity of the one power by relative opposites, and give, as it were, a substratum of permanence, of identity, and therefore of reality, to the shadowy flux of Time. It is Eternity revealing itself in the phænomenon of Time: and the perception and acknowledgment of the proportionality and appropriateness of the Present to the Past, prove to the afflicted Soul, that it has not yet been deprived of the sight of God, that it can still recognize the effective presence of a Father, though through a darkened glass and turbid atmosphere, though of a Father chastising it. And for this cause, doubtless, are we so framed in mind, and even so organized in brain and nerve, that all confusion is painful. (*Biographia*, 2:234)

The sense of before and after then is the sense of continuity given by narrative, but that continuity, to Coleridge's mind, both manifests and participates in "a substratum of permanence, of identity, and therefore of reality." In this justification, Coleridge invokes many of the traditional motives and motifs of autobiography. He sees the narrative record as something that will give permanence and reality to the shadowy flux of time, and he goes so far as to allude to the ultimate model of confessional/ autobiographical writing in his allusion to Augustine's "through a glass darkly."[16] Thus we go from an initially formal justification for the use of narrative (for the purposes of . . . continuity) to the notion that narrative provides a grounding in reality that would seem not to be available even in experience itself.

What is important to note in these two rather different explanations of the goal of Coleridge's use of a narrative form is the possibility that Coleridge's "statement of [his] principles in Politics, Religion, and Philosophy," for which the narrative seems simply to provide a vehicle, is to be, in itself, the means of giving, "as it were, a substratum of permanence and identity, and therefore of reality, to the shadowy flux of time." In Coleridge's notion of a "sense of Before and After" the revelatory power of narrative and of the presentation of "principles" are combined. In constructing a "sense of Before and After" in his narrative, Coleridge thus truly gives us his "metaphysical life *as* [his] life and *in* [his] life."

In order to understand more fully how it is that Coleridge's autobiographical narrative and the statement of his principles can be said to coincide, one must turn to the specific qualities of autobiographical narrative that Coleridge might see as being so amenable to the statement of his principles. This understanding is to be found in Coleridge's efforts to resolve the contradictions inherent in the genre of autobiography itself. While Coleridge claims to have presented a conventional narrative, clearly he has not, and the "proportionality and appropriateness of Past to Present" that he seeks to present in his narrative are indeed fabricated rather than perceived.[17] But it must be noted that such fabrication is the status of autobiography itself, a narrative which cannot "conclude" as do conventional narratives, but indeed must simply end. In this regard, we might conclude that Coleridge does no more or no less than every autobiographer in trying to close a narrative in which he can never write the last word. But Coleridge's fabrication of an ending goes farther than a mere sleight of hand that tries to figure resolution in the face of undeniable confusion. He cannot write the last word of his narrative, but he can figure a place in the text in which the reader might properly "read" that word that Coleridge himself cannot write.

It would seem to be no coincidence that Coleridge's figuring of the reading of this "word" is presented in the context of another instance in which he distinguishes between his "personal life" and his literary life. But rather than provide yet more evidence that the *Biographia* is something other than an autobiography, this distinction points out the way in which our own critical efforts to ground Romantic autobiography, to isolate it, in some unique realm of the "personal" have led us away from an understanding of autobiography precisely as a "literary" life. Coleridge both makes and dissolves the distinction between a personal and literary life when considering that the object of his writing is directed toward a particular audience:

> This has been my Object, and this alone can be my Defence—and O! that with this my personal as well as my LITERARY LIFE might conclude! the unquenched desire I mean, not without consciousness of having earnestly endeavored to kindle young minds, and to guard them against the temptation of Scorners.[18] (*Biographia*, 2:247)

Certainly Coleridge engages here in the usual defense of the autobiographer, claiming that he is not motivated to write his life by self-interest, but hopes that his narrative will be of benefit to others. This claim is all the more defensive for Coleridge in that he has sought to correct the errant accounts of him that he believes have been constructed by others. However, the element of this defense that affords us an insight into Coleridge's formulation of the literary life lies in its sense of what the "young minds" may do or be capable of doing having been "kindled" by Coleridge's endeavor to fulfill his desire. Coleridge hopes to have given these young minds the evidence that will affirm their faith in the "scheme of Christianity" by showing that faith is but the continuation of reason. Coleridge's image of this continuity between faith and reason is the image of the continuity of day into night:

> The Day softens away into sweet Twilight, and Twilight, hushed and breathless, steals into the Darkness. It is Night, sacred Night! the upraised Eye views only the starry Heaven which manifests itself alone: and the outward Beholding is fixed on the sparks twinkling

in the aweful depth, though Suns of other Worlds, only to preserve
the Soul steady and collected in its pure *Act* of inward Adoration to
the great I AM, and to the filial Word that re-affirmeth it from Eternity to Eternity, whose choral Echo is the Universe. (*Biographia*,
2:247–48)

In placing a description of this "pure act of inward adoration"
in the context of his desire to kindle young minds, Coleridge is
not simply silencing the text in a sublime monument of words.[19]
Rather he is presenting a figure which the young mind must
read, and the pure act of inward adoration is not the silence that
is the ending (rather than the conclusion) of the text, but the
silence that opens up the space for the "inward act" of reading.

This is not a space that is simply opened to the freeplay of
the reader. Coleridge provides a space in which the reader, in
accordance with a specified framework, is to bring Coleridge's
literary life to the conclusion that he cannot write. His efforts to
contain this space and to make the reading of his life into a
proper account of himself operate within the more or less clear
framework that is apparent in Coleridge's attention to the notion
of the proper and productive reading of "history" in general.[20]

That Coleridge's discussion of what constitutes "authentic history" should emerge in the context of his chapter (10) on his
opinions in religion and politics is both ironically appropriate
and convenient. In his efforts to represent himself as being entirely consistent in his political positions, Coleridge explains
how it was that he arrived at his judgments of political events,
particularly in his writing for the *Morning Post* and the *Courier*:

On every great occurrence I endevoured to discover in past history
the event, that most nearly resembled it. I procured, wherever it was
possible, the contemporary historians, memorialists, and pamphlet-
eers. Then fairly subtracting the points of difference from those of
likeness, as the balance favored the former or the latter, I conjectured
that the result would be the same or different. (*Biographia*, 1:218)

In making claims as to the accuracy and appropriateness of his
analysis of "great occurrences," Coleridge nonetheless cannot
refrain from defending himself against the charge of defensiveness. He says that he mentions instances when he believed
his judgments to be correct:

from the full persuasion that, armed with the two-fold knowledge of history and the human mind, a man will scarcely err in his judgement concerning the sum total of any future national event, if he have been able to procure the original documents of the past together with authentic accounts of the present, and if he have a philosophical tact for what is truly important in facts, and in most instances therefore for such facts as the DIGNITY OF HISTORY has excluded from the volumes of our modern compilers, by the courtesy of the age entitled historians.[21] (Biographia, 1:219)

In the Biographia Coleridge attempts both to demonstrate and to represent a kind of authentic history that will represent the authentic temporal predicament of the author, while at the same time transforming that predicament so as to render it a form of self-knowledge that need not be negative.[22] This demonstration and representation may be characterized in terms of a process of reading. The "authentic account" is produced by a process of selection that involves what Coleridge calls a "philosophical tact for what is truly important in facts" (Biographia, 1:219), what in effect constitutes a critical "reading" of the facts.[23] The strategies of reading involved in such a philosophical tact confront the series of disruptions and displacements that constitute "authentic temporality," but rather than simply make a coherent account of these disruptions, Coleridge himself uses strategies of displacement and disruption that are designed to provide a lesson in reading, in the construction of an authentic history. Thus autobiographical writing is practiced as a propadeutic toward itself, not because Coleridge is unable to present a "true" account of himself, but because authenticity cannot be found in the facts of his life, or at least those facts that have been "tactlessly" read by others, but in the reading of them that he both performs and demonstrates.[24] This lesson in reading with philosophical tact follows the same form as that lesson with which Coleridge hopes to "kindle young minds," and which he sees as the object of his writing of his literary life. In the affirmation that faith is but the continuation of reason, "the upraised Eye views only the starry Heaven . . . the outward Beholding is fixed on the sparks twinkling in the aweful depths . . . only to preserve the Soul steady and collected." In the act of reading with philosophical tact, the "outward Beholding" is fixed upon "original documents" and "authentic accounts of the present" in order "to preserve the Soul steady and collected in its pure *Act* of inward Adoration . . . to the filial WORD," the act of producing an authentic history that demonstrates the reading process whereby it was constructed, and by which the truth that is not found within its author is to be discovered.

Having asserted that the *Biographia* is perhaps most authentically autobiographical at the moments when narrative disruptions undermine the narrative coherence conventionally associated with autobiographical writing, there is some appropriateness in turning to a chapter of that work that Coleridge himself considered digressive. Coleridge's subtitle for chapter 10 identifies it as:

> A chapter of digressions and anecdotes, as an interlude preceding that on the nature and genesis of the imagination or plastic power—On pedantry and pedantic expressions—Advice to young authors respecting publication—Various anecdotes of the author's literary life, and the progress of his opinions and politics. (*Biographia*, 1:168)

In giving the chapter the status of an interlude, Coleridge indicates that it represents a break or change in the nature of the presentation, but he also affirms that the digressions and anecdotes have a coherence in and of themselves, that of a dramatic or musical interlude. The apparent digressiveness of the chapter constitutes a strategic design in Coleridge's construction of his literary life.

Chapter 10 of the *Biographia* narrates a crucial phase in Coleridge's life as a "man of letters" and in doing so approximates with relative fidelity the conventions of traditional autobiographical narrative. However, Coleridge adapts and transforms the autobiographical form to establish a specific form of textual authority over his literary life. The most recent editors of the *Biographia* suggest that this chapter "may have been an abortive or false start on what finally became Chapter 13" and that "the digressionary nature of Chapter 10 would then not have been planned deliberately" (*Biographia*, 1:168n). Given what we know about Coleridge's habits of composition, this evaluation of chapter 10 is not hard to accept. However, regardless of whether or not the digressive nature of the chapter was planned, we are still left with what it accomplishes as a narrative, which is something much more than just filling up pages or diverting Coleridge from the chapter on the Imagination which he finds so difficult to write. Although chapter 10 is indeed digressive, it nonetheless has a discernible narrative thread that is quite significant to the overall project of the *Biographia*. Coleridge's acknowledgment of the chapter's digressive nature may thus be seen as indicative of a strategy in which digression serves as the means of producing textual coherence and authority.

On the one hand, the best approximation of coherence in chapter 10 may be that suggested by its underlying theme—a very familiar one in the *Biographia*—Coleridge's self-justification and his correction of erroneous accounts of him constructed by others. The topics of his digressions and anecdotes can be gathered rather easily under this heading. The topics are: both the necessity and impossibility of coining new words; the hazards of a publishing career (both an admission of Coleridge's failures and a justification of his practices as a publisher and a writer); an account of a moral and religious crisis that Coleridge experiences; the events of his studies in Germany; and the moral implications of Coleridge's writings and their relation to the events of the day. Each topic follows out the theme of self-justification. Coleridge is accused of pedantry for continually coining new words, so he shows that this accusation is itself the product of pedantry. Coleridge uses the example of his "failed" periodical to show that this failure was the result of poor tactics in enlisting subscribers and the problems of publication itself and not because of any problem with his work itself. Coleridge is faced with negative conjecture about the nature of his political sentiments and activities—his disloyalty to his nation—and he shows the occasion of this conjecture to be an instance of the highest sort of loyalty. Coleridge's period of study in Germany may appear to have been a flight from the difficulties of his life in England and a squandering of the Wedgwood annuity, but Coleridge shows that it is one of the most important events of his intellectual life. Finally, Coleridge addresses various misrepresentations of his politics by showing that "the progress of his opinions and politics" is marked by a constancy in both opinion and political stance. He asserts that his political writings are not partisan in nature, but are philosophical readings of the events of the day, a reading of and through what he calls "authentic history."[25]

The counterpart to the thematic continuity of Coleridge's digressions is the fairly consistent chronological continuity of the anecdotes, which, when discerned, demonstrates how Coleridge seeks to exploit the status of autobiography as a literary life and to establish authority over his own textual productions. Although Coleridge presents some fairly conventional (conservative) advice in chapter 11 about the hazards of becoming "a mere man of letters" and represents himself as little better than the prime negative example, this account of "authorship" is not Coleridge's only word on the subject. Indeed, the advice in chapter 11 needs to be read in terms of Coleridge's practices as a writer, which he describes in chapter 10 and which he demonstrates in the process of constructing those descriptions.

Within and through the digressions and anecdotes of chapter 10, Coleridge presents a fairly well-developed narrative of his forays into public print in his periodicals *The Watchman* and *The Friend* and in his writing for the *Morning Post*. In broad terms, Coleridge outlines the events of his life from approximately 1796 through 1802. There are two significant choices that Coleridge makes in constructing his account of this period. The first is that while this is a period in which poetry is such a significant force in Coleridge's life, he touches upon this subject only collaterally, as it bears upon his political opinions. Indeed, his account of this crucial phase of his literary life focuses almost exclusively on his prose writings. Second, he chooses not to mention his relationship with Wordsworth except in anecdotes about their being suspected of being spies. These omissions may be explained on the grounds of Coleridge's having relinquished claim to the title of poet (albeit in regret and dejection) and his more than full treatment of Wordsworth elsewhere in the *Biographia*. However, the strategic omission of Wordsworth and the subject of poetry (particularly Coleridge's own) at this point in the narrative also concerns, and more essentially, what Coleridge seeks to accomplish in representing his life as a writer of prose.[26]

In his references to *The Watchman* and *The Friend*, it might seem that Coleridge simply is providing the grounding examples for the advice that he will give in chapter 11. He prefaces his account of *The Watchman* with the severe injunction that an author should never consider publishing by any other means than "the trade" (i.e., by the usual mechanisms of production involving publishers and booksellers). That is nominally the lesson that is to be learned from Coleridge's account of his naive efforts to canvass for subscribers to *The Watchman*. However, within this narrative another story emerges. It is the story of how Coleridge's composition of his literary life provides the means of re-appropriating and gaining authority over texts which have the power to reduce him to "a mere man of letters."

In describing his journey in 1796 to canvass for subscribers to *The Watchman*, Coleridge claims that those who met him then:

> will bear witness for me, how opposite even then my principles were to those of jacobinism or even of democracy, and can attest to the strict accuracy of the statement which I have left on record in the 10th and 11th numbers of THE FRIEND. (*Biographia*, 1:184)

Aside from being a fairly revisionary account of his politics, this claim is based on a complex act of textual re-appropriation and reproduction.[27] The numbers of *The Friend* to which Coleridge refers as evidence of the consistency of his political opinions are themselves a reprinting in 1809 of an essay that originally appeared in the *Morning Post* in 1802. While Coleridge is trying to defend himself against the charges of youthful radicalism and of later apostasy (a highly conventional strategy of the autobiographer), he is above all trying to bring under his authority those writings of his that he is most concerned have not been read properly by others.

This textual re-appropriation could result simply from Coleridge's notorious habit of re-using previously written texts as a way of generating something—anything—to put into print, especially in the case of *The Friend*. Indeed, one would not want to dispute the fact that Coleridge's efforts to "fill up" *The Friend* sometimes found him reaching in any and all directions for copy.[28] However, as much as this practice grew out of necessity, it also followed a design, one that is somewhat more materially grounded than the "method" of *The Friend* that Christensen has analyzed.[29] This design is evident from the beginning in that Coleridge envisioned his writings for *The Friend* as involving at least in part a compilation of material from his "memorandum books" and an opportunity of bringing together thoughts and ideas that he had been contemplating in the course of his "literary" career.[30] Furthermore, an earlier citation in the *Biographia* of *The Friend* that led Coleridge to reflect on the status of that periodical as a "published" work indicates that Coleridge very much defines publication in terms of distribution and the status of a text as a thing that has been read. One of Coleridge's digressions in chapter 10 that leads to his account of his work on *The Friend* grows out of Coleridge's initial discussion of the issue of pedantry and the coining of new words. Coleridge attests to the necessity of making precise distinctions between the meanings of related words and cites as an example his efforts in *The Friend* to discriminate the terms Reason and Understanding:

> To establish this distinction was one main object of THE FRIEND; if even in a biography of my own literary life I can with propriety refer to a work, which was printed rather than published, or so published that it had been well for the unfortunate author, if it had remained in manuscript! I have even at this time bitter cause for remembering that, which a number of my subscribers have but a trifling reason for forgetting. (*Biographia*, 1:175)

Coleridge's psychological as well as financial well-being might have been far better had he not undertaken *The Friend*, and that of his friends would certainly have been better.[31] As far as his literary well-being is concerned, however, the case is entirely different. First of all, as a text that can scarcely be said to be published, *The Friend* has the advantage of not having been fully subjected to the authority of a readership.[32] Indeed, early on in the *Biographia*, Coleridge himself makes note of this advantage after citing his own definition of the nature of Genius from *The Friend*:[33]

> As "the Friend" was printed on stampt sheets, and sent only by post to a very limited number of subscribers, that author has felt less objection to quote from it, though a work of his own. To the public at large indeed it is the same as a volume in manuscript. (*Biographia*, 1:82n)[34]

Coleridge can in propriety quote from his own work because it has not been made the property of a reading public.[35] Second, the even greater advantage of the work's manuscript status is that it is all the more readily available to Coleridge who can take it up and be, as it were, its first reader, thus establishing his own proper possession of the text and demonstrating the model of reading whereby it shall be read by others.

Through the re-appropriation of these texts, Coleridge gives a lesson in the sort of reading that is necessary to construct authentic history, and that lesson is constituted in his own practice as reader who claims authority over his own texts in the act of reading them.[36] In this context then, Coleridge's defense, in chapter 10, of his writing for the *Morning Post* and the quality of his assessments of events of the day is not simply a tale of self-justification. Rather, this narrative becomes the subtext of his defense of his politics, and the two together constitute the strategy whereby Coleridge establishes authority over his own life specifically as a textual entity.

This effort at rescuing texts and thereby the self constituted by those texts has been designated by Jerome Christensen as the work of the "machine that runs on itself," which Coleridge invents as a counter to the printing press that Herder imagines as turning the writer, as man of letters, into a mere compositor.[37] In characterizing this machine, Christensen focuses on the redemptive image that Coleridge presents in the note in which he translates the passage from Herder. After presenting his translation of the passage, Coleridge continues:

> To which I may add from myself, that what medical physiologists affirm of certain secretions, applies equally to our thoughts; they too must be taken up again into the circulation, and be again and again re-secreted in order to ensure a healthful vigor, both to the mind and to its intellectual offspring. (*Biographia*, 1:231)

This image of intellectual activity as being organic provides the typical Romantic counter to the threat of mechanization, especially as it is manifest in the debasement of language through the limitless reproduction afforded by the development of print culture. But Coleridge's solution is not simply a retreat into organic intellectual activity and the ineffable word. As much as print and publication are a threat to his authority, he nonetheless seeks a means by which he may avail himself of their power without having to sacrifice his own authority to that power. In dramatizing his reading of his own texts by reproducing them, he is transposing the mechanical processes of publication into the intellectual constructions of reading. In trying to validate such a transposition, Coleridge addresses the issue of the relationship of the book as such to the intellectual activity that it may be said to "embody."

If chapter 11 of the *Biographia* constitutes Coleridge's advice on how to avoid all of the errors which he himself committed as a writer, it is possible to consider chapter 10 as a parallel tale to chapter 11, perhaps with the two constituting commentaries on one another. While chapter 11 advises aspiring authors what to do in order to gain the authority and power as a writer that Coleridge feels he has lost, chapter 10 tells the story of how Coleridge managed, in spite of his many failures and mistakes, to maintain that authority, albeit unrecognized as a result of faulty reading. At the conclusion of chapter 10, Coleridge presents his most heated defense of his writings against the charge of idleness and non-productivity by suggesting that "the book" is not the proper measure of one's success both as a writer and as an intellectual:

> Even if the compositions, which I have made public, and that too in a form the most certain of an extensive circulation, though the least flattering to an author's self-love, had been published in *books*, they would have filled a respectable number of volumes, though every passage of merely temporary interest were omitted. . . . But are books the only channel through which the stream of intellectual usefulness can flow? Is the diffusion of truth to be estimated by publications; or publications by the truth which they diffuse or at least contain. (*Biographia*, 1:220)

Coleridge goes on from here to make an appeal for his defense to those whose minds had been "excited into activity" through conversation and letters and to those who had attended his many lectures.[38] Although it may seem that Coleridge takes refuge from the threat of the dead letter in the presence and immediacy of the spoken word, there nonetheless seem to be two ways in which the authority of intellectual productions is to be maintained. The first is found in the immediacy of the spoken word, but there also is a second which is found in writings that are not published in books, or at least that operate by way of textual mechanisms that prevent the author's word from being transformed into unequivocal property of an alien reader. This mechanism operates by the process of textual re-appropriation and reproduction in which Coleridge takes on the role of the reader of his own textual productions and thereby generates the model by which his texts are to be read. It is Coleridge's presence as reader in the text that gives life to the machine.

Perhaps one of Coleridge's most formidable "public" and critical readers was William Hazlitt. However, Hazlitt also produced one of the more famous testimonies to Coleridge's ability to "kindle young minds" in his more or less sympathetic account of Coleridge in "My First Acquaintance with Poets." Although this essay may represent a significant revision of Hazlitt's earlier attacks on Coleridge, it also owes much to Hazlitt's very scathing reviews of Coleridge's Statesman's Manual and Biographia. And although these reviews attack Coleridge for what amounts to his having devised and practiced the strategies of writing/reading that I have analyzed above, Hazlitt also provides an apt demonstration of the efficacy of the strategies of textual appropriation and re-appropriation that Coleridge seeks to practice.

Hazlitt's review of the Statesman's Manual appeared in The Examiner on 29 December 1816 and focused much of its critical energy on Coleridge's designation of the audience that he seeks to address in his "Lay Sermon."[39] In the course of the "sermon," Coleridge claims that his title page announces that the work is directed "exclusively ad clerum" and is not meant to be addressed to the "promiscuous audience" that he associates with what he has come to refer to as the "Reading Public."[40] In his review, Hazlitt points out that no such announcement appears on the title page of The Statesman's Manual (rather the work is addressed to "the higher classes of society"), and quotes at length Coleridge's discussions of the "misgrowth" of the Reading Public. Taking aim on Coleridge's reputation for announcing future works and then not producing them (at this point the Biographia is prominently among these "announced" works), Hazlitt refers to the title page that is printed in contrast to "that which is not printed" (Hazlitt, Works, 7:125). Coleridge's failure to produce promised works was a familiar target in Hazlitt's attacks on Coleridge. However, because Hazlitt's reference to the "unpublished" title page that Coleridge "produces" by reading it into the context of the sermon is made in the context of the critique of Coleridge's denigration of the Reading Public, it also may be seen as a well-designed reference to Coleridge's own "promiscuous reading."

Furthermore, the passage alludes to Hazlitt's own exercise of reading habits that are very similar to Coleridge's, particularly in Hazlitt's anticipatory review of *The Statesman's Manual*.

The actual review had been preceded by an anticipatory review on 8 September 1816. Hazlitt justified his review of a book that had not been published by citing the "repeated newspaper advertisements" (Hazlitt, *Works*, 7:114) announcing the upcoming publication of *The Statesman's Manual*. The fact that the work did not appear as these announcements declared it would also gave Hazlitt the grounds for his characteristc attack on Coleridge's failure to produce promised works. Hazlitt, however, takes his attention to Coleridge's unpublished works one step further by declaring:

> We see no sort of difference between his published and his unpublished compositions. It is just as impossible to get at the meaning of one as at the other. . . . Each of several works exists only in the imagination of the author and is quite inaccessible to the understanding of his readers. . . . We can give just as good a guess at the design of this Lay-Sermon, which is not published, as of *the Friend*, the Preliminary Articles in *the Courier*, *the Watchman*, the *Conciones ad Populum*, or any other courtly or popular publications of the same author. (Hazlitt, *Works*, 7:114–15)

Many readers of *The Friend* would have agreed with Hazlitt's assertion that Coleridge's unpublished works could not be any more unreadable that those that he had published.[41] In his version of the common complaint, however, Hazlitt suggests that these unpublished works could, in effect, be "read," and he proves that it is possible to do so by producing a review of a work that was "written before the Discourse that it professes to criticize had appeared in print, or probably existed anywhere but in repeated newspaper advertisements (Hazlitt, *Works*, 7:114). Indeed, Hazlitt succeeds in "reading" *The Statesman's Manual* by producing a collection of what he believes to be the unintelligible positions and opinions that Coleridge has presented in his previous publications (Hazlitt, *Works*, 1:117–18).[42] Certainly it would be ridiculous to suggest that a reader and writer as adept as Hazlitt would be subject to the model of reading that Coleridge prescribes. Nonetheless, by reading the text of Coleridge's previous publications into his anticipatory review of *The Statesman's*

Manual, Hazlitt clearly asserts that he is able to produce the unpublished text, thereby demonstrating the efficacy of Coleridge's own strategies of textual re-appropriation.

Hazlitt himself reinforces the efficacy of the strategy in his second review of *The Statesman's Manual*, which appeared when the work had actually been published. At the outset of this review, which appeared in *The Examiner* on 29 December 1816, Hazlitt declares that having given an account of the work "by anticipation. . . . We have only to proceed to specimens of illustrations of what we have said" (Hazlitt, *Works*, 7:119). Given Hazlitt's masterful "reading" in the previous review of the text of a work that had not been written, it is not surprising that prominent among the illustrations that Hazlitt presents are Coleridge's denigrations of the Reading Public. In his selection of and commentary on these illustrations, Hazlitt shows himself to be very much on the side of the "promiscuous audience" toward whom Coleridge does not want to direct his work.

Hazlitt, however, does not stop with this demonstration to Coleridge of the true dangers of promiscuous reading and is not done with *The Statesman's Manual* until he has written his well-known letter to *The Examiner* on 12 January 1817. It is this letter that provides the textual germ of his almost sympathetic representation of Coleridge in "My First Acquaintance with Poets." Hazlitt writes the letter under the guise of a reader of Hazlitt's own review who complains of realizing that the author of the *Lay Sermon* also was the man whom he had heard preach a gloriously inspiring sermon in 1798 (Hazlitt, *Works*, 7:128–29). The sharp contrast between the sermon preached in 1798 and the sermon written in 1816 is, of course, an occasion for Hazlitt to denounce Coleridge's apostasy. However, the production of a letter that purports to be written by a reader of an author's text, when it is in fact written by the author himself, is clearly a Coleridgean strategy of textual re-appropriation, as is Hazlitt's own re-appropriation of that letter in "My First Acquaintance with Poets." Furthermore, Hazlitt pays a great deal of attention to this strategy in his review of the *Biographia* in the August 1817 edition of *The Edinburgh Review*.

This review touches upon all of the matters that made Coleridge a target of Hazlitt's criticism: his unreadable prose style, his excessive metaphysical speculations, his unrealized poetic genius, and his apostasy. There also are, however, several aspects of the review that establish Hazlitt's fascination with and perhaps even admiration for Coleridge's strategies of textual re-appropriation. One of these is Hazlitt's repeated references, almost a refrain, to the absence of the chapter on the Imagination. Hazlitt makes reference to Coleridge's suppression of the chapter in the first paragraph of the review and returns to the subject at almost every major transition in his more or less chapter-by-chapter examination of the *Biographia*. What Hazlitt returns to over and over again is his notion that much of the *Biographia* is taken up with "a prefatory introduction of 200 pages to an Essay on the difference between Fancy and Imagination" (Hazlitt, *Works*, 16:115). In his final reference to the "suppressed" chapter, Hazlitt remarks:

> As Mr. C. has suppressed his Disquisition on the Imagination as unintelligible, we do not think it fair to make any remarks on the 200 pages of prefatory matter, which were printed, it seems, in the present work, before a candid friend apprised him of the little objection to the appearance of the Disquisition itself. (Hazlitt, *Works*, 16:136)

Contrary to his own assertion, Hazlitt does comment on a great deal of this material, beginning with chapter 4 and leading up to the "suppressed" material that would have constituted chapter 13. As he does in the anticipatory review of *The Statesman's Manual*, Hazlitt structures his reading around that which Coleridge has failed or chosen not to publish. Hazlitt thus chooses not to remark upon the material in the chapters themselves, but upon the status of this material as prefatory to the discussion of Imagination and Fancy, and what Hazlitt reads in this material is primarily Coleridge's failure to produce the projected chapter.

The portion of this material that Hazlitt does not consider as prefatory and that he chooses to quote at great length is taken from chapter 10 of the *Biographia*: Coleridge's account of canvassing for subscribers to *The Watchman*—the same passage that I have identified as an example of Coleridge's strategy of textual re-appropriation (*Biographia*, 1:184). Hazlitt writes that he gives this longest extract from the "narrative part" of the work "out of regard to Mr. C. as well as to our readers . . . which is more likely to be popular than any other part—and is, upon the whole, more pleasingly written" (Hazlitt, *Works*, 16:125). At the outset of the review, Hazlitt had noted that the *Biographia* would have been one of the most popular of Coleridge's productions if he had offered more narrative of this sort. However, Hazlitt is far from quoting Coleridge's work to his advantage in presenting Coleridge's revisionary account of his politics in the 1790s, a subject on which Hazlitt had frequently expressed himself to the great disadvantage of Coleridge.[43] In the context of this narrative that Hazlitt has already "read" so frequently for the public in print that he need not repeat the performance here in his review, we have Coleridge's own performance of textual appropriation in his reference to "the statement [he has] left on record in the 10th and 11th Numbers of *The Friend*" (*Biographia* 1:184 and Hazlitt, *Works*, 16:129). Hazlitt's choice to end his long quotation from the *Biographia* with this assertion may be a coincidence or may simply aim at exposing Coleridge's convoluted reading of previously "published" text into the *Biographia*. Hazlitt, however, also is engaging in precisely the same process of textual re-appropriation that Coleridge has used. As we have noted, the 10th and 11th numbers of *The Friend* reproduce an article of Coleridge's previously published in *The Morning Post*, entitled "Once a Jacobin Always a Jacobin." Hazlitt himself had referred to that article in an essay in *The Examiner* (15 December 1816) entitled "On Modern Apostates" (Hazlitt, *Works*, 7:131–37). Thus by quoting a passage that refers to material that Hazlitt already had analyzed in print, the review of the *Biographia* reproduces Hazlitt's previous reading of Coleridge's essay. Hazlitt accomplishes this complex intertextual act by performing the very process of reading that Coleridge uses in re-appropriating his previously published text by reading it into the *Biographia*.

As has been noted previously, Coleridge concludes chapter 10 of the *Biographia* by turning from the effort to defend his textual productions to appeal to those whose minds had been "excited into activity" through conversations, letters, and lectures. One of those to whom this appeal might be appropriately addressed is William Hazlitt, who testifies to his mind being "excited into activity" by Coleridge's sermon in 1798, both in his letter to *The Examiner* and in the more famous essay which is based on the letter. However, the familiar record of that testimony in "My First Acquaintance with Poets," by virtue of its being a re-appropriation of a previously published text, testifies to another sort of activity of mind excited by Coleridge—the strategy of "promiscuous reading."

Coleridge's suspicion of the Reading Public was founded on all of the prejudices about social rank and education that Hazlitt accused Coleridge of holding. However, the threatening power of the reader seems to be something that Coleridge understood so clearly because he exercised it so well himself and because readers like Hazlitt had exerted this power over Coleridge's own texts. If one tries to reconcile Hazlitt's attacks on Coleridge's writings with the more even-handed and even sympathetic account of Coleridge in "My First Acquaintance with Poets," as many critics have, it may seem to make sense to focus on the distinction that Hazlitt sets up in his letter to *The Examiner*: Coleridge's spoken words have the power to inspire, but his written words do little more than confound any attempt to understand them.[44] Thus the relatively warm account of Hazlitt's acquaintance with Coleridge may be seen as the result of Hazlitt's recalling the power of Coleridge's personal presence without the encumbrance of his writings to weigh it down. However, the paragraphs from the essay that precede those that Hazlitt drew from the letter in writing the essay indicate that it was as much Coleridge's strategies of reading as it was his power of speech that excited Hazlitt's mind into activity and enabled his "understanding [to find] a language to express itself" (Hazlitt, *Works*, 17:107). After identifying itself as a response to the review of *The Statesman's Manual*, the letter to *The Examiner* describes Hazlitt's experience in January of 1798 when he heard Coleridge preach to a Unitarian congregation at Shrewsbury. Following this account, Hazlitt proceeds to express his astonishment (disingenuous, of course) that the preacher of that sermon and the writer of the sermon described in the review could be the same individual. The paragraphs from the letter that describe the masterful effect of the sermon are those that are later incorporated into the essay. Very much in the spirit of Coleridge's revisionary re-reading of his own texts, Hazlitt's testimony to the debt that he owes Coleridge constructs a revised version of the re-appropriated paragraphs from the letter in which Coleridge's sermon is a confirmation of the author's estimation of him rather than a contradiction of it, as it was in the letter to *The Examiner*.

Even in the essay, this encomium to Coleridge does not continue unabated, for after all, this is Hazlitt. But when he resorts to his usually sharp, almost bitter, characterization of Coleridge, Hazlitt does so through the strategy of reproducing a previously published text by reading it into the essay. Hazlitt's description of Coleridge's appearance when they were first introduced is far from flattering. The description of Coleridge's nose, "the rudder of his face, the index of the will, was small, feeble, nothing— like what he has done" (Hazlitt, Works, 17:109), carries with it Hazlitt's more common tone of invective against Coleridge. The allusion to *Tristram Shandy* says little, if anything, to Coleridge's credit, and brings up Hazlitt's usual condemnation of Coleridge's failure to fulfill his genius.[45] However, the complex textual re-appropriation involved in this description rivals any ever performed by Coleridge. The allusion to *Tristram Shandy* is a re-appropriation of a previously published text, that of the anticipatory review of *The Statesman's Manual*. In the original published version of the review, Hazlitt made similar allusions to *Tristram Shandy* when he asserted that Coleridge had no purpose or passions of his own (Hazlitt, Works, 7:117). This allusion, however, was removed when the essay was republished in Hazlitt's *Political Essays* in 1819.[46] Thus when Hazlitt describes Coleridge's physiognomy in the essay in 1823, he reproduces both a previously published text and one that has not been "published." In this case, Hazlitt's assertion about Coleridge's writings proves to be equally true about his own: "We see no sort of difference between his published and his unpublished compositions" (Hazlitt, Works, 7:114).

When Hazlitt testifies in "My First Acquaintance with Poets" that he owes Coleridge for the fact that his understanding found a language in which to express itself, he turns away abruptly from this uncharacteristic statement of praise with the remark: "But this is not to my purpose" (Hazlitt, Works, 17:107). Much the same might be said of the way in which Hazlitt repeats Coleridge's own strategies of textual re-appropriation even while mercilessly criticizing his writing. Although it may not be to Hazlitt's purposes to testify to the efficacy of Coleridge's strategies for constructing a reading of his own texts, Hazlitt is nonetheless drawn to use the same strategies himself, and Coleridge's reading strategies exhibit their power to figure not only in Coleridge's representations of himself, but also in the writings of one of his most promiscuous readers.

6

The Passive Page of a Book

As the above analysis of Coleridge's textual strategies and Hazlitt's readings/reproductions of those strategies have shown, the *Biographia*, as an autobiography, is the textual mechanism by which Coleridge is able to produce a text that he believes can resolve the problematic relationship between the truth of an author's writings and the hazardous mechanisms of publication. Coleridge's failure to have his writing published in books turns from being a sign of his failure as an author to an opportunity to construct a model of authority in which he believes he does not have to relinquish the power of his words to the reader. This is precisely the opportunity of which he avails himself not only in chapter 10, where he makes his most concerted and consistent effort to re-appropriate his own texts, but throughout the *Biographia*.

For Coleridge, the test of a writer's power and authority, the efficacy of his literary life, is very much the conventional test of permanence. However, the means by which he seeks to achieve that permanence involves an attempt to circumvent or at least redefine the power of the reader to bestow that permanence. If Wordsworth may be said to work toward "silencing" the reader of *The Prelude*, Coleridge does not so much silence the reader but construct a complexly intertextual narrative that directs and guides the reading process. But the power of the writer/reader of which Coleridge avails himself in constructing his literary life does not extend to all of his writings. When it comes to his poetry, Coleridge is quite ready to express his regret over having not achieved what he believes would be a poetic work of permanence:

On my own account I may perhaps have had sufficient reason to lament my deficiency in self-controul, and the neglect of concentering my powers to the realization of some permanent work. But to verse rather than to prose, if to either, belongs "the voice of mourning." (*Biographia*, 1:221)

This admission of regret comes at the end of Coleridge's narrative of his literary life in chapter 10, and while there is an equivocation to this expression of regret in the "if either," even this confrontation with the threat to his literary authority turns upon a complex act of re-appropriation. The "voice of mourning" that Coleridge chooses to sound at this point is that of the poem "To William Wordsworth":

> Keen pangs of love awakening as a babe
> Turbulent, with an outcry in the heart,
> And fears self-will'd that shunn'd the eye of hope,
> And hope that scarce would know itself from fear;
> Sense of past youth, and manhood come in vain
> And genius given and knowledge won in vain,
> And all which I had cull'd in wood-walks wild
> And all which patient toil had rear'd, and all
> Commune with thee had open'd out—but flowers
> Strew'd on my corpse, and borne upon my bier
> In the same coffin, for the self-same grave!
>
> S. T. C.
> (*Biographia*, 1:222)[1]

Coleridge might have chosen these lines because they are among some of the most extreme of his various poetic self-lamentations and perhaps some of his most self-pitying. However, the fact that they are addressed directly to Wordsworth, are a response to his poetic power, and are taken from a poem that Coleridge is publishing for the first time in *Sibylline Leaves* is of strategic importance.[2]

First of all, the moment when Coleridge might be said to be giving the most damning evidence against himself of the failure of his literary life, becomes the sign that such failure was indeed only momentary—something that is reinforced by the passage from Petrarch which Coleridge presents following the one from "To William Wordsworth." In this quotation, Petrarch speaks of having "another" face, "a new sort of mind" and a voice that "sounds otherwise." In this sense, the closing gestures of this chapter are an apt conclusion to the narrative of his literary life that the chapter presents. Together, Coleridge's self-quotation and his quotation from Petrarch present the "true" story of Coleridge's literary life, giving the lie to the story that others would read out of and into his life in print. But with the passage from "To William Wordsworth," Coleridge goes even further in establishing the authority of his literary life by availing himself of the strategy of textual appropriation which rescues the poem from the dead letter by reading it into his literary life. And unlike Coleridge's other acts of reappropriation in the *Biographia*, this one is virtually simultaneous with the "original" publication of the poem (in *Sibylline Leaves*), thus making Coleridge's textual machine one that truly runs on the energy that it produces itself.

That Coleridge here chooses to characterize an apparent failure in his literary life with lines from a poem addressed to Wordsworth that attest to the greatness of his poetic powers is also of highly strategic importance in Coleridge's construction of his literary life. As I pointed out in chapter 4, Coleridge's expression of his subjection to Wordsworth's poetic authority is not without significant equivocation. The "prayer" in which Coleridge says he finds himself after hearing Wordsworth recite *The Prelude* is as much an act of self-assertion as it is a song of praise. It is in the *Biographia* that Coleridge carries out most fully that act of self-assertion, and he does so through the very strategies of reading/writing that he uses in constructing his literary life.

It might seem to be a matter of stating little more than the obvious to assert that Coleridge's interpretation in the *Biographia* of Wordsworth's poetic theory and his poetry constitutes an attempt on Coleridge's part to assert his dominance over Wordsworth through his power as a reader of Wordsworth's writings. Both the success and inaccuracy of that reading have been the focus of any number of important critical studies.[3] What I would like to focus on here are the ways in which Coleridge's self-assertive strategies for reading Wordsworth constitute specific strategies of autobiographical construction and operate within Coleridge's general scheme of establishing authority over his own writing through the appropriation and reappropriation of previously published texts. I also believe that this "local" performance of "mastering" the reader of his texts can further establish the efficacy of the general strategy of textual re-appropriation that may seem to be possible only if Coleridge has the good fortune to meet with the "ideal reader" who has the equipment necessary to perform such a reading.[4]

Although many critical accounts of the *Biographia* take the position that Coleridge's construction of an autobiographical narrative is much less an autobiography than it is an occasion for fulfilling his desire to write a critique of Wordsworth, I think that we must recognize that the critique of Wordsworth also is the pretext for the development and performance of specific strategies of autobiographical construction. Wordsworth's poetic theory and his poetry provide the occasion whereby Coleridge can demonstrate his powers as a reader, not just of Wordsworth, but (perhaps more importantly) of himself as well.

The first chapter of the *Biographia* that deals specifically with Wordsworth (chapter 4) is from its very beginning embedded in the context of Coleridge's concern with the powers of reading and an author's potential subjection to that power. Although chapter 4 is Coleridge's first sustained effort in the *Biographia* to examine the tenets of Wordsworth's preface to the *Lyrical Ballads*, Coleridge introduces his discussion of Wordsworth as though it were merely an illustrative example of a larger argument. Coleridge begins the chapter with a characteristic reference to what he believes to be the obvious subject of his writing but which leaves that subject very much in question. He makes his transition from his discussion of Southey in chapter 3 to his discussion of Wordsworth in chapter 4 with this remark:

> I have wandered far from the object in view, but as I fancied to myself readers who would respect the feelings that had tempted me from the main road; so I dare to calculate on not a few, who will warmly sympathize with them. At present it will be sufficient for my purpose, if I have proved, that Mr. Southey's writing no more than my own, furnished the original occasion to this fiction of a *new school* of poetry, and of clamors against its supposed founders and proselytes. (*Biographia*, 1:69)

In spite of Coleridge's apparent confidence to the contrary, there is considerable uncertainty at this point in the narrative as to what "the object in view" is. While that object may be any of the three topics announced in the subtitle and (more or less) pursued in the course of chapter 3 ("The author's obligation to critics, and the probable occasion—Principles of modern criticism—Mr. Southey's works and character"), the one object that has been and continues to remain in view is the reader, and the strongest links between chapters 3 and 4 are Coleridge's references to the hazardous business of having one's writings read by others. In the course of chapter 3, providing the background to and context for his reading of Wordsworth in chapter 4, Coleridge examines these hazards through a somewhat conventional equation of a "universal" literacy, the rise of popular literature, and reviewers' pandering to public tastes.[5] He comes to the heart of the matter with regard to his own strategies of writing when he takes reviewers to task for their criticism of some of Southey's "trivial" poems. Coleridge's primary point is that Southey is fully aware that these are not serious works of poetry and that it is foolish of critics to take him to task as though he were trying to pass the poems off as anything other than "playful."

> I guess that Mr. Southey was quite unable to comprehend, wherein would consist the crime or mischief of printing half a dozen or more playful poems; or to speak more generally, compositions which would be enjoyed or passed over, according as the taste and humour of the reader might chance to be; provided they contained nothing immoral. . . . The merest trifle, he ever sent abroad, had tenfold better claims to its ink and paper, than all the silly criticisms, which prove no more, than that the critic was not one of those, for whom the trifle was written; and than all the grave exhortations to a greater reverence for the public. As if the passive page of a book, by having an epigram or doggrel tale impressed on it, instantly assumed at once locomotive power and a sort of ubiquity, so as to flutter and buzz in the ear of the public to the sore annoyance of the said mysterious personage. (*Biographia*, 1:60–61)

This complaint against critics touches upon two significant elements of Coleridge's conception of readers and reading. The first echoes the "law of reading" that he wishes to lay down in *The Friend*, which states that readers should conduct themselves as do well-behaved guests at a banquet, politely passing over that which does not suit their tastes without commenting on the circumstances of their displeasure (*Friend*, 2:15).[6] In this instance, Coleridge uses this law of reading as a way of pointing out not only the foolishness of reviewers who are not adept enough readers to recognize these trifles for what they are, but also the inherent "lawlessness" of reading that the reviewers and their readers mutually perpetuate in one another. Here Coleridge, however, expands this law by emphasizing the "passive" character of the printed page. It is the passive character of the page that makes the writer subject to that activity of the reader, but here Coleridge is more concerned with what happens or can happen when one is conscious of that passive character. What Coleridge is pointing out, while ridiculing critics for their lack of it, is the significance of the readers' self-consciousness about the activity of reading and the role that it can play in the construction of a text. In this instance Coleridge points out how critics' misconceptions both about the "loco-motive power" of the text and about the passive character of their readership (listeners, rather than readers) generate the sort of lawless reading that cannot see beyond mere trifles and recognize the excellences of a text.

This account of reading and the critique of the lawlessness of reviewers not only provides the immediate context for Coleridge's examination of Wordsworth, it also provides the terms in which Coleridge will conduct that examination. Throughout the chapters on Wordsworth's poetry and poetic theory, Coleridge's conception of the necessity of reading actively and critically and of recognizing the passive character of the printed page serve as the grounds on which Coleridge takes issue with Wordsworth. In a rather ironic way, Coleridge follows his own advice (*Biographia*, 1:61–63) by pointing out the excellences of Wordsworth's poetry rather than focusing solely on its apparent defects. However, in Coleridge's eyes the defect that most needs to be highlighted is a defect of reading; it is not as a poet that Wordsworth fails, but as a reader, especially of his own texts.

In chapter 4, Coleridge's discussion of the *Lyrical Ballads* and Wordsworth's preface lays the groundwork for his later critique of Wordsworth's failure of reading. He does so not by examining the problems in the theory of the preface, but by projecting how the readers of the volume were distracted from the poems themselves by Wordsworth's own highlighting of the peculiar character of some of the poems. Coleridge asserts that the preface itself is responsible for the way in which Wordsworth's poems were read: "In the critical remarks therefore, prefixed and annexed to the 'Lyrical Ballads,' I believe that we may safely rest, as the true origin of the unexampled opposition which Mr. Wordsworth's writings have been since doomed to encounter" (*Biographia*, 1:70–71). As a preliminary to this assertion, Coleridge projects his sense of how the poems would have been read had not these peculiarities been pointed out:

> A careful and repeated examination of these [the two volumes of *Lyrical Ballads* 1800] confirms me in the belief, that the omission of less than an hundred lines would have precluded nine-tenths of the criticism on that work. I hazard this declaration, however, on the supposition, that the reader had taken up, as he would have done any other collection of poems purporting to derive their subjects or interest from the incidents of domestic or ordinary life, intermingled with higher strains of meditation which the poet utters in his own person and character; with the proviso, that they were perused without knowledge of, or reference to, the author's peculiar opinions and that the reader had not had his attention previously directed to those peculiarities. (*Biographia*, 1:69)

When read in light of Coleridge's account in chapter 3 of how reviewers failed in their reading of Southey's trivial poems, this discussion of the *Lyrical Ballads* implies that Wordsworth, like a bad reviewer, has highlighted that which would not have drawn the censure of the reader had it not been marked out for recognition.[7] The further implication is that Wordsworth may suffer from the same misconception as the reviewers in his assumption that the passive page of a book will assume "at once loco-motive power and a sort of ubiquity." And in Wordsworth's concern over such loco-motive power, he composes a preface that indeed does give a sort of "ubiquity" to the peculiarities of his poetic theories which "buzz in the ear of the public," thus drowning out the poems themselves.

In Coleridge's view, it would seem that Wordsworth misapprehends the way in which his poems will be read and miscalculates the power of the effect of his poetic experiments:

> The humbler passages in the poems themselves were dwelt on and cited to justify the rejection of the theory. What in and for themselves would have been either forgotten or forgiven as imperfections, or at least comparative failures, provoked direct hostility when an-

nounced as intentional, as the result of choice after full deliberation. Thus the poems, admitted by *all* as excellent, joined with those which had pleased the far *greater* number, though they formed two-thirds of the whole work, instead of being deemed (as in all right they should have been, even if we take for granted that the reader judged aright) an atonement for the few exceptions, gave wind and fuel to the animosity against both the poems and the poet. (*Biographia*, 1:71)

In spite of Coleridge's attestations to Wordsworth's poetic genius in the rest of the chapter, as far as the preface is concerned, Wordsworth comes off as an even more foolish and misguided reader than the reviewers who insist upon taking Southey's "trifles" seriously.[8] They are simply foolish in pointing out "defects" that are (according to Coleridge) obviously not meant to be seen as anything else, and the damage that they do is to place those so-called defects in the forefront of the reader's mind without pointing out any of the excellences of the work. Wordsworth is by implication all the more foolish in that he highlights the peculiarities of his opinions and thus places those peculiarities in the forefront of the mind of a reader who would not have otherwise gone looking for, and therefore found, the peculiar defects with which his poems were charged.[9]

This critique of Wordsworth's failure as a reader, or at least his failure to comprehend the nature of reading and the passive character of the printed page, does not end with Coleridge's apparent effort to re-focus attention on the poems rather than on the preface. His very efforts to attest to Wordsworth's poetic genius end up offering the counter-example of his own strategies as a reader and the way in which these strategies can give him authority over his own texts, even in the face of the passive character of the printed page. Although Coleridge suggests that Wordsworth's best strategy might have been to trust in the power of his poetic genius to defend his poetic experiments (or to trust that his readers will pass over the peculiarities of his poetry "in silence, as so much blank paper," *Biographia*, 1:74), Coleridge himself adopts and demonstrates a much more active strategy for establishing textual authority. Whereas Wordsworth's best defense is a blank page, Coleridge's is the overwritten page produced through textual re-appropriation.

I already have examined this strategy in some detail in my discussion of how, in chapter 4 of the *Biographia*, Coleridge appropriates from *The Friend* the definition of genius that he applies to Wordsworth.[10] Now with an understanding of the context in which that re-appropriation takes place, it becomes apparent that Coleridge's strategy operates at two levels. On the one hand its basic function is to make Coleridge into the reader of his own texts and provide the model by which his text is to be read. On the other hand it seeks to establish the efficacy of his conception and performance of reading by presenting it as a counter-example to Wordsworth's misconceptions and miscalculations about the nature of reading. In effect Coleridge's account of Wordsworth's poetic genius opens the space in which Coleridge can establish his own genius not only as a reader of Wordsworth's poetry but as a writer who can establish textual authority through his powers as a reader—something that Wordsworth, according to Coleridge, has failed at in the preface. Whereas Wordsworth is advised to rely on his reader (having faith in his own poetic genius) to forget or forgive his failures, to treat them as so many blank pages, Coleridge demonstrates his ability to take the forgotten pages of his own failures and turn them into the means of generating textual authority.

When Coleridge proceeds with his examination of Wordsworth's poetry and poetic theory in subsequent chapters of the *Biographia*, his emphasis on Wordsworth's defects as a reader/writer becomes more and more explicit. Rather than simply faulting Wordsworth for his misconceptions about how his poetry will be read, Coleridge seeks to demonstrate that Wordsworth is even a faulty reader of his own writing who cannot recognize the gap between the "object" that he has in mind and what his words indeed "authorize." In his critique of Wordsworth's preface, Coleridge does much more than just criticize Wordsworth's poetic theory. The terms in which Coleridge offers this critique seek to establish not only the efficacy of Coleridge's poetic theory, but also of his strategies to establish textual authority.

In chapter 14, Coleridge expands upon his assertion that Wordsworth's preface was the source of the negative criticism of his poetry. Rather than simply assert, as he had in chapter 4, that the "peculiar" opinions of the preface had misdirected the readers of the poems, Coleridge now argues that the opinions of the preface are not just "peculiar," but erroneous:

> With many parts of this preface in the sense attributed to them and which the words undoubtedly seemed to authorize, I never concurred; but on the contrary object to them as erroneous in principle, and as contradictory (in appearance at least) both to other parts of the same preface, and to the author's own practice in the greater number of his poems themselves. (*Biographia*, 2:9–10)

Coleridge's equivocations about what the words of the preface "seemed to authorize" and the "appearance" of contradiction would seem to indicate that he gives Wordsworth the benefit of the doubt as to whether or not his readers might be guilty of misreading his preface. However, Coleridge's subsequent examinations of the preface in chapters 17 and 19 leave little doubt that it is Wordsworth who fails in the writing of the preface because he does not recognize the "true" import of his own words. Thus he fails as a reader not only of what it is that the words of the preface do indeed authorize, but of the poems themselves about which the preface purports to theorize. Coleridge's stated motivation for his extended discussion of Wordsworth's poetic theory is that of setting the record straight: "Considering it [the preface] as the source of a controversy, in which I have been honored more, than I deserve, by the frequent conjunction of my name with his [Wordsworth's], I think it expedient to declare once and for all, in what points I coincide with his opinions, and in what points I altogether differ" (*Biographia*, 2:10). But his critique is not simply a matter of setting out his own opinions and pointing to their conjunctions with and differences from those of Wordsworth. Rather, Coleridge ultimately seeks to distinguish himself from Wordsworth as a reader who has the power not only to establish his own textual authority, but to reestablish the authority of Wordsworth's poetic genius by correcting his erroneous readings of his own poems.

Coleridge's criticism of the specific tenets of Wordsworth's preface turns upon the issue of what the words of the preface authorize and the "right" interpretation of them:

> My own differences from certain supposed parts of Mr. Wordsworth's theory ground themselves on the assumption, that his words had

been rightly interpreted, as purporting that the proper diction for poetry in general consist altogether in a language taken, with due exceptions, from the mouths of men in real life, a language which actually constitutes the natural conversation of men under the influence of natural feeling. (*Biographia*, 2:42)

There may be considerable debate as to whether or not Coleridge's interpretation of the words of the preface is the correct one, but there can be little doubt as to the way in which he is positioning himself here as a reader of Wordsworth's text. When Coleridge refers to "certain supposed parts of Wordsworth's theory," the matter of supposition is not, as one would usually assume, a matter of a theory having been erroneously attributed to Wordsworth by another. Rather it is a matter of Wordsworth having supposed his theory to be one thing when indeed it was another. The problem with the preface is not that Wordsworth's words have been misread, but that he misreads them himself.

This point is made all the more clear when Coleridge tries to establish what he believes to be the "real" object of Wordsworth's preface. Again Coleridge focuses on the problem of what Wordsworth's words authorize, but highlights the issue of faulty reading and interpretation all the more. In expressing his doubts that Wordsworth ever practiced the theory of poetry that his preface appears to advance, Coleridge states, "I cannot, and do not, believe that the poet did ever himself adopt it [the exclusive style of the real language of men] in the unqualified sense, in which his expressions have been understood by others, and which indeed according to all the common laws of interpretation they seem to bear" (*Biographia*, 2:90). After going to great lengths to suggest that Wordsworth's "real object" was the beauty of the aptness of expression and the establishment of a *lingua communis*, which Coleridge finds already present in English poetry from its "first dawn," Coleridge once again points out that this theory is one that he has read into or out of the faulty reading that Wordsworth presents in his preface: "And let it be remembered too, that I am now interpreting the controverted passages of Mr. W.'s critical preface by the purpose and object, which he may be supposed to have intended, rather than by the sense which the words themselves must convey, if they are taken without this allowance" (*Biographia*, 2:99).[11] To this point in his critique of Wordsworth's preface, Coleridge has confined himself to examining the ways in which Wordsworth fails as a writer because of his faulty reading of both his own poems and of the import of his own words in the preface. However, Coleridge's lesson in reading goes several steps further when it comes to his long deferred critical evaluation of Wordsworth's poetry.[12] And it is here that his construction of his literary life reaches its ultimate embodiment.

After having expanded upon his earlier critique of the critical practices of literary reviewers in chapter 21, Coleridge again proceeds to offer himself as the exemplary critical reader by examining the defects and excellences of Wordsworth's poetry. This time, rather than demonstrate his acute skills as a reader by finding the origin of genius in Wordsworth's earliest writings as he had done in chapter 4, Coleridge focuses more closely on following out the method of critical practice that he has been delineating in previous chapters. Coleridge's analysis of the defects and excellences of Wordsworth's poetry culminates in a series of intricate textual maneuvers that completes the process of Coleridge's reading lesson for Wordsworth. These strategies commence with Coleridge's declaration that Wordsworth is "capable of producing . . . the FIRST GENUINE PHILOSOPHICAL POEM." This declaration is not without the usual ambivalent qualification that echoes in most of Coleridge's extravagant praise of Wordsworth, presented here by the disclaimer that it is not for Coleridge to "prophesy" what "Mr. Wordsworth *will* produce" (*Biographia*, 2:156). The distinction between what Wordsworth will produce and what he is capable of producing is very much dependent upon his powers as a reader of his own texts. Coleridge also directs his attention to Wordsworth's "admirers and advocates," particularly their admiration for Wordsworth's "SIMPLICITY" (*Biographia*, 2:158).

Finally, in what may appear simply to be an effort to make a transition to the previously published material with which he pads out the too-short manuscript, Coleridge says that he wishes "to present himself to the Reader as [he] was in the first dawn of [his] literary life":

> When Hope grew round me, like the climbing vine,
> And fruits and foliage not my own seem'd mine!
>
> (*Biographia*, 2:159)

As a transition to the cobbled together material from "Satyrane's Letters" and the critique of *Bertram*, this quotation from "Dejection: An Ode" is admittedly weak and unconvincing, but it has a certain virtue and strength when considered in the context of the culmination of Coleridge's reading of Wordsworth.

First of all it would seem nearly impossible to ignore the significance of Coleridge's having chosen to quote a poem in which he so intimately detailed his sense of his own weakness as a poet and which marks so clearly his sense of his difference from Wordsworth. This connection is made all the more significant by the prominent role played in the poem by the quality of "simplicity." And most significantly of all, this quotation inaugurates a highly strategic instance of textual re-appropriation that not only calls upon the general Reader whom Coleridge addresses, but quite specifically calls upon Wordsworth as reader.

The process of textual appropriation taking place here is greatly complicated by the compositional and publishing history of "Dejection." The particular lines which Coleridge quotes remain the same throughout this history, but the implied addressee or designated reader changes with the occasions on and forms in which the poem is produced. There are different sets of "associations" for the different readers of these lines. In addition to the reading that Coleridge sets up in this specific context, he also points the general Reader to the two published versions of "Dejection:" that which appeared in the *Morning Post* on 4 October 1802 and that which appears in *Sibylline Leaves*. Beginning with the latter, we again may note Coleridge's strategy (as illustrated in Coleridge's quotation of "To William Wordsworth" in chapter 10) of simultaneously "publishing" a work and gaining authority over that text through an act of textual re-appropriation that takes over the function of the reader. In this particular instance Coleridge first of all constructs the reading of the poem as it appears in *Sibylline Leaves*, which identifies the poem as representing a particular stage of his literary life. But by presenting a quotation from this poem at this point in the *Biographia*, Coleridge also re-marks the connection between the poem as now addressed to the "Lady" and the *Morning Post* version, addressed to the "lofty poet" Edmund. Thus Coleridge makes the link between his analysis of Wordsworth's poems and "Dejection" stand out in the seemingly mechanical transition to the material that he had to add to the manuscript of the *Biographia* in order to make it into an attractively saleable object. Although it may be somewhat speculative to make much of Coleridge's revisions of the poem in and of themselves and of the possibility that his readers might be expected to recognize these revisions and their significance, it is nonetheless quite plausible to consider the way in which these revisions would have been particularly apparent to Wordsworth, both because of his connection with the various circumstances involved in the composition and publication of the poem and because of his familiarity with the longer, more personal, and unpublished version of the poem, "A Letter to ———."[13]

From the very beginning, "A Letter to ———" and its subsequent revisions as "Dejection: An Ode" had a very specific significance for Wordsworth. That Coleridge begins the verse letter to Sara as a response to the first four stanzas of Wordsworth's "Intimations" is well known, and certainly Coleridge is calling upon this association in his quotation from his own poem at the close of his analysis of Wordsworth's poetry. Indeed, Wordsworth's "Ode" is so prominent in Coleridge's account of both the defects and excellences of Wordsworth's poetry that it is not hard to imagine that Coleridge's citation of "Dejection" at this point serves as something of a gloss on that critical reading. But there are personal as well as poetic matters to be examined here in considering the sort of reading that Coleridge sets up for Wordsworth in citing the lines from "Dejection."

Coleridge begins writing "A Letter to ———" on the evening of Sunday, 4 April 1802, the last day of a stay by William and Dorothy Wordsworth with Coleridge at Keswick. For Wordsworth, this visit marks the time at about which he has decided to wed Mary Hutchinson and also has concluded that it will be necessary to go to France to see Annette Vallon and his daughter Caroline.[14] The occasion of the poem's composition need not be associated with Wordsworth's activities in bringing his domestic life into order, except for the fact that Coleridge chose to publish "Dejection" in the *Morning Post* on Wordsworth's wedding day, which also was Coleridge's wedding anniversary.[15] In addition to the complicating circumstances of composition and publication, the subject of the verse letter and of its subsequent revision as "Dejection" have to make Wordsworth's reading of the poem all the more complex and disturbing.[16]

The publication of "Dejection" on Wordsworth's wedding

day is in and of itself problematic at a rather basic level: that of the appropriateness of presenting a delineation of one's own dejected state as a tribute to a friend on his wedding day. However, the revisions of the original verse letter, with which Wordsworth was quite familiar, clearly move the poem away from its personal, melancholy lamentations toward a tribute to the spirit and the power of Joy that is Edmund's (the name under which Coleridge addresses Wordsworth in the *Morning Post* version of "Dejection") and which leads the poet to this wish for Edmund:

> With light heart may he rise,
> Gay fancy, cheerful eyes
> And sing his lofty song, and teach me to rejoice!
> O EDMUND, friend of my devoted choice,
> O rais'd from anxious dread and busy care,
> By the immenseness of the good and fair
> Which thou see's evr'y where
> Joy lifts thy spirit, joy attunes thy voice,
> To thee do all things live from pole to pole,
> Their life the eddying of thy living soul!
>
> (126–35)

But as much as these revisions mark more clearly and perhaps more successfully the poet's effort to move from absorption in his own dejection to rejoicing in the joy of his friend (the first five lines are some of the few that are newly written for "Dejection"), it would be difficult to imagine that Wordsworth could read this poem without also seeing in it the huge rift in the text (graphically represented in the *Morning Post* by a series of lines of asterisks and the explicit statement "The sixth and seventh stanzas omitted") that leaves unwritten but not unrepresented Coleridge's distressing account of his own marriage. Even in the original verse letter, Coleridge cannot help but speak of that which he wishes he could leave unspoken. Having written of each visitation of misfortune that "suspends, what Nature gave me at my Birth / My shaping spirit of imagination!" Coleridge nonetheless goes on to note:

> I speak not now of those habitual Ills,
> That wear out Life, when two unequal minds
> Meet in one House, and two discordant Wills—

> This leaves me, where it finds,
> Past cure and past Complaint! A fate Austere,
> Too fixed and hopeless to partake of Fear!

(242–47)

These lines and the poem as a whole were disturbing enough to William as well as Dorothy when Coleridge first repeated them to Wordsworth and his sister on 21 April 1802.[17] But when they were so distinctly elided in the published version of the poem, they could not help but be present to Wordsworth; this is one of the most explicit instances in which it is clear that Coleridge figures a reading in the text that Wordsworth cannot help but follow out, or at least follow it out in order to resist it.[18] Other of Coleridge's revisions of the verse letter also highlight the way in which a very complex reading is figured for Wordsworth in the conclusion of chapter 22.

Aside from excising the very personal lines discussed above, Coleridge's revisions of the verse letter for "Dejection" involve a fairly radical re-ordering of the poem. The first three stanzas of "Dejection" in the *Morning Post* repeat the first fifty lines of "A Letter to ———" almost exactly, but then Coleridge abruptly jumps to the final stanza of "A Letter to ———." In the verse letter Coleridge had given the account of his "heartless mood" that concluded:

> I may not hope from outward Forms to win
> The Passion and the Life, whose Fountains are within!
> Those lifeless Shapes, around, below, above,
> O dearest Sara! what can they impart?
> Even when the gentle Thought, that thou, my Love,
> Art gazing now, like me
> And see'st the Heaven, I see,
> Sweet Thought it is—yet feebly stirs my Heart.

(50–57)

In converting his ambivalent love letter in verse into an equally ambivalent poem of tribute to Wordsworth, Coleridge clearly must find an alternative to the rather sentimental image of being joined to his beloved by their both gazing at "Heaven."[19] But when he chooses in "Dejection" to follow his pronouncement that "I may not hope from outward Forms to win / The Passion and the Life, whose Fountains are within!" with a new stanza, taken from the end of the verse letter, he is doing much more than just changing the poem from a love letter to a tribute to Wordsworth.

The lines that had been the conclusion and general summing up of "A Letter to ———" become in "Dejection" a specific account of why Coleridge cannot "hope from outward Forms to win / The Passion and the Life, whose Fountains are within":

O EDMUND! we receive but what we give,
And in our life alone does Nature live:
Ours is her wedding-garment, ours her shroud!
And would we aught behold, of higher worth,
Than that inanimate cold world, *allow'd*
To the poor loveless ever-anxious crowd,
Ah from the soul itself must issue forth,
A light, a glory, a fair luminous cloud
Enveloping the earth—
And from the soul itself must there be sent
A sweet and potent voice, of its own birth,
Of all sweet sounds the life and element!
O pure of heart! Thou need'st not ask of me
What this strong music in the soul may be?
What, and wherein it doth exist,
This light, this glory, this fair luminous mist,
This beautiful and beauty-making pow'r?
Joy, virtuous EDMUND! joy, that ne'er was given,
Save to the pure, and in their purest hour,
Joy, EDMUND! is the spirit and the pow'r,
Which wedding Nature to us gives in dow'r
    A new earth and new Heaven
Undream'd of by the sensual and the proud—
Joy is the sweet voice, Joy the luminous cloud—
    We, we ourselves rejoice!
And thence flows all that charms or ear or light,
All melodies the echoes of that voice
All colours a suffusion from that light.

(48–75)

As an account of Coleridge's loss of his shaping spirit of Imagination, this stanza does present a tribute to Wordsworth as one whose purity has been retained and with whom the power and spirit of Joy remains. But if we look more closely at this delineation of imaginative power, the clear demarcation between Coleridge's conception of imagination and that of Wordsworth becomes apparent.[20]

Coleridge is identifying the circumstances behind his own dejection and loss of imaginative power when he asserts that "we receive but what we give / And in our life alone does Nature live!" [emphasis mine], but the strategic shift to the first person plural at this point in the poem serves to identify Wordsworth/ Edmund as subject to the possibility of such loss as well. When read as a response to the first four stanzas of Wordsworth's Intimations ode (as the various allusions direct us to read it), this stanza offers a direct formulation of that which Wordsworth's poem is struggling to delineate—the question of whether or not the celestial light that is so elusive has its source in him or in Nature. The answer that Wordsworth evolves in his completion of the ode is a complex and equivocal one, but there can be little doubt that Coleridge's direct and unequivocal location of the life of Nature in the individual soul presents Wordsworth with a response that runs contrary to his own conceptions of the source of the "life" of Nature. This poetic difference is the one that we see laid out explicitly in Coleridge's reading of *The Prelude* in "To William Wordsworth" when he says of Wordsworth "power streamed from thee, and thy soul received / The light reflected, as a light bestowed."[21] Thus in the context of all of the other equivocal aspects of Coleridge's "tribute" to a fellow poet, the re-ordering of the stanzas of the verse letter brings to the center of the poem and to the center of Wordsworth's attention a theory of the nature of poetic imagination and its source in Nature that runs quite contrary to Wordsworth's own conception of his poetic power.

Finally, among the few lines added to the verse letter in "Dejection" are those that record the most explicit tribute to Edmund/ Wordsworth as a poet, but they do so in terms that will carry a set of disturbing associations when "Dejection" is published in *Sibylline Leaves* and is brought to Wordsworth's attention with the quotation that concludes chapter 22 of the *Biographia*. The way in which Coleridge picks and chooses among and adds to the concluding lines of the verse letter to construct the concluding lines of "Dejection" is the result of his need to rearrange the rhyme scheme in order to construct the three couplets that close

"Dejection." In this process, the lines "O simple spirit, guided from above, / O lofty Poet, full of light and love," when newly written for the poem, provide him with one of those three couplets that the rhyme scheme of the verse letter could not. It is clear as well that the addition of the lines serves to reinforce Coleridge's adaptation of the love letter to Sara Hutchinson as a tribute to Wordsworth's poetic power. But even in this context, without the negative associations with simplicity that the *Biographia* sets up, these lines are disturbing.

These associations are set up in stanza 5 of "Dejection" when Coleridge characterizes his own experience of Joy and the suspension of his powers of Imagination:

> Yes, dearest EDMUND, yes!
>> There was a time when, tho' my path was rough,
>>> This joy within me dallied with distress,
>> And all misfortunes were but as the stuff
>>> Whence Fancy made me dreams of happiness:
>> For hope grew round me, like a twining vine,
>> And fruits and foliage, not my own, seem'd mine.
>> But now afflictions bow me down to earth:
>> Nor care I, that they rob me of my mirth,
>>> But O! each visitation
>> Suspends what nature gave me at my birth,
>>> My shaping spirit of Imagination.
>
> (76–87)

The most obvious reason that Coleridge can have no Joy is that afflictions, both physical and psychological, are visited upon him and rob him of the possibility of experiencing Joy. The less apparent cause of this loss, however, may have its source in Coleridge's realization that "in our life alone does Nature live." Because of this realization, he must conclude that even his experiences of Joy were not his own and only seemed to be so. In this context, Coleridge's alignment of his own Joy with the operations of "Fancy" is quite significant. The afflictions that now bow Coleridge "down to earth" are the specific physical and psychological afflictions that he experiences and that the verse letter presents so explicitly, but one of these afflictions also may be his painful recognition that Joy may be nothing more than an illusion that is constructed out of Fancy, that happiness is merely a dream, and that the "shaping spirit of Imagination" may be a power of maintaining fanciful allusions. At least that is what Coleridge feels the gift the Nature, which indeed gives nothing, has given him.

The stanzas which surround this account of Coleridge's loss of the shaping spirit of Imagination make it clear that there are alternatives to this scenario of the degeneration of Imagination into Fancy, and it is particularly clear that these alternatives are readily available to those like Edmund/William who are "pure." That possibility is made prominent in the blessing that concludes "Dejection," but the echoes of the possibly illusory and fanciful quality of Joy are present as well. The characterization of Edmund/William as a simple spirit picks up these echoes from the poet's blessing which he bestows on his friend: "With light heart may he rise / Gay fancy, cheerful eyes." The term *fancy* does not take on its full Coleridgean import until much later, but even in this context, in which Coleridge has delineated how Fancy gave him a mere "dream of happiness," the negative implications pertain. Thus when the poet says of his friend "Joy lifts thy spirit, Joy attunes thy voice" the potentially fanciful quality of this Joy lingers over the lines, and while the friend's singing of his "lofty song" may be able to teach the poet to rejoice, there is something about Joy and Fancy that the poet may teach his friend as well.

When Coleridge quotes the lines from "Dejection" at the end of chapter 22, these associations become all the more prominent for Wordsworth both because of the negative characterization of simplicity with which Coleridge concludes his analysis of the "excellences" of Wordsworth's poetry and because of the very explicit way in which Coleridge has marked out his disagreement with Wordsworth about the nature of and the relationship between Fancy and Imagination in various parts of the *Biographia*. Also, Coleridge's placement of the quotation from "Dejection" for Wordsworth to read at this point in the narrative of his literary life makes the disagreement over the nature of poetic power that is highlighted in his revisions of the verse letter all the more prominent. If the version of "Dejection" that Coleridge published in the *Morning Post* on the day of Wordsworth's wedding was a disturbing one for him to read, then that published in *Sibylline Leaves* would have been all the more so. Thus Coleridge not only sets up Wordsworth to read the analysis of his poetry in light of the associations called up by the citation of "Dejection," he also sets him up to read the version of the poem published in *Sibylline Leaves* in light of the theories set forth in the *Biographia*. Coleridge makes the texts into glosses upon one another and maintains authority over his texts by figuring in them a reading that Wordsworth cannot author for himself.

The one addition that Coleridge makes to the poem when he publishes it in *Sibylline Leaves* consists of a series of lines that had been in previous, privately circulated versions of the poem (although not included in the *Morning Post* version in October 1802), but which were not published until 1817.[22] Like the omitted lines of the verse letter, which occupied the same position in that poem—following the declaration of Coleridge's loss of his "shaping spirit of Imagination"—these lines are of a rather personal nature and would no doubt have been left out of "Dejection" in 1802 to avoid making public the details of a private lamentation:

> For not to think of what I needs must feel,
> But to be still and patient, all I can;
> And haply by abstruse research to steal
> From my own nature all the natural Man—
> This was my sole resource, my only plan:
> Till that which suits a part infects the whole,
> And now is almost grown the habit of my Soul.
>
> (87–93)

Although one may conclude that in 1817 Coleridge was able to acknowledge the escapist impulse and potential destructiveness of his metaphysical pursuits more directly than he was able to do in 1802, the narrative of the *Biographia* tells a different story entirely—that of the productive power of metaphysical pursuits. Nonetheless, perhaps we can account for the inclusion of these lines in *Sibylline Leaves* by suggesting that now that Coleridge has told the story of what his metaphysical speculations have produced, it is no longer so difficult to acknowledge their destructiveness in an effort to "steal / From [one's] own nature all the natural Man." More importantly, however, these lines provide a means of recognizing the way in which Wordsworth both follows out and struggles against the reading that Coleridge figures for him in his text.

By including these lines in the version of the "Dejection" that is published in *Sibylline Leaves*, Coleridge is not introducing something new to Wordsworth. The lines are present in the privately circulated versions of the verse letter to which Wordsworth had access.[23] However, in making public what had previously been private and by drawing attention to his doing so by quoting from the poem in the *Biographia*, Coleridge is calling to Wordsworth's attention the way in which he had characterized Coleridge's metaphysical speculations in *The Prelude*.[24] When Coleridge includes these lines in "Dejection" in 1817 he is not simply acknowledging that his metaphysical speculations were inimical to his poetic creativity, but rather he is pointing Wordsworth's reading of the poem back to *The Prelude* in such a way as to appropriate Wordsworth's text, figuring it for him to read, in the context of Coleridge's own critique of Wordsworth's theories of poetic creativity and imagination.

The general strategy of textual appropriation that Coleridge develops in order to confront the problem of textual authority is particularly appropriate to the predicament of the Romantic autobiographer. On the one hand, it re-situates the problematic division of subject and object that is peculiar to autobiographical writing, the division between the self that writes and the self that is written about. What is written about is not some past self that can never be made fully present and can be only re-presented in language. Coleridge's strategies of textual re-appropriation make a life of his texts. But this life is not the mere literary life of a man of letters because in reproducing his own texts, Coleridge figures in them a reading of those texts that works against the reader's own attempts to appropriate the textual self he constructs.

The second part of this strategy, the attempt to circumvent the appropriation of the text by the reader, would seem to have its limits. Indeed, my accounts of the way in which Coleridge constructs a reading of his writings in chapter 10 of the *Biographia* depend upon the existence of a reader who is capable of recognizing all of the intertextual complexities of Coleridge's re-appropriations. If this general application of the strategy were Coleridge's only effort to construct such a reading, then our account of the efficacy or even existence of such a strategy might not move beyond interesting speculation. However, when he directs this strategy at a specific reader like Wordsworth, Coleridge's power to re-appropriate his own texts, to assert his authority over them, and to circumvent the reader's efforts to appropriate that authority are demonstrated quite effectively. Given the abundance of textual associations that Coleridge constructs for Wordsworth, it would seem that even if Wordsworth were to resist the reading that is figured for him in the *Biographia*, he would nonetheless have to acknowledge and confront that reading. And while Coleridge's general ability to extend this textual authority to the Reading Public as a whole may be open to question, it is, however, certain that his autobiography is structured by the desire to exercise this ability, and thus, by becoming a writer in a biographia literaria, to be the author of a life.

7

Perpetual Self-Duplication

F$_{\text{EW}}$, if any, would dispute the assertion that chapter 13 of the *Biographia* stands at the center of the problematic history and status of Coleridge's literary life. Coleridge himself is caught in the midst of this problem when in September of 1815 he must send his manuscript to the publishers, but sees no way of completing the chapter on the Imagination that he has projected.[1] Literary critics find themselves in the midst of this problem when they must confront the fictional letter from "a friend" that is produced as an expedient means of solving Coleridge's problems.[2] And finally, Coleridge's failure to produce this theory, except by presenting the "main result" of the deferred chapter, leaves every reader to face up to fact that the majority of what Coleridge does write about his theory of the Imagination consists of the plagiarisms, "borrowings," and translations that constitute chapter 12. By no means can these issues be resolved by an account of Coleridge's text as an autobiographical production. However, by attending to the strategies of autobiographical writing that are inscribed within this text we can come to an understanding of what it is that chapter 13 *does* produce, rather than simply seeing it as a sign of Coleridge's failure to produce.

The first strategic element of autobiographical writing that Coleridge inscribes in his theory of Imagination is the designation of an ideal reader. At the end of chapter 12, concluding what in his headnote he calls a "series of requests and premonitions concerning the perusal or omission of the chapter that follows" (*Biographia*, 1:232), Coleridge makes one final point before proceeding to "the nature and genesis of the imagination" (*Biographia*, 1:293). Coleridge addresses Wordsworth's discussion of the imagination in his 1815 preface to his *Poems*.[3] The process involved here of textual appropriation and re-appropriation becomes highly complex. Coleridge begins by quoting his own assertions about Imagination and Fancy from Southey's *Omniana*, then goes on to quote Wordsworth's disagreement in the 1815 preface with these assertions, and this quotation itself contains a quotation from the passage that Coleridge already has cited. In one sense, this complex of quotations within quotations is simply an example of the procedure of literary criticism in which we continually inscribe the commentaries and opinions of earlier critics within our own. However, Coleridge concludes his address to Wordsworth's commentary by identifying Wordsworth's error in failing to distinguish Fancy from Imagination and by designating him as just the sort of reader that Coleridge would wish to have:

> I am disposed to conjecture, that he [Wordsworth] has mistaken the co-presence of fancy with imagination for the operation of the latter singly. A man may work with two very different tools at the same moment; each has its share in the work, but the work effected by each is distinct and different. But it will probably appear in the next chapter, that deeming it necessary to go back much further than Mr. Wordsworth's subject required or permitted, I have attached a meaning to both fancy and imagination, which he had not in view, at least while he was writing that preface. He will judge. Would to heaven that I meet with many such readers. (*Biographia*, 1:294)

In and of itself this address to Wordsworth's account of imagination and fancy may constitute little more than Coleridge's effort to establish his own priority over those with whom he disagrees. This priority is to be found in Coleridge's choosing "to go back much further than Mr. Wordsworth's subject required." However, when read in conjunction with my earlier examination (chapter 6) of the production of Wordsworth's reading of Coleridge's text, this wish to meet with readers such as Wordsworth is quite appropriate and hardly disingenuous. As one whose reading processes have been structured by Coleridge's textual appropriations and re-appropriations, Wordsworth is indeed an ideal reader. Any effort on Wordsworth's part to take possession through reading of Coleridge's text will have to be equivocal at best. Additionally, when we consider this designation of Wordsworth as the wished-for reader in conjunction with the stated purpose of chapter 12—to advise the reader on the "perusal or omission of the chapter that follows"—and the fortuitous appearance of the friend's letter in chapter 13, we can begin to see how Coleridge's strategies of self-representation impinge upon and may even be inscribed within his theory of the Imagination.

Admittedly, there is some confusion and even debate as to whether the chapter that Coleridge refers to in the headnote to chapter 12 is that which follows when Coleridge presents the grounds for his theory of Imagination in chapter 12 itself, or if the cautionary advice refers to the chapter which Coleridge, on the advice of his "friend," does indeed omit—what would have been the "whole" of chapter 13.[4] However, if we allow ourselves to consider that the chapter to be perused or omitted is indeed chapter 13, then Coleridge's strategies of appropriation and re-appropriation in producing the text of the self may be seen to intersect in a very significant way with his theory of the Imagination.

The options that Coleridge's advice to "the unknown reader" offers are to "either pass over the following chapter altogether, or read the whole connectedly" (*Biographia*, 1:233–34). If, as I have suggested, we are assuming that the chapter to be passed over or read connectedly is chapter 13, then the explanation that Coleridge offers for giving this advice is quite telling:

> The fairest part of the most beautiful body will appear deformed and monstrous, if dissevered from its place in the organic Whole. Nay, on delicate subjects, where a seemingly trifling difference of more or less may constitute a difference in *kind*, even a *faithful* display of the main and supporting ideas, if yet they are separated from the forms by which they are at once cloathed and modified, may perchance present a skeleton indeed: but a skeleton to alarm and deter. (*Biographia*, 1:234)

This characterization of the act of displaying "main and supporting ideas . . . separated from the forms by which they are at once cloathed and modified" would seem to render chapter 13 "deformed and monstrous." However, the designation of Wordsworth as an ideal reader and the production of another such reader in the "friend" provides Coleridge with the opportunity to make advantageous use of the monstrosity of his text by producing a skeleton that will indeed alarm and deter.

As it turns out, Wordsworth and the "friend" who sends the cautionary letter to Coleridge have much more in common than his belief that they are both properly equipped to judge his text. In describing the effect of reading the chapter on the imagination, the "friend's" letter offers up an analogy that implicates Wordsworth in that reading in a highly complex way:

> The effect on my feelings, on the other hand, I cannot better represent, than by supposing myself to have known only our light airy modern chapels of ease, and then for the first time to have been placed, and left alone, in one of our largest Gothic cathedrals in a gusty moonlight night of autumn. 'Now in glimmer, and now in gloom;' often in palpable darkness not without a chilly sensation of terror; then suddenly emerging into broad yet visionary lights with coloured shadows, of fantastic shape yet all decked with holy insignia and mystic symbols. (Biographia, 1:301)

The editors of the Biographia interpret this passage as alluding to Wordsworth's Prelude.[5] But even if we question the strength of this apparent allusion, the analogy of the Gothic cathedral nonetheless calls up Wordsworth's description of The Recluse and its relation to The Prelude with the same analogy.[6] The defensive strategy of Coleridge's allusions to Wordsworth is perhaps all too obvious, but the complexity of the ways in which Wordsworth is implicated in this letter goes far beyond mere defensiveness.

First of all, at a moment when Coleridge is offering an explanation as to why he will not present the theory of the Imagination toward which the whole work has been building, he makes a point of alluding to the great "philosophic poem" that Wordsworth announced in his 1814 preface to The Excursion, but which he has yet to produce. Second, within that allusion Coleridge quotes ("now in glimmer, now in gloom") from Christabel, his poem that was to have appeared in the 1800 Lyrical Ballads but which was left out because Coleridge could not bring it to a satisfactory conclusion, thereby leading Wordsworth to put his poem "Michael" in its place. Finally, Coleridge repeats and reinforces the strategy, which I have previously analyzed (chapter 6), by having the letter from the "friend" use lines from "To William Wordsworth" to characterize the impression left by Coleridge's chapter on the Imagination:

*Yet after all, I could not but repeat the lines which you had quoted
from a MS. poem of your own in the FRIEND, and applied to a work
of Mr. Wordsworth's though with a few of the words altered:*

      ——— An orphic tale indeed,
      A tale *obscure* of high passionate thoughts
      To *a strange* music chaunted! (*Biographia*, 1:302)

In addition to the reading of the connection of Coleridge's deferred chapter to Wordsworth's *Prelude* (and *The Recluse*) that
is constructed here for Wordsworth to perform, there also is the
reference to *The Friend* that places this complex of allusions
and quotations in the context of the extended lesson in reading
that Coleridge produces in that work.[7] However, this linking of
Wordsworth and the friendly letter-writer of chapter 13 would
not go much beyond being just another version of Coleridge's
efforts to produce in Wordsworth the ideal reader of his text
were it not for another way in which the connection between
chapters 12 and 13 are forged. And this link is forged by yet
another set of textual re-appropriations.

    Coleridge's effort in the "theses" of chapter 12 to posit a prin-
ciple that will constitute a "self-grounded" truth that is "uncon-
ditional and known by its own light" (*Biographia*, 1:268) leads
him to the assertion that this principle is indeed "the SUM or I
AM." At one level, Coleridge may simply be engaging in the mad
scramble to finish the manuscript by borrowing from whatever
appropriate sources are at hand, in this case Schelling.[8] The language of thesis 6 may plagiarize, borrow, echo, or translate that
of Schelling, but it is the inscription in that language of the
strategies of self-representation and the re-inscription of that language in the definition of the Imagination in chapter 13 that is
important to our understanding of the autobiographical ground
of the definition of the Imagination. Thesis 6 states that:

    This principle, and so characterised manifests itself in the SUM or
I AM; which I shall hereafter indiscriminately express by the words
spirit, self, and self-consciousness. In this, and in this alone, object
and subject, being and knowing, are identical, each involving and
supposing the other. In other words, it is a subject which becomes
subject by the act of constructing itself objectively to itself; but which
never is an object except for itself, and only so far as by the very

same act it becomes a subject. It may be described therefore as a perpetual self-duplication of one and the same power into object and subject, which presuppose each other, and can exist only as antithesis. (*Biographia*, 1:272–73)

In terms of the problematic status of autobiographical writing, the language of Thesis 6 could not be more appropriate. Producing the self in writing is the activity of a subject becoming a subject "by the act of constructing itself objectively." However, in this activity, the self/subject is "never an object except for itself." Writing can produce self-consciousness but it cannot guarantee the reading of the other. Thus in order for the autobiographer (Coleridge) to maintain the objective status of self-consciousness that autobiographical writing attempts to achieve, he finds that he must engage in a process of perpetual self-duplication. Thus we have Coleridge's continual reappropriation of his own texts, as well as those of others.

The possibility of arriving at some satisfying end to this process of perpetual self-duplication is what Coleridge attempts to inscribe in the definition of the Imagination. Perhaps this definition could not be more familiar to us than it already is, but our preoccupation with its place in the Romantic account of the imagination has left little room for a consideration of its place in an account of Romantic strategies of self-representation. Coleridge begins his definition by stating:

The IMAGINATION then, I consider as primary or secondary. The primary IMAGINATION I hold to be the living Power and prime Agent of all human Perception, and as a repetition in the finite mind of the eternal act of creation in the infinite I AM. (*Biographia*, 1:304)

In one sense, Coleridge's assertion that the primary Imagination is a repetition of the eternal act of creation in the infinite I AM highlights the status of the finite mind that is "never an object except for itself" and can gain knowledge of its own being only in a process of "perpetual self-duplication." However, the definition of the primary Imagination does provide a ground for this knowledge in asserting that human perception has as its stable origin the eternal act of creation of the infinite I AM. In terms of traditional autobiographical writing, which also are the terms of scripture, the finite human word is ultimately grounded in the divine Word.

When Coleridge turns to the secondary imagination, he makes an effort to bring this perpetual process under the direction of the conscious will, and it is at this point that we see Coleridge re-inscribing the language of Thesis 6 into his account of the Imagination. The terminology that Coleridge uses here leaves little choice but to read the definition as an elaboration of the process whereby the subject makes itself into an object.

> The secondary I consider as an echo of the former, co-existing with the conscious will, yet still as identical with the primary in the *kind* of its agency, and differing only in the *degree* and in the *mode* of its operation. It dissolves, diffuses, dissipates, in order to re-create, or where this process is rendered impossible, yet still at all events it struggles to idealize and unify. It is essentially *vital*, even as all objects (*as* objects) are essentially fixed and dead. (*Biographia*, 1:304)

Without our entering directly into the debate over whether Coleridge gives a place of greater importance to either the primary or the secondary Imagination, it is readily apparent that Coleridge equates the secondary Imagination with poetic activity.[9] The "kind of its agency" in which the secondary Imagination is identical with the primary, would seem to be its repetition in a finite form of the identity of being and knowing that is the eternal act of creation. The difference in its "degree and . . . mode of its operation" would seem to be in its acts of dissolving, diffusing, and dissipating "in order to recreate." Thus in the secondary Imagination, we come up against Coleridge's assertion in chapter 12 that the act whereby the subject constructs itself objectively to and for itself is "a perpetual self-duplication of one and the same power into object and subject, which presuppose each other and can exist only as antithesis." The secondary Imagination is the site of perpetual self-duplication, and the acts of dissolving, diffusing, and dissipating are those of textual appropriation and re-appropriation by which Coleridge objectifies his own reading of the self that he produces in writing and thereby objectifies the reading of the other in his text. What Coleridge is asserting, in effect, is that the secondary Imagination, the poetic faculty, consciously engages in the perpetual process of the subject making itself an object to and for itself; and because it engages in the process of textual appropriation and re-appropriation, the poetic Imagination's effort "to idealize and unify" is, at bottom, an autobiographical act. The consciously chosen task of the poetic imagination is to produce the self in writing.

Although the essentially autobiographical nature of poetic activity is defined in what Coleridge does produce of his theory of Imagination and his textual appropriations and re-appropriations are explained as a strategy of autobiographical writing, the finite character of human perception and the resultant poetic activity are still problematic. It is by turning to the nature of language itself that Coleridge will draw upon the power of the infinite I AM in which being and knowing, being and act, co-inhere. He does so in the writings that were to have constituted at least one part of his "Logosophia," which is projected in the *Biographia* and is the work in which the "friend" advises that Coleridge locate the deferred chapter on the Imagination.[10]

As Coleridge defines it in the *Logic*, the "verb substantive" is essentially the "finite form" of the infinite I AM. Coleridge derives the notion of the "verb substantive" from those who theorized that the origin of the Greek language can be traced to the verb "to be." Rather than seeing language as originating in nouns, in the naming of objects, Coleridge supports the idea, at least in part, that language originates in the verb that combines both being and act, the verb "to be":

> All words express either being or action, or the predominance of one over. In philosophical grammar, they are either substantives, or verbs, or as adnouns and adverbs express the modification of one by the other. But the verb substantive ("am," *sum*, εἰμι) expresses the identity or coinherence of being and act. It is the act of being. All other words therefore may be considered as tending from this point, or more truly from the mid-point of the line, the *punctum indifferentiae* representing the *punctum identitatis*, even as the whole line represents the same point as produced or polarized. (*Logic*, 16–17)

This notion of the verb substantive has been said to represent a middle position between a materialist account of the origin of language in the noun, such as Locke's argument in the *Essay on Human Understanding*, and that of idealists who propose the verb as the origin of language.[11] By making this link between language and human consciousness, however, Coleridge is attempting to resolve more than just the opposition of two philosophical systems; he is attempting to define the relationship between language and thought. More specifically, he is seeking to identify in the origin of language the repetition of the eternal act of creation that is the infinite I AM. Also, when the definition of the verb substantive is read in terms of the definition of the Imagination in the *Biographia*, imaginative activity and linguistic production are identical as well.

The importance of Coleridge's identification of imaginative activity with linguistic production to our understanding of autobiography as the production of the self in writing becomes apparent when Coleridge turns in the *Logic*, as he did in the *Biographia*, to a discussion of the I AM as a "self-grounded" truth and principle of certainty. However, rather than turning to the infinite I AM as the ultimate source of certainty, he posits the possibility of such certainty in language itself, and he does so by means of the verb substantive:

> The *verb substantive* or first form in the science of grammar brings us the highest possible evidence of its [the I AM as principle of being and knowing] truth. For what is a fact of all human language is of course a fact of all human consciousness. The verb (*verbum*), the word is of all possible terms the most expressive of that which it is meant to express, an act, a going forth, a manifestation, a something which is distinguishable from the mind which goes forth in the word, yet inseparable therefrom; for the mind goes forth in it, and without the mind the word would cease to be a word, it would be a sound. (*Logic*, 82)

Just as the I AM represents the perfect coinherence of being and knowing, the verb substantive represents the coinherence of mind and word—each distinguishable from one another, but totally necessary to one another. If the mind goes forth in the word, then it is indeed a word; if not, it is mere sound. In the terminology of autobiographical representation that we have been using, if the self is produced in the text, then the text is the self; if not it is a mere collection of marks subject to the reading of another. Here we are faced with the question of what guarantees the production of the self in the text.

In attempting to address this question, we are led back to Thesis 6 of chapter 12 of the *Biographia*, which is inscribed in the definition of the imagination. But as it is re-appropriated in the text of the *Logic*, it also is read into the structure of the verb substantive, thus representing the process of "perpetual self-duplication" in a rather different form:

> The principle thus characterised manifests itself in the εἰμι, *sum*, or "I am," which we shall hereafter express indiscriminately by the words "mind", "self", or "self-consciousness," the preference being at once determined and explained by the context. In this, and in this alone, object and subject, being and knowing, are identical, each involving and supposing the other; it is a subject which becomes a subject in and by the very act of making itself its own object, or to familiarise ourselves gradually with the technical language of our science, it is a subject which becomes subject by the act of constructing itself objectively to and for itself; but which never is nor can be an object except for itself, and only so far an object as by the very same act and in the same indivisible moment it becomes a subject. (*Logic*, 84)

Once Coleridge's use of the I AM as a grounding principle of certainty is located within a theory of language that identifies its origin in the verb substantive, the description of "the subject which becomes subject by the act of constructing itself objectively" as a "perpetual self-duplication of one and the same power into object and subject" is revised. Even more emphatically than in the *Biographia*, Coleridge asserts that the subject "never is nor can be an object except for itself." However, rather than describing the I AM as perpetual self-duplication, Coleridge describes the mechanism by which this objectivity for itself is made possible. The subject is "only so far an object as by the very same act and in the same indivisible moment it becomes a subject." The subject has the status of object by the same act and in the same indivisible moment that it becomes a subject. Again, in the terminology of autobiography that we have been using, the self is produced in the text in the indivisible moment that is the act of reading performed in and through writing.

The means by which Coleridge seeks to capture this indivisible moment is that of making the act of writing a process of textual re-appropriation. The author-function that would make Coleridge's literary life into mere marks on the page by dividing the word from the mind and making it the property of an alien reader is put into the service of Coleridge's authority when he writes himself as the reader of his own text. Throughout the *Biographia* we see how Coleridge asserts this power to author the author-function by using re-appropriated texts as the means of constructing a reader whose act of reading is a repetition of Coleridge's own I AM.

I believe that the particularly Romantic nature of the textual production of the self can be seen in the way in which the central text of the Romantic Imagination, Coleridge's definition of the imagination, has inscribed within it the strategies of autobiographical representation that we have seen in both Coleridge and Wordsworth's writings. This study has explored the ways in which Coleridge's strategies of self-representation address the threat posed by the power of the reader. In Hazlitt's readings of Coleridge's texts, we also have explored the way in which a particularly powerful reader is implicated in and drawn to repeat those strategies. Aside from the general phenomenon of the Romantic suspicion of the reading "public," we find in both Wordsworth and Coleridge's writing very specific expressions of concern over the "promiscuous" habits of these readers. Wordsworth's own distinction between "the Public" and "the People" makes quite clear why the text that produces the self for Wordsworth would require the act of reading its own reading to be inscribed within the poem itself.[12] Although we can view Wordsworth and Coleridge's denigrations of the Reading Public in a traditional and conservative light, as does Hazlitt with his charges of apostasy, we find that Coleridge's remedy to this problem is not a means of escape or direct negation of promiscuous reading, but is a strategic practice of it.

In the manuscript of the *Logic,* Coleridge returns to the subject of the Reading Public and treats the subject in much the same spirit that he had in the *Biographia* and the *Lay Sermons.* However, in this instance Coleridge focuses on the specific effect that this phenomenon has had on language use:

> Among the consequences of the overbalance of the commercial spirit
> . . . from the gradual neglect of all the austerer studies; the long
> eclipse of philosophy, the transfer of that name to physical and psy-
> chological empiricism, and the non-existence of a learned and philo-

sophic class, constituting a *publicum in publico* . . . we have had frequent occasion to lament the vague and equivocal import of the terms and phrases which we are obliged to use in philosophic disquisition, and which yet we cannot use without awakening the meaning engrafted on them by the market, or at least the confused state of apprehension, which the wearing out of the original impress and superscription by promiscuous handling is too well calculated to reproduce. Some advantage, however, will be derived from this inconvenience if it should work a conviction of examining into the original meanings of the words we have occasion to use, to compare these with what we ourselves actually meant, and thus to understand with a clearness and distinctness which cannot fail to produce a correspondent effect on our practice "the full force of the words *propriety* of language." (*Logic*, 150)

Here Coleridge both states the threat to self-representation that promiscuous readers pose and presents the solution to that problem.

The words used in the textual production of the self are doubly under this threat of the Reading Public in that their meanings are subject to promiscuous interpretation, but they also have the meaning of the market engrafted upon them that makes them the possession of whoever purchases the book that is the literary life. The original impress and superscription of these words is worn out not only by the promiscuous handling of their meanings, but also of text that becomes the possession of the purchaser/reader. Coleridge's answer to this problem, however, is to derive some advantage from that "inconvenience" by producing in his practice "the full force of the words *propriety* of language." It is the full force of this propriety that Coleridge invokes as he re-appropriates his own textual productions and thereby constructs his reader in his text.

That the full force of the "propriety of language" for the Romantics was, at best, tenuous is indisputable. The attempt to author the author-function that is Romantic autobiography could not stand up for long against the commodifying forces of textual production. But perhaps that is the very reason that the possession of textual production in autobiography was so central to the project of Romanticism.

Notes

Introduction

1. A particularly telling example of this continual effort of the criticism to autobiography to define itself can be gathered by comparing James Olney's introductions to two collections of essays on autobiography. See *Autobiography: Essays Theoretical and Critical* (Princeton: Princeton University Press, 1980), 3–27; and *Studies in Autobiography* (New York: Oxford University Press, 1988), xiii–xvii. The time span between the dates of publication of these two collections is relatively short, so it may not seem unusual that both collections provide occasions on which Olney announces that "autobiography's time has come." However, the essays presented in the two collections indicate that the timeliness of autobiography studies was rather different in 1988 (or 1985, the year in which the conference was held from which the essays are collected) from what it was in 1980. The first set of essays focuses on tracing the trajectory of autobiography studies from its "origins" in the 1950s up to the stirrings of the challenge to autobiographical studies posed by poststructuralist theories of language and of subjectivity. The second collection takes this challenge more or less as its starting point, but nonetheless treats this present "moment" as though it were the same one that gave rise to the first collection.

2. Again examples from Olney's two collections are telling in this regard. See Elizabeth Bruss, "Eye for I: Making and Unmaking Autobiography in Film" in *Autobiography*, 268–320, and Paul John Eakin," Narrative and Chronology as Structures of Reference and the New Model Autobiographer" in *Studies in Autobiography*, 32–41. Relevant works cited by Eakin are: Philippe Lejeune, "L'ordre du re'cit dans *les Mots* de Sartre" in *Le pacte autobiographique* (Paris: Seuil, 1975), 197–243; and John Sturrock, "The New Model Autobiographer," *New Literary History* 9 (1977): 51–63.

3. Clearly these theories have posed an extreme challenge to all literary interpretation, but especially to autobiography because such theories are based in a radical account of how the subject comes to be "embodied" in writing. Olney identifies the attention to the subject of autobiography (the "autos" of autobiography) as the basis for the early criticism of autobiography (*Autobiography*, 19–22).

4. Jerome Christensen, *Coleridge's Blessed Machine of Language* (Ithaca: Cornell University Press, 1981), and *Practicing Enlightenment: Hume and the Formation of a Literary Career* (Madison: University of Wisconsin Press, 1987).

5. Frances Ferguson, *Wordsworth: Language as Counter-Spirit* (New Haven: Yale University Press, 1977).

6. John Klancher, *The Making of English Reading Audiences, 1790–1832* (Madison: University of Wisconsin Press, 1987).

7. Lucy Newlyn, *Coleridge, Wordsworth, and the Language of Allusion* (Oxford: Oxford University Press, 1986); Paul Magnuson, *Coleridge and Words-*

worth: *A Lyrical Dialogue* (Princeton: Princeton University Press, 1988); Gene W. Ruoff, *Wordsworth and Coleridge: The Making of the Major Lyrics 1802–1804* (New Brunswick, N.J.: Rutgers University Press, 1989).

8. Michel Foucault, "What Is an Author?" in *Textual Strategies*, ed. Josua V. Harrari (Ithaca: Cornell University Press, 1979), 148.

9. Lucy Newlyn, *Coleridge, Wordsworth, and the Language of Allusion*; Paul Magnuson, *Coleridge and Wordsworth: A Lyrical Dialogue*; Gene W. Ruoff, *Wordsworth and Coleridge: The Making of the Major Lyrics 1802–1804*.

Chapter 1. The Writing of Autobiography in Romanticism

1. Among those critics whose conceptions of autobiography I would call traditional, the works of some of the most prominent are: Georges Gusdorf, "Conditions and Limits of Autobiography" in *Autobiography*, 28–48; Georg Misch, *A History of Autobiography* (Cambridge: Harvard University Press, 1951); Roy Pascal, *Design and Truth in Autobiography* (Cambridge: Harvard University Press, 1960); James Olney, *Metaphors of the Self* (Princeton: Princeton University Press, 1972); Karl Weitraub, "Autobiography and Historical Consciousness," *Critical Inquiry* 1 (1975): 821–48 and *The Value of the Individual: Self and Circumstance in Autobiography* (Chicago: University of Chicago Press, 1978); William Spengemann, *The Forms of Autobiography* (New Haven and London: Yale University Press, 1980); Philippe Lejeune, *Le pacte autobiographique* (Paris: Editions du Seuil, 1975).

2. Jacques Lacan, *Ecrits*, trans. Alan Sheriden (New York: W. W. Norton & Co., 1977), 297–98.

3. Ibid., 50.

4. The psychoanalytic theory of Lacan does more than just reintroduce us to what has been a staple of the study of autobiography—that the self knows itself in and through the process of presenting its own narrative, the idea that the writing of the life "completes" the life. By identifying the structure of the unconscious with that of language, Lacan cancels out the possibility of holding some element in the process of self-representation outside of the processes of language. In this way, a central, inner self cannot be placed outside of the process of signification because that inner self, indeed if it can even be called that, is formed by the very structures through which the subject is attempting to represent itself. Writing is not simply what the subject does in the effort to represent its essence; writing is what the subject participates in at all times by the nature of the very process of constituting itself in and through language.

5. Jacques Derrida, *The Ear of the Other: Otobiography, Transference, Translation*, ed. Christie V. Mcdonald, trans. Peggy Kamuf (New York: Schocken Books, 1985), 50–51. Derrida's representation here of the autobiographical text as a speech act is rather complex and involves a crossing of speech and writing that is purposeful, playing upon his notion of the textuality of all linguistic production. This characterization of autobiographical writing as speech is very different from the use of speech act theory as a grounding for a theory of autobiography. For further consideration of this issue, see my discussion of the work of Elizabeth Bruss below.

6. Derrida generalizes his account of autobiographical writing to all texts in this way: "It is rather paradoxical to think of an autobiography whose signature is entrusted to the other, one who comes along so late and is so un-

known. . . . Every text answers to this structure. It is the structure of textuality in general. A text is signed only much later by the other. And this testamentary structure doesn't befall a text as if by accident, but constructs it. This is how a text always comes about" (*Otobiographies*, 51). I, however, wish to add to this general account of textuality the notion that the other who signs the text later has very specific historical and cultural coordinates, which may be defined in terms of Foucault's notion of "the mode of existence, circulation, and functioning of certain discourses within a society." See "What Is an Author?" in *Textual Strategies*, ed. Josua V. Harrari (Ithaca: Cornell University Press, 1979), 148.

7. Avrom Fleishman, *Figures of Autobiography* (Berkeley: University of California Press, 1983), 32.

8. A more interesting use of the notion of self-alteration may be found in Eugene Stelzig's "Coleridge in *The Prelude*: Wordsworth's Fiction of Alterity," *Wordsworth Circle* 18 (Winter 1987): 23–27.

9. In trying to conceive of a way in which representation may be seen as less threatening and more enabling, Fleishman seems to miss the point that Derrida's notion of the supplement reveals certain flaws in the theory of a unified subject of consciousness. Accounts of Derrida's notion of supplementarity may be found in "The Supplement of Origin" in *Speech and Phenomenon*, trans. David B. Allison (Evanston, Ill.: Northwestern University Press, 1973), 88–89; *Of Grammatology*, trans. Gayatri Spivak (Baltimore: Johns Hopkins University Press, 1974), 144–45.

10. This redemptive reading is particularly apparent in critical accounts of Wordsworth's poetry. Among those critics whose work I cite and take issue with in my discussions of Wordsworth in chapters 2 and 3 are the following: Timothy Bahti, "Wordsworth's Rhetorical Theft," in *Romanticism and Language*, ed. Arden Reed (Ithaca: Cornell University Press, 1984), 86–124; David Haney, "The Emergence of the Autobiographical Figure in *The Prelude*, Book 1," *Studies in Romanticism* 20 (Spring 1981): 33–63; J. Douglas Kneale, *Monumental Writing: Aspects of Rhetoric in Wordsworth's Poetry* (Lincoln: University of Nebraska Press, 1988).

11. Fleishman, *Figures*, 33.

12. Fleishman's efforts to read autobiography as a discourse of restoration (reincarnation?) has affinities to the argument that Hartman makes in offering what he calls his "counter statement" to Derrida in *Saving the Text* (Baltimore: Johns Hopkins University Press, 1981), 121ff.

13. Elizabeth W. Bruss, *Autobiographical Acts: The Changing Situation of a Literary Genre* (Baltimore: Johns Hopkins University Press, 1976); Jean Starobinski, "The Style of Autobiography" in *Autobiography*, ed. James Olney (Princeton: Princeton University Press, 1980), 73–83.

14. Starobinski, "Style," 76.

15. Emile Benveniste, *Problemes de linguistique generale* (Paris, 1966), 242. Cited by Starobinski, "Style," 76.

16. Starobinski, "Style," 75.

17. Bruss, *Autobiographical Acts*, 10–11.

18. Ibid., 11.

19. Bruss tries to qualify the degree to which the reader may resist the author's choices among the variables available within the "rules" as to the functions that an autobiography must perform by asserting that "'discovery' [of new ways of intelligibility aside from those employed by the author] and

'modification' occur only when the attention is already engaged and responsible for what it finds" (11). This responsibility is governed ultimately by the
autobiographer's "act" and the reader's "tacit knowledge of the roles(s) . . .
assigned in the act" (11).

20. Elizabeth L. Eisenstein, *The Printing Press As an Agent of Social Change*
(Cambridge: Cambridge University Press, 1979); Martha Woodmansee, "The
Genius and the Copyright: Economic and Legal Conditions of the Emergence of
the 'Author,'" *Eighteenth Century Studies* 17 (Summer 1984): 425–48; Jerome
Christensen, *Practicing Enlightenment*, particularly chapter 6, "The Commerce
of Letters," 120–200. For an exploration of this issue which focuses specifically
on the writing of autobiography in the eighteenth century, see Felicity Nussbaum, *The Autobiographical Subject: Gender and Ideology in Eighteenth-
Century England* (Baltimore and London: Johns Hopkins University Press,
1989). Also, a very useful account of various critical examinations of the role
played by historical and cultural circumstance in the construction of concepts
of self is presented by Paul John Eakin in *Fictions in Autobiography* (Princeton:
Princeton University Press, 1985), 191–201.

21. Foucault, "What Is an Author?" 148.

22. Ibid., 148. For a fuller discussion of the significance of this period of
history as one in which there occurs a "mutation of Order into History," see
Foucault's *The Order of Things* (New York: Random House, 1970), 220–21.

23. Jerome Christensen, *Practicing Enlightenment* (Madison: University of
Wisconsin Press, 1987), 4.

24. Foucault, *The Order of Things*, 221.

25. One way of characterizing this situation in which Romantic authors find
themselves is provided by the very productive term *Romantic irony*. Among
the range of the different accounts of Romantic irony that I have found useful
are: Paul de Man, "The Rhetoric of Temporality" in *Interpretation: Theory and
Practice*, ed. Charles Singleton (Baltimore: Johns Hopkins University Press,
1969), 173–209 and *Blindness and Insight* (New York: Oxford University Press,
1971); Micheal G. Cooke, *The Romantic Will* (New Haven and London: Yale
University Press, 1976); David Simpson, *Irony and Authority in Romantic Poetry* (Totowa, N.J.: Rowman & Littlefield, 1979); Anne Mellor, *English Romantic
Irony* (Cambridge: Harvard University Press, 1980); Tilottama Rajan, *Dark
Interpreter: The Discourse of Romanticism* (Ithaca and London: Cornell University Press, 1980); and Frederick Garber, *Self, Text, and Romantic Irony*
(Princeton: Princeton University Press, 1988). My exploration of the strategies
that Romantic writers construct in order to come to terms with the divided
subject of autobiography is very much grounded in these accounts of Romantic
irony, particularly those of de Man, Simpson, and Rajan. However, my work
goes beyond simply examining the way in which irony provides the means by
which to figure the self in a text; rather it explores the way in which Romantic
autobiographers sought to control the way in which that figure might be read.

26. Foucault, "What Is an Author?" 159.

27. M. H. Abrams, *Natural Supernaturalism: Tradition and Revolution in
Romantic Literature* (New York: W.W. Norton & Co., 1971), 83.

28. A significant exception to the usual practice of citing Augustine's *Confessions* as a model for English autobiography may be found in Linda Peterson's
Victorian Autobiography (New Haven and London: Yale University Press,
1986), 2–4. Peterson takes "the spiritual autobiographies of the late seventeenth
and eighteenth centuries, rather than the *Confessions*, to be influential in the

development of English forms of the genre" of autobiography (195n). In part, Peterson's questioning of the Augustinian model of autobiographical discourse is based on her conception of autobiography as a "hermeneutic" form which "distinguishes itself as a genre by the act of interpretation rather than the act of presentation" (4). It is precisely this activity of interpretation and the pressing need for it occasioned by the emergence of the "author-function" that I focus on in my account of Romantic strategies of self-representation.

29. Abrams, *Natural Supernaturalism*, 89.

30. Paul Jay, *Being in the Text* (Ithaca and London: Cornell University Press, 1984), 31.

31. One aspect of Jay's analysis of Augustine's confrontation with the divided subject of autobiography has been quite useful to me. In his examination of the problematic break in Augustine's narrative between "the retrospective narration of [his] life (Books 1–9) and the introspective exegetical portions that follow (Books 10–14)," Jay points out the crucial relationship between "narrative recollection and discursive analysis" (24, 29). In the latter of these two modes, Jay sees a "meditation on the philosophical problems underlying literary self-representation" (31). In the terms that I am using to examine autobiographical writing, this relationship can be characterized as one in which Augustine uses the second part of his text to construct a reading of the first part. But the nature of this reading also marks the crucial difference between Augustine's confessions and Romantic autobiography in that Augustine's discursive analysis, his reading of the process of self-representation, finally avails itself of a grounding in the Word of God (the scriptures).

32. Christensen, *Practicing Enlightenment*, 9.

33. Giambattista Vico, *The Autobiography of Giambattista Vico*, trans. Max Harold Fisch and Thomas Goddard Bergin (Ithaca and London: Cornell University Press, 1944), 2. All references to this work are drawn from this edition and are cited in the text parenthetically.

34. Vico himself saw the *Autobiography* as a narration of the history of the *New Science*, but the way in which he complicates that narrative indicates that it needs to be read as something other and more than a presentation of the *New Science* in another form. For a reading of Vico's *Autobiography* that examines it as an explication of the *New Science*, see Michael Sprinker, "Fictions of the Self: The End of Autobiography" in *Autobiography: Essays Theoretical and Critical*, ed. James Olney, 326–29.

35. The "lies" appear in a review of the *New Science* in the book notices of the Leipzig *Acta [Eruditorum]* for August 1727 (*Autobiography*, 187).

36. For discussions of Vico's principle of *verum factum*, see Max H. Fisch, "Vico and Pragmatism" in *Giambattista Vico An International Symposium*, eds. Giorgio Tacliacozzo and Hayden V. White (Baltimore: Johns Hopkins University Press, 1969), 405–14; Jeffrey Barnouw, "The Relation between the Certain and the True in Vico's Pragmatist Construction of Human History," *Comparative Literature Studies* 15 (June 1978): 242–64; and James C. Morrison, "Vico's Principle: *Verum* is *Factum*," *Journal of the History of Ideas* 39 (October–December 1978): 579–95.

37. For discussions of Vico's theory of knowledge, see Bergin and Fisch's introduction to *The New Science of Giambatista Vico*, ed. and trans. Thomas Bergin and Max Harold Fisch, revised and abridged ed. (Ithaca: Cornell University Press, 1970), xxxv–xxxviii. Also see Hayden White, "The Tropics of History: The Deep Structure of the *New Science*" in *Giambatista Vico's Science*

of Humanity, ed. Giorgio Tagliacozzo and Donald Philip Verene (Baltimore: Johns Hopkins University Press, 1976), 65–66. For discussions of Vico's *Autobiography* as an application of the *New Science*, see Bergin and Fisch's introduction to the *Autobiography* (7), and Benedetto Croce, *The Philosophy of Giambatista Vico*, trans. R. G. Collingwood (New York: Russell & Russell, 1964), 266. All further references to the *New Science* are presented in the text by page and paragraph number and are taken from *The New Science of Giambattista Vico*, trans. Thomas Goddard Bergin and Max Harold Fisch (Ithaca: Cornell University Press, 1948).

38. According to the *OED*, the term *autobiography* is first used by Southey in 1809. For a correction of this citation that identifies William Taylor as having used the word *autobiography* in 1797, see James M. Good, "William Taylor, Robert Southey, and the Word 'Autobiography,'" *The Wordsworth Circle* 12 (Spring 1981): 125–27.

39. Christensen, *Practicing Enlightenment*, 120–200.

Chapter 2. The Subsidiary to Preparation

1. William Wordsworth, *The Prelude: 1799, 1805, 1850*, eds. Jonathan Wordsworth, M. H. Abrams, and Stephen Gill (New York: W.W. Norton & Co, 1979), book 1, lines 9–15. Unless indicated otherwise, this and all subsequent references to this poem are taken from the 1805 *Prelude* and are designated in the text by book and line numbers.

2. See Charles J. Rzepka, *The Self as Mind: Vision and Identity in Wordsworth, Coleridge, and Keats* (Cambridge: Harvard University Press, 1986), 31–99, for an account of Wordsworth's poetic career as an effort to "place" himself in the world.

3. Mary Jacobus's analysis of Wordsworth's use of apostrophe in *The Prelude* deals with this desire for transcendence and the strategies whereby Wordsworth seeks to achieve it. See "Apostrophe and Lyric Voice in *The Prelude*" in *Lyric Poetry*, ed. Chaviva Hosek and Patricia Parker (Ithaca: Cornell University Press, 1985), 167–81.

4. For an account of the distinction between origins and beginnings, see Edward Said, *Beginnings: Intention and Method* (Baltimore: Johns Hopkins University Press, 1975), 174–75, as well as 44–46 on *The Prelude* as a poem of beginnings.

5. Kenneth Johnston's account of the *The Prelude* and *The Recluse* downplays the significance of *The Prelude* as an autobiography, but his reading of the relationship between the two works in their various stages of composition has offered me significant guidance in the construction of my reading of *The Prelude*. See Kenneth Johnston, *Wordsworth and The Recluse* (New Haven: Yale University Press, 1984), especially 119–216.

6. My understanding of the compositional history of *The Prelude* is primarily drawn from the account provided by Jonathan Wordsworth, M. H. Abrams, and Stephen Gill in *The Prelude: 1799, 1805, 1850*. Significant information has also been provided by Stephen Parrish's introduction to *The Prelude, 1798–1799* (Ithaca: Cornell University Press, 1977). The first 54 lines of the 1805 *Prelude* were composed just at the time when Wordsworth was completing the 1799 *Prelude*. The lines that follow these and precede "Was it for this. . . ." (1.55–271) are composed in early 1804.

7. Jonathan Arac has traced a line in the revisions of the 1805 *Prelude* in the final 1850 version of the poem that demonstrates a process of what he calls "reading asunder." See "Bounding Lines: *The Prelude* and Critical Revision," *boundary 2* 7 (1979): 31–48. In a brief suggestion at the beginning of his article, Arac offers the observation that the 1805 *Prelude* is naturally seen as a "spinning out of material to stand between parts that were originally compacted together" (31). I argue that the relationship between the 1799 *Prelude* and the 1805 is similar to that outlined by Arac in reading the revisions of 1805 in 1850, and I have taken the lead provided by this reading of the revisions to suggest a similar "reading asunder" of the two-part *Prelude* and 1805.

8. Johnston, *Wordsworth*, 53–78.

9. Ibid., 81–99.

10. Ibid., 183.

11. See below for a more detailed account of Coleridge's role as auditor in *The Prelude*. Also see Frank D. McConnell, *The Confessional Imagination: A Reading of Wordsworth's Prelude* (Baltimore: Johns Hopkins University Press, 1974) 27–39. McConnell examines the issue of audience from the point of view of the rhetorical structure of the confession as a genre.

12. Jacobus, "Apostrophe," 173–76.

13. J. Douglas Kneale offers another version of Wordsworth's "uneasiness" with the privileging of "voice," in "Wordsworth's Image of Language: Voice and Letter in *The Prelude*," *PMLA* 101 (1986): 351–61. Kneale, unlike Jacobus, keeps the categories of voice and letter rather discreet, opting for an account of the way in which they play off from one another in *The Prelude*, rather than adopting what seems to me to be the more accurate line that Jacobus takes in accounting for the way in which the seemingly exclusive categories continually and strategically intersect.

14. Certainly the members of Wordsworth's circle could "read" *The Prelude*, and Coleridge is among the most prominent of those who can and do read it. But as my analysis of Coleridge's role in *The Prelude* presented below will make clear, Wordsworth was always conscious of the need to control the reader of *The Prelude*, and in many ways he managed to withhold the poem from being "read" even by those who had access to the text.

15. William Wordsworth, *Wordsworth: Poetical Works*, ed. Ernest de Selincourt (London: Oxford University Press, 1936), 589.

16. Perhaps the most prominent treatment of the "mighty maze" of *The Prelude's* narrative is that of Geoffrey Hartman in *Wordsworth's Poetry* (New Haven: Yale University Press, 1964), 163–207. Critics who treat these beginnings specifically as aspects of autobiographical writing are David Haney, "The Emergence of the Autobiographical Figure in *The Prelude*, Book 1," *Studies in Romanticism* 20 (Spring 1981): 33–63; and Paul Jay, *Being in the Text: Self-Representation from Wordsworth to Roland Barthes* (Ithaca: Cornell University Press, 1984), 33. Johnston's account of the beginnings of *The Prelude* divides the lines preceding the 1799 beginning, "Was it for this. . . .", into three parts: the "glad preamble" (1–54), the post-preamble or topical introduction (55–156), and the introduction proper (157–271), and he reads these beginnings as a three-part movement that serves to ground the vague referent of the 1799 opening (123–31).

17. See Susan Wolfson, *The Questioning Presence: Wordsworth, Keats, and the Interrogative Mode in Romantic Poetry* (Ithaca: Cornell University Press, 1986). Wolfson presents an account of the way in which the 1814 Preface

"obscures the history of delay" that surrounds *The Prelude* and *The Recluse* in her examination of the interrogative mode as a strategy in Wordsworth's autobiographical writing (134ff).

18. The link between reading and writing in Wordsworth is instructively explored by Geoffrey Hartman, "Words, Wish, Worth: Wordsworth" in *Deconstruction and Criticism*, ed. Harold Bloom (New York: Seabury Press, 1979), 177–216.

19. Johnston categorizes and examines these themes in some detail (127–31). See also James Chandler, *Wordsworth's Second Nature: A Study of the Poetry and Politics* (Chicago: University of Chicago Press, 1984). Chandler links Wordsworth's inability to proceed with these themes to a basic flaw in the poet's conception of "freedom" as it manifests itself in the glad preamble's assertion of the poet's freedom to fix his residence where he will (192–93). Chandler's reading of *The Prelude* chronicles Wordsworth's education about the nature of this flaw as he moves from a Rousseauistic model of nature to a Burkean model of "second nature."

20. Abrams, *Natural Supernaturalism*; Hartman, *Wordsworth's Poetry*, 208–59. In the political vein, I have in mind Chandler's reading in *Wordsworth's Second Nature* that admirably seeks to link the "literary" crisis of book 1 to the political and moral crises of books 9–11 in an account of *The Prelude* as recording "the discipline of a poet's mind" (184–215).

21. Paul de Man's account of the relationship between epitaph and autobiography offers an important alternative to the account of Romantic autobiography as visionary transcendence. See "Autobiography as De-facement," *MLN* 94 (1979): 925. Although I agree to a certain extent with critics like Paul John Eakin who take the position that de Man's insistence upon stripping the illusion from reference from autobiography leads to an all-too-totalizing view of the self as being displaced by the text, I believe that de Man nonetheless presents a very useful account of the threat that writing constitutes to the self. See Paul John Eakin, *Fictions in Autobiography* (Princeton: Princeton University Press, 1985), 184–91.

22. See Chandler, *Wordsworth's Second Nature*, 187ff; Wolfson, *The Questioning Presence*, 146ff; Stephen Parrish, Introduction to *The Prelude, 1798–99* (Ithaca: Cornell University Press, 1977), 6ff; Johnston, *Wordsworth and The Recluse*, 62ff; Jonathan Wordsworth, *Borders of Vision*, 36ff.

23. David Haney suggests the line of argument that I have adopted here in asserting that "the figure of the poet's life [emerges] as a solution" to the problematic narrative. However, Haney's sense that this solution "alters the poet's graveward journey" seems to me to underestimate the degree to which the "death" of the project of a poetry of self-presented truth figures in this solution (Haney, "Emergence," 48). Mary Jacobus's account of the lyric voice in *The Prelude* would suggest that the turn involved in the rhetorical question about the power of the murmurs of the Derwent constitutes a "poetic self-immersion" standing as an alternative to the "poetic self-assertion." In Jacobus' terms, the rhetorical move here would constitute "the fiction of a poetry that originates in Nature, [which] like the voice of the Derwent, ensures continuity while providing a safely trans-subjective voice in which the poet's own can be merged ("Apostrophe," 170). Again, my addition to this account would be to point out the way in which the rhetorical question embodies both such a self-immersion and the self-assertion that it seeks to reject. Finally, J. Douglas Kneale makes an argument similar to Jacobus's with regard to Wordsworth's voice merging

with that of Nature (353), but does not construct nearly so cogent an argument
as does Jacobus with regard to the significance of this voice in relation to
Wordsworth's larger poetic project.

24. Johnston, *Wordsworth*, 62.

25. Timothy Bahti reads these episodes as accomplishing a "rhetorical
theft." See "Wordsworth's Rhetorical Theft" in *Romanticism and Language*, ed.
Arden Reed (Ithaca: Cornell University Press, 1984), 86–124.

26. Bahti explores the significance of the situation of "hanging" (98–99),
drawing on analyses of the Boy of Winander passage (*Prelude* 5.389ff.) particularly Paul de Man, "Wordsworth and Hölderlin" in *The Rhetoric of Romanticism* (New York: Columbia University Press, 1984); 47–65; and Cynthia Chase,
"The Accidents of Disfiguration: Limits to Literal and Rhetorical Reading in
Book V of *The Prelude*," *Studies in Romanticism* 18 (1979): 547–65.

27. Hartman, "Words, Wish, Worth: Wordsworth," 194. Haney is very instructive in his use of this notion from Hartman to support his assertion that
Wordsworth "uses his perception of Nature's relation to his childhood as a
figure for his own relation to his past" (59).

28. See my discussion above of the preference for the secondary echo over
the immediate voice and the related reference to Mary Jacobus on apostrophe
and the lyric voice.

29. This is the sound of "silent reading" which Jacobus identifies as the goal
of Wordsworth's substitution of the "'WORD'—lasting but inaudible except to
the mind—for an epic theme" ("Apostrophe," 181).

30. Bahti, "Rhetorical Theft," 121.

31. Both McConnell and Haney, each with a slightly different emphasis,
focus on the integrative function of voice, textualized or otherwise, that absorbs
and transforms the "blank desertion" (McConnell, *Confessional*, 98; Haney,
"Emergence," 59).

32. With a rather different emphasis, Susan Wolfson (*Questioning Presence*,
160–62) also examines this sequence of apostrophes, and concludes with regard to the rhetorical question posed to the "presences of Nature" that the
question "foreclose[s] uncertainty with an expanded predicate that in effect
precludes any need for counter-assertion by recovering the presences in question" (162). This foreclosure of uncertainty is at the base of the self-presence
that Wordsworth achieves in figuring in the reading/writing of the self the
dividedness of the autobiographical subject.

33. The force with which these expectations operate in *The Prelude* will be
examined in much greater detail in chapter 4. This passage also stands as the
conclusion of the 1799 *Prelude*, and I think that the new context provided by
the 1805 revisions could be read in a similar manner to that in which I read
the re-contextualization of the original opening of 1799 ("Was it for this. . . .").

34. Arac, "Bounding Lines," 84. While the address to Coleridge that precedes these lines had been the closing lines of the 1799 *Prelude*, these are
added in 1804 in order to bring book 1 to a close, further emphasizing the
differences between 1799 and 1805 in terms of their status in Wordsworth's
effort to write the self.

Chapter 3. The Surface of Past Time

1. M. H. Abrams, *Natural Supernaturalism* (New York: Norton, 1971); Geoffrey Hartman, *Wordsworth's Poetry* (New Haven: Yale University Press, 1964);

Earl R. Wasserman, "The English Romantics: The Grounds of Knowledge" in *Romanticism: Points of View*, eds. Gleckner and Enscoe (Princeton: Princeton University Press, 1962); Jonathan Wordsworth, *William Wordsworth: The Borders of Vision* (Oxford: Oxford University Press, 1982).

2. See Hartman, *Wordsworth's Poetry*, 223–25; Kenneth Johnston, *Wordsworth and The Recluse* (New Haven: Yale University Press, 1984), 136–38; and Charles Rzepka, *The Self as Mind* (Cambridge: Harvard University Press, 1986), 56–62. Also, see Paul Magnuson, *Coleridge and Wordsworth: A Lyrical Dialogue* (Princeton: Princeton University Press, 1988), 84–95, for a discussion of "The Discharged Soldier" as a response to Coleridge's "Rime of the Ancient Mariner."

3. See Jonathan Wordsworth, *William Wordsworth: The Borders of Vision* (Oxford: Oxford University Press, 1982), 334–35. Professor Wordsworth calls this passage the "truest" of Wordsworth's retrospects and points out the image's representation of the narrative as non-sequential. Although I might partially agree with Professor Wordsworth that the passage seems to assert that there may be no point in trying to get at "objective memory," I want also to suggest that the poet may indeed be indicating that there is a point in *not trying*. See Theresa M. Kelley, *Wordsworth's Revisionary Aesthetics* (Cambridge: Cambridge University Press, 1988), 97–98, for an account of this passage as a decisive moment in Wordsworth's definition of his aesthetic project in *The Prelude*.

4. Wasserman, "The English Romantics: The Grounds of Knowledge," 334.

5. The linguistic and/or textual nature of this passage was pointed out and analyzed by Eugenio Donato in a seminar conducted at the University of California at Irvine in the winter of 1982. In another context Donato has compared Wasserman's accounts of the relationship between subject and object in Romantic accounts of perception to the argument made by Paul de Man in "The Intentional Structure of Romantic Imagery" in *Romanticism and Consciousness*, ed. Harold Bloom (New York: Norton, 1970), 65–77. See Eugenio Donato, "Divine Agonies: Of Representation and Narrative in Romantic Poetics," *Glyph* 6 (1979): 104. The relationship between perception and language in Wordsworth's poetry is also developed in another context by Frances Ferguson, *Language as Counter-Spirit* (New Haven: Yale University Press, 1977), 126–54.

6. Johnston, *Wordsworth and the Recluse*, 136.

7. Charles Rzepka draws explicit connections between the encounter with the discharged soldier and Wordsworth's efforts in the 1800 Preface to the *Lyrical Ballads* to create his own ideal audience and thereby assure that his works will not be misread (*Self as Mind*, 62–71). I have extended Rzepka's point to try to expose the way in which the "others" in Wordsworth's poetry can almost always be seen as figures of readers.

8. Rzepka, *Self as Mind*, 60–62.

9. *Lyrical Ballads*, eds. R. L. Brett and A. R. Jones (London: Routledge, 1968), 249.

10. *The Prose Works of William Wordsworth*, eds. W. J. B. Owen and Jane Worthington Smyser, 3 vols. (Oxford: Clarendon Press, 1974), 3.84.

11. Rzepka, *Self as Mind*, 64–65.

12. Johnston offers a very suggestive account of why Wordsworth may have chosen to place books 7 and 8 before the France books; see Johnston, *Wordsworth and the Recluse*, 158–73. Also on the relationship between books 7 and 8, see Jonathan Wordsworth, *The Borders of Vision*, 279–307.

13. Lines 43–50 of book 7 can definitely be identified as having belonged to

book 8, and the editors of *The Prelude 1799, 1805, 1850* speculate that by implication, lines 1–50 can be so identified as well (518–19).

14. *The Prelude 1799, 1805, 1850*, 519. Wordsworth is said in the original opening of book 8 "to gloss over" this entire experience.

15. I rely on David Simpson's account of these three stages in the construction of my argument and particularly his discussion of the final stage, which involves a "second look." See *Wordsworth and the Figurings of the Real* (London: Macmillan, 1982), 54–58.

16. It is also an especially important word in Wordsworth's narrative of his experiences in France. The account of London spectacles serves as an important pretext to the reading of France that Wordsworth constructs in *The Prelude*. See Mary Jacobus, "'That Great Stage Where Senators Perform': Macbeth and the Politics of Romantic Theatre," *Studies in Romanticism* 22 (Fall 1983): 353–87.

17. This development of "stagecraft" has been attributed to the licensing act which severely limited the way in which contemporary events could be represented on the stage. In effect, accurate scenic depiction was substituted for the banned verbal representation of politically sensitive materials. Also, see Jacobus, "The Politics of Romantic Theatre," (353–74) for an account of Burke's use of theatrical metaphors in *Reflections on the Revolution in France* and Wordsworth's complex working out of his "anti-theatrical bias" in *The Prelude*.

18. Simpson, *Figurings of the Real*, 54.

19. See Donald H. Reiman, "The Beauty of Buttermere as Fact and Romantic Symbol," *Criticism* 26 (Spring 1984): 139–70 for an account of the facts of Mary Robinson's life and the ways in which these facts were treated not only by William Wordsworth, but also by Dorothy Wordsworth, Coleridge, the Lambs, and De Quincey.

20. As Geoffrey Hartman asserts, this reflection is itself a "performance within the context of Wordsworth's narrative" in that it "enters the narrative as a special event" (*Wordsworth's Poetry*, 236).

21. Ibid.

22. This process of embalming by nature and Wordsworth's own embalming of the maid and the boy in his narrative offers an account of the dark and threatening side of the parallel relation between Nature and imagination, the transcendent version of which is represented in the ascent of Mount Snowdon in book 13. See below for my further development of this connection.

23. The image of the board as stage is added in the 1850 *Prelude* (7.358n).

24. Johnston considers the narrative of book 7 in terms of Wordsworth's problematic efforts to attend responsibly to the "real" world according to the terms of the *Recluse* project (162–63).

25. For pertinent readings of this passage see Hartman, *Wordsworth's Poetry*, 238–42; Jay, *Being in the Text: Self-Representation from Wordsworth to Roland Barthes* (Ithaca: Cornell University Press, 1894), 90–91; Frances Ferguson, *Wordsworth: Language as Counter-Spirit*, 138–46; and Jonathan Wordsworth, *The Borders of Vision*, 300–304. See also Theresa M. Kelley, *Wordsworth's Revisionary Aesthetics*, 111. Kelley examines the contrast between Wordsworth's account of the blind beggar and all of the other spectacles of London in terms of their status as "sublime" figures. Kelley's account of Wordsworth's efforts to manage the sublime in the London books indicates some of the important ways in which this management involves a process of "reading" (109–15).

26. Ferguson comments on how the account of the blind beggar exhibits a conversion from images of externality (Wordsworth as passive spectator) to an

image of "startling internality" (*Language as Counter-Spirit*, 143). Although I cannot fully assent to Ferguson's later assertion that it is at this point in Wordsworth's narrative that "the primacy of the human (rather than of nature) begins to assert itself," I nonetheless fully assent to and follow her lead in her assertion that "the 'Blind Beggar' episode operates both as an insight into the alienness of external form and as testimony to the power of external form for creating the very possibility of internality" (145). I would go on to assert, as I do as my reading of *The Prelude* proceeds, that Wordsworth's means of confronting this apparent paradox is his construction of self in and through the reading that constitutes the writing of the self.

27. Hartman notes the way in which Wordsworth takes the position that the over-stimulation of the urban scene has the effect of putting the imagination to sleep. The judgment that Hartman sees Wordsworth as making about all descriptive poetry, that it is the product of mere memory and not imagination, is clearly a judgment Wordsworth makes not so much about descriptive poetry in general but about his own narrative at this particular point (*Wordsworth's Poetry*, 240).

28. Johnston analyzes this "weakness" in Wordsworth's argument (*Wordsworth and the Recluse*, 165–71). A similar account of Wordsworth's failure in his attempts to establish a sense of connection between himself and his fellow human beings is registered in Jonathan Wordsworth's account of book 8 (*Borders*, 281–95).

29. Simpson sees the beholder of the spectacles as being invited briefly to occupy a position of mastery (*Figurings*, 56). Although Simpson does to some degree acknowledge the illusory nature of this mastery, his concern with the violent oscillation of mastery and slavery seems to elide the significant way in which this "mastery" is in itself problematic.

30. Paul Jay compares Wordsworth's procedure of repeating key scenes in his narrative to Kierkegaadian notions of repetition. Although Jay does note Wordsworth's process of constructing a "pretext," he does not focus on the relationship between writing and reading in the construction of the self in the sense that I have tried to do here. See Paul Jay, *Being in the Text*, 79ff.

Chapter 4. To Thee the Work Shall Justify Itself

1. There are any number of recent examinations of both the personal and poetic relationship between Wordsworth and Coleridge. Accounts of this relationship as one of mutual sympathy may be found in these analyses of the theme of intellectual love in *The Prelude*: Francis Christensen, "Intellectual Love: The Second Theme of The Prelude," *PMLA* 80 (1965): 69–75; and Frances Ferguson, *Wordsworth: Language as Counter-Spirit* (New Haven: Yale University Press, 1977), 148–54. Recent studies that emphasize the tension between Coleridge and Wordsworth as represented in *The Prelude* are: James Chandler, *Wordsworth's Second Nature: A Study of the Poetry and Politics* (Chicago: University of Chicago Press, 1984), 235–65; Thomas McFarland, *Romanticism and the Forms of Ruin* (Princeton: Princeton University Press, 1981), 56–103 and "Wordsworth on Man, on Nature, and on Human Life," *Studies in Romanticism* 21 (Winter 1982): 601–18; Lucy Newlyn, *Coleridge, Wordsworth, and the Language of Allusion* (Oxford: Oxford University Press, 1986). William H. Galperin examines Wordsworth and Coleridge's representations of one another in terms of Coleridge's concept of "desynonymization" in "'Desynonymizing' the Self in Wordsworth and Coleridge," *Studies in Romanticism* 26 (Winter 1987):

513–26. Eugene Stelzig has directly addressed Coleridge's role as auditor in *The Prelude* in "Coleridge in *The Prelude*: Wordsworth's Fiction of Alterity," *The Wordsworth Circle* 28 (1987): 23–27. Although Stelzig presents an important and compelling account of Wordsworth's address to Coleridge as an "enabling fiction that allows Wordsworth to take full charge of himself and his intended impact as a poet" (24), he does not fully take into account the depth and dimension of Coleridge's presences as a "reader" that I seek to address here. Paul Magnuson's account of Coleridge and Wordsworth's "lyrical dialogue" highlights significant elements in the exchange between Coleridge and Wordsworth that I examine here. See Paul Magnuson, *Coleridge and Wordsworth: A Lyrical Dialogue* (Princeton: Princeton University Press, 1988).

2. Harold Bloom's model for mapping the anxiety of influence has an important bearing on my analysis. See *Anxiety of Influence* (London: Oxford University Press, 1973) and *A Map of Misreading* (London: Oxford University Press, 1975). However, the limitations of Bloom's system in analyzing the influence of contemporaries on one another points up the need for an understanding of the role of the contemporary as a potentially threatening reader. The limitations of Bloom's theory are apparent in his own analysis of Coleridge's "misreading" of Wordsworth in "Dejection: An Ode" and "To William Wordsworth." See *Figures of Capable Imagination* (New York: Seabury Press, 1976), 14. When Bloom considers Coleridge's "misreading" of Wordsworth, he immediately transposes it into a mutual revisionary reading by both Wordsworth and Coleridge of Milton. Bloom states that "both poems misread Milton as sensitively and desperately as they do Wordsworth; the meaning of 'Dejection' is in its relation to 'Lycidas' as much as in its relations to the 'Intimations' Ode, even as the poem 'To William Wordsworth' assimilates *The Prelude* to *Paradise Lost*" (*Figures*, 14). Bloom's theory of influence insists upon a linear view of intertextual relations that does not account for the interplay of reading and writing that I am examining in the works of Coleridge and Wordsworth. Recently, W. J. T. Mitchell has addressed issues that are similar to those I raise here. See "Influence, Autobiography, and Literary History: Rousseau's *Confessions* and Wordsworth's *The Prelude*," *ELH* 57 (1990): 643–64.

3. My account of Wordsworth's struggle with Coleridge as reader is informed by Bakhtin's notion of dialogic discourse. In Bakhtin's terms, I would characterize Wordsworth's attempt as an effort that seeks to extinguish the "internal dialogization of discourse" in the way that Bakhtin asserts all poetic discourse seeks to do. See M. M. Bakhtin, *The Dialogic Imagination*, trans. Caryl Emerson and Michael Holquist, ed. Michael Holquist (Austin: University of Texas Press, 1981), 284–88.

4. McFarland, "Wordsworth on Man," 606–10.

5. While a "bourne" is a terminal point or a goal, it is also a stream, a meaning that fits well with the stream imagery throughout the poem, but which can also be implicated in Wordsworth's account of the impossibility of parceling out one's intellect by "geometric rule": "Who shall point as with a wand, and say / 'This portion of the river of my mind / Came from yon fountain?'" (2.213–15).

6. See my discussion in chapter 3 of books 7 and 8 for an account of Wordsworth's own efforts to preserve himself from the corruption of the "haunts of men."

7. Most critical attention to Wordsworth, science, and geometry has focused on book 5 and the Arab dream and Wordsworth's conception of the relationship

between science and poetry. See Jane Worthington Smyser, "Wordsworth's Dream of Poetry and Science: *The Prelude*, V," *PMLA* 71 (March 1956): 269–75; Geoffrey Hartman, *Wordsworth's Poetry* (New Haven: Yale University Press, 1964), 228–31; J. Hillis Miller, "The Stone and the Shell: Problems of Poetic Form in Wordsworth's Dream of the Arab" in *Mouvements Premiers* (Paris: Librairie José Corti, 1972), 140, 144; Timothy Bahti, "Figures of Interpretations, The Interpretation of Figures: A Reading of Wordsworth's Dream of the Arab," *Studies in Romanticism* 18 (Winter 1979): 617; Mary Jacobus, "Wordsworth and the Language of Dream," *ELH* 46 (Winter 1979): 642; Theresa M. Kelley, "Spirit and Geometric Form: The Stone and the Shell in Wordsworth's Arab Dream," *Studies in English Literature 1500–1900* 22 (Autumn 1982): 563–82; Nicholas Roe, *Wordsworth and Coleridge: The Radical Years* (Oxford: Oxford University Press, 1988), 223–33. Although the general pattern of criticism that portrays Wordsworth as opposing science to poetry as a mode of knowledge would seem to fit my argument about Coleridge's threatening presence fairly well, I believe Kelley's argument about Wordsworth's desire for a unified concept of geometric and poetic truth best accounts for the kind of ambivalences that I examine in Wordsworth's representation of Coleridge.

8. See Kelley, "Spirit and Geometric Form," 570–80. The alteration and development in Wordsworth's attitude toward science that Kelley traces are quite significant with regard to Wordsworth's representation of Coleridge in *The Prelude*. The alternating suspicion (2.469–75) and praise (6.135–59, 178–87) of geometry and mathematics follows much the same alternating pattern of Wordsworth's account of Coleridge that I am tracing here. Also, Paul Magnuson's reading of the "Dream of the Arab" (*Lyrical Dialogue*, 320–23) has an important bearing on the exchange between Wordsworth and Coleridge that I analyze here.

9. "To William Wordsworth," 18–19. This and all subsequent quotations of Coleridge's poetry are taken from *Samuel Taylor Coleridge*, ed. H. J. Jackson (Oxford: Oxford University Press, 1985).

10. The most prominent sites of this debate, of course, are found in Wordsworth's "Intimations Ode" and Coleridge's "Dejection" and in Wordsworth's 1815 preface to his *Poems* and the *Biographia Literaria*.

11. In contrast to my emphasis on defense and negation, Chandler views Wordsworth's address here to Coleridge as being designed to offer him guidance (*Wordsworth's Second Nature*, 239–42).

12. This is the source of Wordsworth's "failure" in book 8 to establish a plausible line of love of Nature leading to love of man. See chapter 3 above for references to this failure; also see Johnston, *Wordsworth and The Recluse* (New Haven: Yale University Press, 1984), 165–73 for an account of this problem in relation to *The Recluse*.

13. Nicholas Roe sees Wordsworth's interest in mathematics as serving to predispose him to Coleridge's notions about the One Life as the proper alternative and corrective to errors of Godwinian rationalism (*Wordsworth and Coleridge*, 223–33).

14. See Alan Grob, "Wordsworth and Godwin: A Reassessment," *Studies in Romanticism* 6 (Winter 1967): 98–119. Grob's account of Wordsworth's repudiation of an abstract Godwinian methodology, while remaining committed to an essentially Godwinian "rational benevolence," describes an ambivalence on Wordsworth's part that parallels his ambivalence toward Coleridge, which I examine here.

15. See Newlyn for an account of the specific ways in which Wordsworth and Coleridge each constructed their own arguments against Godwinian rationalism (*Language of Allusion*, 5–12).

16. Nicolas Roe sees Wordsworth's study of mathematics as a bridge between his rejection of Godwin and his adoption of Coleridge's philosophy of the One Life. See *The Radical Years*, 229.

17. Interestingly, it is not the "five-book" *Prelude* that Wordsworth gives to Coleridge. Wordsworth had seemed to intend to give the completed five-book poem "to Coleridge," but had subsequently decided to expand it. In giving Coleridge the incomplete poem, he withholds his full narrative from Coleridge's power as a reader, but he also gives him a text upon which Coleridge can project the completion in his own reading. For the account of Wordsworth's construction of the five-book *Prelude*, see *The Prelude 1799, 1805, 1850* (516–517) and Jonathan Wordsworth, "The Five-Book *Prelude* of Early Spring 1804," *JEGP* 76 (1977): 1–25. Johnston suggests that Wordsworth dismantled the five-book *Prelude* because of "his need to keep on writing to Coleridge" (*Wordsworth and The Recluse*, 110).

18. For a very useful account of the differences in the general atmosphere at Cambridge between the time when Wordsworth was there (1787–January 1791) and when Coleridge attended (October 1791–1794), see Roe, *The Radical Years*, 15–23. Roe's account of Wordsworth's relative detachment from politics at Cambridge in a time when radical thought and support for the revolution were more or less the order of the day offers another avenue for examining Wordsworth's revision of Coleridge's history at Cambridge. Wordsworth's revisionary account of Coleridge seems to have a significant connection to his absorption in the political ferment that was generated when the reaction against radicals at Cambridge set in.

19. Ferguson, *Language as Counter-Spirit*, 148.

20. In reading *The Prelude* in the context of the *Recluse* project, Johnston follows the line that would see the monument not as a memorial, but as the embodiment of the work that will be completed when Coleridge's race is run (*Wordsworth and The Recluse*, 214–16). In terms of Wordsworth's hope for Coleridge's and his own future work, this reading would seem to be entirely appropriate, but given the problematic nature of the entire *Recluse* project, it also is necessary to see the misgivings and ambivalence that are inherent in Wordsworth's looking forward to getting on with *The Recluse*.

21. The double quotation embodied in these lines emphasizes the way in which Coleridge is represented as receding. Lines 431–52 closely allude to *1799* 2.478–88, which are themselves a revision of Coleridge's letter of September 1799 in which he projects for Wordsworth plans for a poem in blank verse that might form part of *The Recluse*. See *The Prelude 1799, 1805, 1850*, 26n.

22. In 1805 the death that Wordsworth projects for Coleridge is a figurative one, while in 1850 the literal and the figurative have merged. However, the subsumption of Coleridge's voice and power as reader operates in either case. Jonathan Wordsworth's reading of these concluding lines (*Borders*, 337–39) focuses too exclusively on the strength of the bond between Wordsworth and Coleridge. The poignancy that Professor Wordsworth notes in the hollow "millenarian assertions" of these lines point toward the same sort of assertions that Coleridge will try to make in *The Friend*, but based on a rather different set of "principles" than those which guide Wordsworth. Thus I would suggest that the poignancy of these lines is as much the result of Wordsworth's sense of

this basic difference between himself and Coleridge as it is of the fact that Coleridge and Wordsworth's time as "prophets of nature" has passed.

23. This and other details of the account of Coleridge's work on *The Friend* are taken from Barbara E. Rooke's Introduction to *The Friend* (London and Princeton: Princeton University Press, 1969), *The Collected Works of Samuel Taylor Coleridge* 4, 1:xxv–xxxvi. All further citations from *The Friend* are from this edition and are presented in the text.

24. *Collected Letters of Samuel Taylor Coleridge*, ed. Earl Leslie Griggs, 6 vols. (Oxford and New York: Oxford University Press, 1956–71), 2.1036. Cited by Rooke in her introduction to *The Friend*, 1:xxxvi.

25. Letter to Humphrey Davey 14 December 1808, *Collected Letters* 3.143; cited by Rooke, *The Friend*, 1:xxxvi–xxxvii.

26. Coleridge admits this failing in the prospectus to *The Friend*, but seems to present his habitual failure to complete his plans as a strength:

> Waiving the Mention of all private and accidental Hindrances, I am inclined to believe, that this Want of Perseverance has been produced in the Main by an Over-activity of Thought, modified by a constitutional Indolence, which made it more pleasant to me to continue acquiring, than to reduce what I acquired to a regular Form. (*Friend* 2.16)

27. Letter to Thomas Poole 31 May or 1 June 1809, *Letters of William and Dorothy Wordsworth; The Middle Years*, ed. Ernest de Selincourt, rev. Mary Moorman and Alan G. Hill, 2 vols. (Oxford: Oxford University Press, 1969–71), 1.328. Cited by Rooke, (*Friend* 1:lii), who notes that Wordsworth advised Poole to burn the letter.

28. In particular, Coleridge's work on *The Friend* follows not long after the rift between Coleridge and Wordsworth over whether or not the members of Wordsworth's household were "overlooking" Sara Hutchinson's correspondence with Coleridge and trying to discourage her relationship with him.

29. Petrarch, *De vita solitaria*. The translation is Coleridge's.

30. For a very useful account of the radical past that Coleridge often seems to be trying to forget or revise, see Nicolas Roe, *The Radical Years*, especially part. 145–56.

31. The source of this quotation cannot be traced. It appears at the end of the first number of *The Friend* just before the presentation of the prospectus (*Friend* 2:15) in the Latin "original." The translation is Coleridge's and is presented in the notes of the 1812 edition of *The Friend* (1:15–16).

32. This image of reader as guest is especially significant in that during some of the time that Coleridge was writing *The Friend*, he was a guest of the Wordsworths', and part of the tension between Coleridge and Wordsworth at this time had to do with the apparent toll exacted on Sara Hutchinson in her efforts to help Coleridge get on with his work. See Rooke's introduction to the *The Friend* for an account of Sara's involvement in Coleridge's work (1:lxxii).

33. In this respect it is important to acknowledge that Coleridge's account of the latitude allowed to the reader by the serial publication of *The Friend* is, in itself, clearly self-serving. Although the reader is given time to reflect and "digest," Coleridge is also given the time that he needs to accommodate his own habits of deferral and procrastination. The defense involved in Coleridge's conception of the active reader is explored more fully in the discussion of the *Biographia Literaria* in chapter 5 below, which considers Coleridge's notion of the "passive page" (*Biographia* 1:60).

34. Although Bloom notes this revisionary aspect of Coleridge's poem, he

nonetheless views Coleridge as succumbing to Wordsworth's poetic power; see *The Visionary Company* (Ithaca: Cornell University Press, 1971), 229–31. Bloom's reading is accurate if we assume that Coleridge is trying to surpass Wordsworth as a poet, but if we see the struggle between Wordsworth and Coleridge in terms of Coleridge's efforts to assert himself as a reader and not a poet, the outcome is rather different. Galperin's account of "To William Wordsworth" gives a more proper estimation of the self-assertion involved in Coleridge's homage to Wordsworth. Galperin states that Coleridge writes the poem "less as an arbiter of taste than a respondent on whom the latter's [Wordsworth's] greatness depends" ("'Desynonymizing,'" 518). Although Galperin's reading of the poem advances a general argument that is quite similar to my own, in advancing his analysis of the "desynonymization" of the self, he does not always pay close attention to the specific intersections between "To William Wordsworth" and Wordsworth's poetry, particularly the sections of *The Prelude* to which I refer and the "Intimations Ode."

35. See Theresa M. Kelley, *Wordsworth's Revisionary Aesthetics* (Cambridge: Cambridge University Press, 1988), 157–58 for an account of aesthetic management in the "Intimations Ode." Also, Kelley's account of the differences between Wordsworth's notions of the sublime and those of Kant have important bearing on the difference between Coleridge and Wordsworth. See particularly 30–31. Coleridge's revisionary quotation of Wordsworth's poem takes Wordsworth's negotiation with sublimity away from the intuitive and the imaginative into the Kantian realm of the rational.

36. Galperin, "'Desynonymizing,'" 518–19.

37. Walter Jackson Bate, *Coleridge* (New York: Macmillan, 1968), 121. Also see Galperin ("'Desynonymizing,'" 519) for a discussion of the significance of this prayer.

Chapter 5. The Sense of Before and After

1. Kenneth Johnston's account of the relationship between *The Recluse* and *The Prelude* bears out this notion, particularly with regard to the 1805 *Prelude*. See Kenneth Johnston, *Wordsworth and The Recluse* (New Haven and London: Yale University Press, 1984), 100–118. One can argue, however, that in the latter stages of revision, after Wordsworth has ceased to work toward *The Recluse*, he did envision *The Prelude* as an autobiography in formal terms, but one that was not to be published in his own lifetime. I would take this also as evidence of Wordsworth's ambivalence toward the autobiographical status of the poem.

2. Prominent among the numerous critical accounts of these issues are Kathleen Wheeler, *Sources, Processes, and Methods in Coleridge's Biographia Literaria* (Cambridge: Cambridge University Press, 1980); Lawrence Buell, "The Question of Form in Coleridge's *Biographia Literaria*," *ELH* 46 (1979): 399–416; Daniel Mark Fogel, "A Compositional History of the *Biographia Literaria*," *Studies in Bibliography* 30 (1977): 219–34; George Watson, Introduction to *Biographia Literaria*, ed. George Watson (London: J.M. Dent & Sons, 1975), ix–xxii; Norman Fruman, *Coleridge, The Damaged Archangel* (New York: George Braziller, 1971), 69–107; J. Shawcross, ed., Introduction to *Biographia Literaria* (Oxford and London: Oxford University Press, 1907), lv–lxxvii; W. J. Bate, editor's Introduction to *Biographia Literaria*, ed. James Engell and W. J.

Bate, 2 vols. (Princeton: Princeton University Press, 1983), *The Collected Works of Samuel Taylor Coleridge* 7, xli–lxvii.

3. Jerome Christensen, *Coleridge's Blessed Machine of Language* (Ithaca: Cornell University Press, 1981), 96–117.

4. Ibid., 104.

5. It is not so much that Christensen's assertion that the *Biographia* is not an autobiography is in error, but rather that most definitions of autobiography are too narrow to accommodate the sort of writing that Coleridge uses to construct the *Biographia*.

6. Christensen, *Blessed Machine*, 119–20.

7. Watson, Introduction to *Biographia*, xiii–xiv; Earl Leslie Griggs, ed., *Letters of Samuel Taylor Coleridge*, 6 vols. (Oxford and New York: Oxford University Press, 1956–71), 5:578n, 579n; D. M. Fogel, "A Compositional History of the *Biographia Literaria*," 226–28.

8. For the relevant discussion of the status of the preface, see Jacques Derrida, "Outwork, Prefacing" in *Dissemination*, trans. Barbara Johnson (Chicago: University of Chicago Press, 1981), 1–59.

9. For a discussion of the autobiographical predicament in these terms, see Louis Marin, "The 'I' as Autobiographical Eye: Reading Notes on a few Pages of Stendahl's *Life of Henry Brulard*," *October* 9 (1979), 66–67.

10. See Fogel, "Compositional History," 232–33.

11. The topic is mentioned in the titles to both chapters 10 and 11 of the *Biographia*. Samuel Taylor Coleridge, *Biographia Literaria*, eds. James Engell and W. J. Bate, 2 vols. (Princeton: Princeton University Press, 1983), *The Collected Works of Samuel Taylor Coleridge* 7, 168, 223. Unless otherwise noted, all subsequent references to Coleridge's *Biographia Literaria* are taken from this edition.

12. An appropriate example in this regard can be found by comparing Jerome Christensen's use of the term "literary life" (*Blessed Machine*, 118–85) and that of W. J. Bate (Editor's Introduction to *Biographia Literaria*, lvi).

13. Christensen, *Blessed Machine*, 120.

14. *The Notebooks of Samuel Taylor Coleridge*, Vol. 1, text, ed. Kathleen Coburn (New York: Pantheon Books, 1957–), entry no. 1515.

15. See Watson, Introduction to *Biographia Literaria*, xx.

16. Augustine, *The Confessions of St. Augustine*, trans. John K. Ryan (New York: Doubleday & Co., 1960), 181. Augustine's allusion is to I *Corinthians* 13:12.

17. Christensen quotes this phrase from the first paragraph of the Conclusion (2:234) to the *Biographia* (*Blessed Machine*, 180) in support of his assertion that Coleridge's text "ends" but its "conclusion is suspicious."

18. Coleridge is speaking of the object of all of his endeavors in general, which he says have been aimed toward "showing that the scheme of Christianity, as taught in the liturgy and homilies of our Church, though not discoverable through human reason, is yet in accordance with it." (*Biographia*, 2:247).

19. Christensen reads this passage precisely as evidence of such a silencing (*Blessed Machine*, 181). However, the passage of Coleridge's Conclusion that precedes this one and contextualizes it is not examined by Christensen.

20. Jerome McGann presents an important account of Coleridge's "explicitly historicized" theoretical view in *The Beauty of Inflections: Literary Investigations in Historical Method and Theory* (London: Oxford University Press, 1985), 143–50. See also Elinor Shaffer, *"Kubla Khan" and The Fall of Jerusalem*

(Cambridge: Cambridge University Press, 1975), chap. 1–3 (cited in McGann, 145).

21. In an essay published in the *Courier*, 15 December 1809, Coleridge contends that "trifling incidents" reveal the true character of men, and the omission of them makes modern histories less valuable as materials for philosophic recollection. Samuel Taylor Coleridge, *Essays on His Times*, ed. David V. Erdman, 3 vols. (Princeton: Princeton University Press, 1978) *The Collected Works of Samuel Taylor Coleridge* 3:58–59.

22. Paul de Man, "The Rhetoric of Temporality" in *Interpretation: Theory and Practice*, ed. Charles Singleton (Baltimore: Johns Hopkins University Press, 1969), 191.

23. This understanding of the nature of history and the way in which it is both produced and read does follow the lines of an understanding of history as "figural." However, Coleridge's attempts in the *Biographia* to resolve the conflict between "authentic" temporality and self-mystification are not simply a matter of his engaging in a sort of figural interpretation. For a discussion of such figural interpretation see Erich Auerbach, "Figura" in *Scenes from the Drama of European Literature* (Minneapolis: University of Minnnesota Press, 1984), 49–60.

24. As discussed above, Coleridge also has some doubts as to the decision making processes which determine what does and does not qualify as a fact that is worthy of the "dignity of history."

25. See the discussion above of Coleridge's notion of reading with "philosophical tact."

26. Chapter 6 examines Coleridge's extended examination of Wordsworth's poetry and his account of his own poetic "failure."

27. The revisionary nature of this assertion is noted by John Thelwall in the margin of his copy of *Biographia*. See Nicholas Roe, *Wordsworth and Coleridge: The Radical Years* (Oxford: Oxford University Press, 1988), 5. See also (cited by Roe, 5) B. Pollin and R. Burke, "John Thelwall's Marginalia in a Copy of Coleridge's *Biographia Literaria*," *Bulletin of the New York Public Library* 74 (1970): 81.

28. For an account of Coleridge's difficulties in producing *The Friend*, see the Editor's Introduction to *The Friend*, 2 vols. (Princeton: Princeton University Press, 1969) *The Collected Works of Samuel Taylor Coleridge* vol. 4, 1:liii-lxvi. See also Deirdre Coleman, *Coleridge and The Friend (1809–1810)* (Oxford: Oxford University Press, 1988), especially chap. 2.

29. Christensen, *Blessed Machine*, "The Method of *The Friend*," 186–269.

30. Prospectus to *The Friend*, 2:16–20.

31. See the above discussion of *The Friend* in chapter 4.

32. This "advantage" does grow out of a very real failure to find the audience that Coleridge envisioned for *The Friend*. For a discussion of *The Friend's* Quaker readership see Coleman, 80–106. For a discussion of the reading public during the Romantic period, see Jon Klancher, *The Making of English Reading Audiences, 1790–1832* (Madison: University of Wisconsin Press, 1987).

33. See Christensen, *Blessed Machine*, 124–32. As with the quotation from *The Friend* in chapter 10, cited above, this text has also been appropriated from and in other contexts: *Notebooks* (1.1622), October 1803 and *The Statesman's Manual* in *The Lay Sermons*, ed. R. J. White (Princeton: Princeton University Press, 1972) *The Collected Works of Samuel Taylor Coleridge* 6:25. When Coleridge cites this definition of genius, he refers to Wordsworth as an example

of someone who exhibits such genius. In chapter 6, I examine in more detail how Coleridge uses the strategy of textual reappropriation in his representation of Wordsworth in the *Biographia*.

34. The note is Coleridge's own.

35. See *Biographia*, 1.82–83 for Coleridge's account of how the originally synonymous words, *propriety* and *property*, have become desynonymized since the time of Charles I. Although I agree with Christensen (*Blessed Machine*, 139) that Coleridge's desire for authority requires the synonymity of these words and involves a nostalgia for "the last age of sovereignty," I would argue that Coleridge seeks to use the mechanism of textual production itself as the means of establishing this authority. Thus Coleridge sees the literary text as a specific form of property which retains its synonymity with propriety.

36. See Klancher (chapter 5) for a discussion of Wordsworth and Coleridge's efforts to "forge" a new audience for their works.

37. Christensen, *Blessed Machine*, 167. For Coleridge's quotation from and translation of Herder, see *Biographia*, 1.231.

38. See Klancher (152) for an account of Coleridge's gratification at recognizing faces from his lectures in the audience of *Remorse* and his desire to constitute a "personal public."

39. William Hazlitt, *The Complete Works of William Hazlitt*, ed. P. P. Howe, 21 vols. (London: J. M. Dent & Sons, 1930–34), 7.119–128. All further references to Hazlitt's writing are taken from this edition and are designated by volume and page number.

40. Samuel Taylor Coleridge, *The Lay Sermons*, ed. R. J. Patton (Princeton: Princeton University Press, 1972) *The Collected Works of Samuel Taylor Coleridge* 6:35–36. For a well-developed account of the reading public during the Romantic period and specific discussion of Coleridge and Wordsworth's effort to direct and form their readers, see Klancher, *The Making of the English Reading Audiences, 1790–1832*.

41. For an account of the many complaints about the unreadability and obscurity of *The Friend*, see Barbara Rooke's introduction to Samuel Taylor Coleridge, *The Friend*, 2 vols. (Princeton: Princeton University Press, 1969) *The Collected Works of Samuel Taylor Coleridge* vol. 4, 1:lix–lxii.

42. Most of Hazlitt's allusions are to *The Friend*.

43. In addition to his reviews of Coleridge's works, Hazlitt made Coleridge and his politics the target of at least six essays in *The Examiner* and *The Morning Chronicle* during the time between the first "review" of *The Statesman's Manual* (September 1816) and the review of the *Biographia* (August 1817).

44. Accounts of the relationship between the letter and the subsequent essay (published six years later) tend to focus on Hazlitt's tempering, with time, his harsh judgments of Coleridge. See Bill Ruddick, "Recollecting Coleridge: The Internalization of Radical Energies in Hazlitt's Political Prose," *The Yearbook of English Studies* 19 (1989): 243–55; and Stanley Jones, "First Flight: Image and Theme in a Hazlitt Essay," *Prose Studies* 8 (1985): 35–47. I argue that while Hazlitt's harsh treatment of Coleridge may be tempered, his strategy for reading Coleridge, which he adopts from Coleridge himself, remains the same.

45. The allusion is identified and discussed by Geoffrey Carnall in "The Impertinent Barber of Baghdad: Coleridge as the Comic Figure in Hazlitt's Essays" in *New Approaches to Coleridge*, ed. Donald Sultana (Totowa, N.J.: Barnes & Noble, 1981), 38–47.

46. P. P. Howe suggests that Hazlitt may have removed the sentence in defer-
ence to his friend Charles Lamb who thought it a "horrible license" (Hazlitt,
Works, 7:381n).

Chapter 6. The Passive Page of a Book

1. Lines 65–75 of "To William Wordsworth."
2. See chapter 4 above for a discussion of the strategic importance of this
poem in relation to *The Prelude*.
3. For accounts of Coleridge's criticism of Wordsworth in the *Biographia*
and the way in which it has been received in the critical tradition, see Don
Bialostosky, "Coleridge's Interpretation of Wordsworth's Preface to *Lyrical Ballads*," *PMLA* 93 (October 1978): 912–24; and Richard Gravil, "Coleridge's
Wordsworth," *The Wordsworth Circle* 15 (Spring 1984): 38–46.
4. See Jon Klancher, *The Making of English Reading Audiences, 1790–1832*
(Madison: University of Wisconsin Press, 1987), 150–70 for an account of Coleridge's construction of an "ideal reader" through the institution of the clerisy.
5. *Biographia*, 1:48, 57. In a note to the text, Coleridge distinguishes between the activity that he would give the name of reading and the activity of
the "devotees of the circulating libraries" (1:48). This account of contemporary
habits of reading is similar to Wordsworth's attack on the tastes of the reading
public in the preface to the *Lyrical Ballads*.
6. See chapter 4 above for an account of "the Friend" as reader.
7. The parallels between the reviewer's account of Southey's poems and
Wordsworth's misapprehension of how his poems might be read are further
enforced by Coleridge's echoing of the previous chapter when he calls it an
injustice to criticize the defects of isolated poems "instead of passing over
them in silence, as so much blank paper, or leaves in a bookseller's catalogue;
especially, as no one pretends to have found immorality or indelicacy" (*Biographia*, 1:74).
8. Indeed, Coleridge's exaggerated praise of Wordsworth's early poems (*Biographia*, 1:77, 80) may be seen more as an effort to follow his own dictum in
passing over defects and highlighting excellences than as an effort to establish
Wordsworth's early genius. Lucy Newlyn sees this exaggerated praise as being
linked to Coleridge's political, rather than poetic, affinities with Wordsworth
at the time of their first acquaintance. See *Coleridge, Wordsworth, and the
Language of Allusion* (Oxford: Oxford University Press, 1986), 3–5.
9. It must be granted that Coleridge clearly misses (perhaps deliberately)
Wordsworth's point in that Coleridge insists upon seeing the "humbler passages" as defects when Wordsworth certainly would not. This basic disagreement over poetic theory becomes more explicit in Coleridge's critique of
Wordsworth's preface in chapter 14 of the *Biographia*.
10. Chapter 5.
11. It is also significant that Coleridge sees the excellence of Wordsworth's
poetry as consisting in something wholly other than the supposed quality of
style on which his preface focuses, in that Wordsworth's style is not one that
adopts a common language but is rather quite singular and uniquely recogniz-
able (*Biographia*, 2:99).
12. See Kenneth Johnston, *Wordsworth and The Recluse* (New Haven and
London: Yale University Press, 1984), 333–62 for a discussion of the way in
which this evaluation serves as the motivating force behind the *Biographia*.

13. Stephen Parrish's edition of the manuscripts of "Dejection" has been an invaluable aid to my work on this poem. All quotations from the various versions of "Dejection" are taken from this edition, *Coleridge's Dejection*, ed. Stephen Maxfield Parrish (Ithaca and London: Cornell University Press, 1988).

14. See Mark L. Reed, *Wordsworth: The Chronology of the Middle Years* (Cambridge: Harvard University Press, 1975), 157–58.

15. In his reading of "the Dejection dialogue," Paul Magnuson makes the point that, unlike Coleridge's highly personal references in the "Letter," the first four stanzas of the "Intimations Ode" deal exclusively with "Wordsworth's struggle with his writing in 1802 and the unfulfilled promise of 1800." This account of Wordsworth's poem makes all the more remarkable Coleridge's very public positioning of the rather personal associations called up by these lines. See Paul Magnuson, *Coleridge and Wordsworth: A Lyrical Dialogue* (Princeton: Princeton University Press, 1988), 275.

16. While I have not addressed Wordsworth's specific responses to Coleridge's versions of "Dejection," recent critical accounts of this poetic exchange characterize Wordsworth's part in it in such a way as to confirm my account of the role that Coleridge is trying to construct for him. See Lucy Newlyn's analysis of patterns of allusion in "The Leech-gatherer" and "Resolution and Independence" (*Language of Allusion*, 117–37) and Paul Magnuson's analysis of the thematic correspondences between Coleridge's verse letter and Wordsworth's "Resolution and Independence" (*A Lyrical Dialogue*, 308–17).

17. Reed, *Chronology of the Middle Years*, 163. For Dorothy Wordsworth's account of this occasion, see *Journals of Dorothy Wordsworth*, ed. Mary Moorman (Oxford: Oxford University Press, 1971), 113–14.

18. Lucy Newlyn reads Wordsworth's "Leech-gatherer" as an example of just such resistance (*Language of Allusion*, 118). See also Parrish's introduction (12–13) to his edition of "Dejection" for a discussion of the "Leech-gatherer" as a response to Coleridge's poem. Paul Magnuson's account of what I call Wordsworth's resistance focuses on Wordsworth's struggle to extract himself from a poetic dialogue with Coleridge (*A Lyrical Dialogue*, 316–17).

19. Parrish (17) sees this as a fairly easy adaptation for Coleridge to make.

20. The problematic personal context is also apparent in the equation of wedding garment and shroud, and the general abundance of wedding imagery, in a poem published on Wordsworth's wedding day.

21. See chapter 4 above for a fuller account of the corrective nature of this response.

22. See Parrish's introduction to his edition of "Dejection" (7–8) for an account of the circumstances that give rise to these lines.

23. The Dove Cottage Manuscript and the Cornell Manuscript, published in Parrish's edition of the poem(s).

24. See chapter 4 above for an analysis of Wordsworth's representation of Coleridge in *The Prelude*.

Chapter 7. Perpetual Self-Duplication

1. This problem is compounded all the more when Coleridge accedes to the suggestion that the work be made into two volumes and the positioning of chapter 13 creates such complications. See W. J. Bate, Editor's Introduction to the *Biographia Literaria*, lvi–lxv. My discussion of Coleridge's composition of the *Biographia* also draws upon Kathleen Wheeler, *Sources, Processes, and*

Methods in Coleridge's Biographia Literaria (Cambridge: Cambridge University Press, 1980); Lawrence Buell, "The Question of Form in Coleridge's *Biographia Literaria*," *ELH* 46 (1979): 399–416; Daniel Mark Fogel, "A Compositional History of the *Biographia Literaria*" *Studies in Bibliography*, 30 (1977): 219–34.

2. See *Biographia* 300n for Coleridge's admission to having written the letter.

3. See *The Prose Works of William Wordsworth*, ed. W. J. B. Owen and J. W. Smyser (Oxford: Oxford University Press, 1974), 3:30–39.

4. In their notes to the *Biographia*, Engell and Bate leave the question somewhat open, but imply that Coleridge himself may have been uncertain as to what he was referring to as that which might be omitted: "In light of C's headnote to ch 12, 'the following chapter' seems to refer to ch 13. But if C were dictating rapidly, he might not have foreseen how ch 12 would grow to such length and complexity" (*Biographia*, 1:234n).

5. Wordsworth is describing the "great Nature that exists in works / Of mighty poets" (*The Prelude* 5.619–29). The allusion is identified in *Biographia* 301n.

6. "The two Works [*The Prelude* and *The Recluse*] have the same kind of relation to each other . . . as the ante-chapel has to the body of a Gothic church. Continuing this allusion, he [the author] may be permitted to add, that his minor Pieces, which have been long before the Public, when they shall be properly arranged, will be found by the attentive Reader to have such connection with the main Work as may give them claim to be likened to the little cells, oratories, and sepulchral recesses, ordinarily included in those edifices." *The Prose Works of William Wordsworth*, ed. W. J. B. Owen and J. W. Smyser (Oxford: Oxford University Press, 1974), 3:5–6.

7. See chapter 4 above for my discussion of *The Friend* in these terms.

8. For particular accounts of these "borrowings" one can turn to Fruman's indictment of Coleridge in *Coleridge, The Damaged Archangel* (New York: George Braziller, 1971), 101–6, as well as to Engell and Bate's account in the Editors' Introduction to the *Biographia* (lvii, cxiv–cxxvii) and in the editorial notes to chapter 12. Fruman has called the editorial stance of Engell and Bate "on all controversial matters . . . unremittingly defensive, evasive, non-committal or intrusive in ways intended to shape the reader's views along the paths congenial to the editors." See "Aids to Reflection on the New Biographia," *Studies in Romanticism* 24 (Spring 1985): 143.

9. For a relatively recent entry into this debate, see Jonathan Wordsworth, "The Infinite I AM: Coleridge and the Ascent of Being," *The Wordsworth Circle* 16 (1985): 74–84.

10. Samuel Taylor Coleridge, *Logic*, ed. J. R. de J. Jackson (Princeton: Princeton University Press, 1981) *The Collected Works of Samuel Taylor Coleridge* 13. All further references to this work are presented parenthetically in the text. Bate suggests that in Chapter 12 Coleridge takes the opportunity to insert "the philosophical vestibule for the "Logosophia" (*Biographia*, 1:lvi). Jackson identifies Coleridge's *Logic* as one of several treatises that will comprise the "Logosophia" (*Logic*, xl–xli).

11. For an account of Coleridge's struggle with materialist theories of language, see Jackson's introduction to the *Logic* (lxiii). Also see James McKusick, "Coleridge and Horne Tooke," *Studies in Romanticism* 24 (1985): 85–111.

12. See *The Prose Works of William Wordsworth* 3:84.

Bibliography

Abrams, M. H. *Natural Supernaturalism: Tradition and Revolution in Romantic Literature*. New York: W.W. Norton & Co., 1971.

Arac, Jonathan. "Bounding Lines: *The Prelude* and Critical Revision." *boundary 2* vol. 7 (1979): 31–48.

Auerbach, Erich. *Scenes from the Drama of European Literature*. Minneapolis: University of Minnesota Press, 1984.

Augustine, *The Confessions of St. Augustine*. Translated by John K. Ryan. New York: Doubleday and Co., 1960.

Bahti, Timothy. "Figures and Interpretations, The Interpretation of Figures: A Reading of Wordsworth's Dream of the Arab." *Studies in Romanticism* 18 (Winter 1979): 601–27.

———. "Wordsworth's Rhetorical Theft." In *Romanticism and Language*, edited by Arden Reed, 86–124. Ithaca: Cornell University Press, 1984.

Bakhtin, M. M. *The Dialogic Imagination*. Translated by Caryl Emerson and Michael Holquist, and edited by Michael Holquist. Austin: University of Texas Press, 1981.

Barnouw, Jeffrey. "The Revelation between the Certain and the True in Vico's Pragmatist Construction of Human History." *Comparative Literature Studies* 15 (June 1978): 242–64.

Bate, Walter Jackson. *Coleridge*. New York: Macmillan, 1968.

Benveniste, Emile. *Problems in General Linguistics*. Translated by M. E. Meek. Coral Gables, Fla.: University of Miami Press, 1971.

Bialostosky, Don. "Coleridge's Interpretation of Wordsworth's Preface to *Lyrical Ballads*," *PMLA* 93 (October 1978): 912–24.

Bloom, Harold. *Anxiety of Influence*. London: Oxford University Press, 1973.

———. *Figures of Capable Imagination*. New York: Seabury Press, 1976.

———. *A Map of Misreading*. London: Oxford University Press, 1975.

———. *The Visionary Company*. Ithaca: Cornell University Press, 1971.

Bruss, Elizabeth W. *Autobiographical Acts: The Changing Situation of a Literary Genre*. Baltimore: Johns Hopkins University Press, 1976.

Buell, Lawrence. "The Question of Form in Coleridge's *Biographia Literaria*." *ELH* 46 (1979): 399–416.

Carnall, Geoffrey. "The Impertinent Barber of Baghdad: Coleridge as the Comic Figure in Hazlitt's Essays." In *New Approaches to Coleridge*, edited by Donald Sultana, 38–47. Totowa, N.J.: Barnes and Noble, 1981.

Chandler, James. *Wordsworth's Second Nature: A Study of the Poetry and Politics*. Chicago: University of Chicago Press, 1984.

Chase, Cynthia. "The Accidents of Disfiguration: Limits to Literal and Rhetorical Reading in Book V of The Prelude." Studies in Romanticism 18 (1979): 547–65.

Christensen, Francis. "Intellectual Love: The Second Theme of The Prelude." PMLA 80 (1965): 69–75.

Christensen, Jerome. Coleridge's Blessed Machine of Language. Ithaca: Cornell University Press, 1981.

———. Practicing Enlightenment: Hume and the Formation of a Literary Career. Madison: University of Wisconsin Press, 1987.

Coleman, Deirdre. Coleridge and The Friend (1809–1810). Oxford: Oxford University Press, 1988.

Coleridge, Samuel Taylor. Biographia Literaria. Edited by J. Shawcross. 2 vols. Oxford and London: Oxford University Press, 1907.

———. Biographia Literaria. Edited by George Watson. London: J.M. Dent and Sons, 1975.

———. Coleridge's Dejection. Edited by Stephen Maxfield Parrish. Ithaca and London: Cornell University Press, 1988.

———. Collected Letters of Samuel Taylor Coleridge. Edited by Earl Leslie Griggs. 6 vols. Oxford and New York: Oxford University Press, 1956–71.

———. The Collected Works of Samuel Taylor Coleridge. Bollingen Series 75. Princeton: Princeton University Press. Vol. 3, Essays on His Times, edited by David V. Erdman, 1978; Vol. 4, The Friend, edited by Barbara E. Rooke, 1969; Vol. 6 The Lay Sermons, edited by R. J. White, 1972; Vol. 7, Biographia Literaria, edited by James Engell and W. Jackson Bate, 1983; Vol. 13, Logic, edited by J. R. de J. Jackson, 1981.

———. The Notebooks of Samuel Taylor Coleridge, edited by Kathleen Coburn. New York: Pantheon Books, 1957–.

———. Samuel Taylor Coleridge. Edited by H. J. Jackson. Oxford Authors Series, edited by Frank Kermode. Oxford: Oxford University Press, 1985.

Cooke, Micheal G. The Romantic Will. New Haven and London: Yale University Press, 1976.

Croce, Benedetto. The Philosophy of Giambatista Vico. Translated by R. G. Collingwood. New York: Russell & Russell, 1964.

de Man, Paul. "Autobiography as De-facement." MLN 94 (1979): 919–30.

———. Blindness and Insight. New York: Oxford University Press, 1971.

———. "The Intentional Structure of Romantic Imagery." In Romanticism and Consciousness, edited by Harold Bloom, 65–77. New York: Norton, 1970.

———. The Rhetoric of Romanticism. New York: Columbia University Press, 1984.

———. "The Rhetoric of Temporality." In Interpretation: Theory and Practice, edited by Charles Singleton, 173–209. Baltimore: Johns Hopkins University Press, 1969.

Derrida, Jacques. Dissemination. Translated by Barbara Johnson. Chicago: University of Chicago Press, 1981.

———. The Ear of the Other: Otobiography, Transference, Translation. Edited by Christie V. Mcdonald, and translated by Peggy Kamuf. New York: Schocken Books, 1985.

————. *Of Grammatology.* Translated by Gayatri Spivak. Baltimore: Johns Hopkins University Press, 1976.

————. *Speech and Phenomenon.* Translated by David B. Allison. Evanston, Ill.: Northwestern University Press, 1973.

Donato, Eugenio. "Divine Agonies: Of Representation and Narrative in Romantic Poetics." *Glyph* 6 (1979): 90–102.

Eakin, Paul John. *Fictions in Autobiography.* Princeton: Princeton University Press, 1985.

————. "Narrative and Chronology as Structures of Reference and the New Model Autobiographer." In *Studies in Autobiography,* edited by James Olney, 32–41. New York: Oxford University Press, 1988.

Eisenstein, Elizabeth L. *The Printing Press As an Agent of Social Change.* Cambridge: Cambridge University Press, 1979.

Ferguson, Frances. *Wordsworth: Language as Counter-Spirit.* New Haven: Yale University Press, 1977.

Fisch, Max H. "Vico and Pragmatism." In *Giambattista Vico: An International Symposium,* edited by Giorgio Tacliacozzo and Hayden V. White. Baltimore: Johns Hopkins University Press, 1969.

Fleishman, Avrom. *Figures of Autobiography.* Berkeley: University of California Press, 1983.

Fogel, Daniel Mark. "A Compositional History of the *Biographia Literaria.*" *Studies in Bibliography* 30 (1977): 219–34.

Foucault, Michel. *The Order of Things.* New York: Random House, 1970.

————. "What Is an Author?" In *Textual Strategies,* edited by Josua V. Harrari, 141–60. Ithaca: Cornell University Press, 1979.

Fruman, Norman. "Aids to Reflection on the New Biographia." *Studies in Romanticism* 24 (Spring 1985): 141–73.

————. *Coleridge, The Damaged Archangel.* New York: George Braziller, 1971.

Galperin, William H. "'Desynonymizing' the Self in Wordsworth and Coleridge." *Studies in Romanticism* 26 (Winter 1987): 513–26.

Garber, Frederick. *Self, Text, and Romantic Irony.* Princeton: Princeton University Press, 1988.

Good, James M. "William Taylor, Robert Southey, and the Word 'Autobiography.'" *The Wordsworth Circle* 12 (Spring 1981): 125–27.

Gravil, Richard. "Coleridge's Wordsworth." *The Wordsworth Circle* 15 (Spring 1984): 38–46.

Grob, Alan. "Wordsworth and Godwin: A Reassessment." *Studies in Romanticism* 6 (Winter 1967): 98–119.

Gusdorf, Georges. "Conditions and Limits of Autobiography." In *Autobiography: Essays Theoretical and Critical,* edited by James Olney, 28–48. Princeton: Princeton University Press, 1980.

Haney, David. "The Emergence of the Autobiographical Figure in *The Prelude,* Book 1." *Studies in Romanticism* 20 (Spring 1981): 33–63.

Hartman, Geoffrey. *Saving the Text.* Baltimore: Johns Hopkins University Press, 1981.

————. "Words, Wish, Worth: Wordsworth." In *Deconstruction and Criticism,* edited by Harold Bloom, 177–216. New York: Seabury Press, 1979.

———. *Wordsworth's Poetry.* New Haven: Yale University Press, 1964.

Hazlitt, William. *The Complete Works of William Hazlitt.* Edited by P. P. Howe. 21 vols. London: J.M. Dent and Sons, 1930–34.

Jacobus, Mary. "Apostrophe and Lyric Voice in *The Prelude.*" In *Lyric Poetry,* edited by Chaviva Hosek and Patricia Parker, 167–81. Ithaca: Cornell University Press, 1985.

———. "'That Great Stage Where Senators Perform': Macbeth and the Politics of Romantic Theatre." *Studies in Romanticism* 22 (Fall 1983): 353–87.

———. "Wordsworth and the Language of Dream." *ELH* 46 (Winter 1979): 618–44.

Jay, Paul. *Being in the Text: Self-Representation from Wordsworth to Roland Barthes.* Ithaca and London: Cornell University Press, 1984.

Johnston, Kenneth. *Wordsworth and The Recluse.* New Haven: Yale University Press, 1984.

Jones, Stanley. "First Flight: Image and Theme in a Hazlitt Essay." *Prose Studies* 8 (1985): 35–47.

Kelley, Theresa M. "Spirit and Geometric Form: The Stone and the Shell in Wordsworth's Arab Dream." *Studies in English Literature 1500–1900* 22 (Autumn 1982): 563–82.

———. *Wordsworth's Revisionary Aesthetics.* Cambridge: Cambridge University Press, 1988.

Klancher, John. *The Making of English Reading Audiences, 1790–1832.* Madison: University of Wisconsin Press, 1987.

Kneale, J. Douglas. *Monument Writing: Aspects of Rhetoric in Wordsworth's Poetry.* Lincoln: University of Nebraska Press, 1988.

———. "Wordsworth's Image of Language: Voice and Letter in *The Prelude.*" *PMLA* 101 (1986): 351–61.

Lacan, Jacques. *Ecrits.* Translated by Alan Sheriden. New York: W.W. Norton & Co., 1977.

LeJeune, Phillipe. *Le pacte autobiographique.* Paris: Seuil, 1975.

McConnell, Frank D. *The Confessional Imagination: A Reading of Wordsworth's Prelude.* Baltimore: Johns Hopkins University Press, 1974.

McFarland, Thomas. *Romanticism and the Forms of Ruin.* Princeton: Princeton University Press, 1981.

———. "Wordsworth on Man, on Nature, and on Human Life." *Studies in Romanticism* 21 (Winter 1982): 601–18.

McGann, Jerome. *The Beauty of Inflections: Literary Investigations in Historical Method and Theory.* London: Oxford University Press, 1985.

McKusick, James. "Coleridge and Horne Tooke." *Studies in Romanticism* 24 (1985): 85–111.

Magnuson, Paul. *Coleridge and Wordsworth: A Lyrical Dialogue.* Princeton: Princeton University Press, 1988.

Marin, Louis. "The 'I' as Autobiographical Eye: Reading Notes on a Few Pages of Stendahl's *Life of Henry Brulard.*" *October* 9 (1979), 65–79.

Mellor, Anne. *English Romantic Irony.* Cambridge: Harvard University Press, 1980.

Miller, J. Hillis. "The Stone and the Shell: Problems of Poetic Form in Wordsworth's Dream of the Arab." In *Mouvements Premiers*, 125–47. Paris: Librarie José Corti, 1972.

Misch, Georg. *A History of Autobiography*. Cambridge: Harvard University Press, 1951.

Mitchell, W. J. T. "Influence, Autobiography, and Literary History: Rousseau's *Confessions* and Wordsworth's *The Prelude*." *ELH* 57 (1990): 643–65.

Morrison, James C. "Vico's Principle: Verum is *Factum*." *Journal of the History of Ideas* 39 (Oct.–Dec. 1978): 579–95

Newlyn, Lucy. *Coleridge, Wordsworth, and the Language of Allusion*. Oxford: Oxford University Press, 1986.

Nussbaum, Felicity. *The Autobiographical Subject: Gender and Ideology in Eighteenth-Century England*. Baltimore and London: Johns Hopkins University Press, 1989.

Olney, James. *Metaphors of the Self*. Princeton: Princeton University Press, 1972.

————, ed. *Autobiography: Essays Theoretical and Critical*. Princeton: Princeton University Press, 1980.

————, ed. *Studies in Autobiography*. New York: Oxford University Press, 1988.

Pascal, Roy. *Design and Truth in Autobiography*. Cambridge: Harvard University Press, 1960.

Peterson, Linda. *Victorian Autobiography*. New Haven and London: Yale University Press, 1986.

Pollin, Burton R., and Redmond Burke. "John Thelwall's Marginalia in a Copy of Coleridge's *Biographia Literaria*." *Bulletin of the New York Public Library* 74 (1970): 73–94.

Rajan, Tilottama. *Dark Interpreter: The Discourse of Romanticism*. Ithaca and London: Cornell University Press, 1980.

Reed, Mark L. *Wordsworth: The Chronology of the Middle Years*. Cambridge: Harvard University Press, 1975.

Reiman, Donald H. "The Beauty of Buttermere as Fact and Romantic Symbol." *Criticism* 26 (Spring 1984): 139–70.

Roe, Nicholas. *Wordsworth and Coleridge: The Radical Years*. Oxford: Oxford University Press, 1988.

Ruddick, Bill. "Recollecting Coleridge: The Internalization of Radical Energies in Hazlitt's Political Prose." *The Yearbook of English Studies* 19 (1989): 243–55.

Ruoff, Gene W. *Wordsworth and Coleridge: The Making of the Major Lyrics 1802–1804*. New Brunswick, N.J.: Rutgers University Press, 1989.

Rzepka, Charles J. *The Self as Mind: Vision and Identity in Wordsworth, Coleridge, and Keats*. Cambridge: Harvard University Press, 1986.

Said, Edward. *Beginnings: Intention and Method*. Baltimore: Johns Hopkins University Press, 1975.

Shaffer, Elinor. *"Kubla Khan" and The Fall of Jerusalem*. Cambridge: Cambridge University Press, 1975.

Simpson, David. *Irony and Authority in Romantic Poetry*. Totowa, N.J.: Rowman and Littlefield, 1979.

———. *Wordsworth and the Figurings of the Real.* London: Macmillan, 1982.

Smyser, Jane Worthington. "Wordsworth's Dream of Poetry and Science: *The Prelude*, V." *PMLA* 71 (March 1956): 269–75.

Spengemann, William. *The Forms of Autobiography.* New Haven and London: Yale University Press, 1980.

Sprinker, Michael. "Fictions of the Self: The End of Autobiography." In *Autobiography: Essays Theoretical and Critical*, edited by James Olney, 321–42. Princeton: Princeton University Press, 1980.

Starobinski, Jean. "The Style of Autobiography." In *Autobiography: Essays Theoretical and Critical*, edited by James Olney, 73–83. Princeton: Princeton University Press, 1980.

Stelzig, Eugene. "Coleridge in *The Prelude*: Wordsworth's Fiction of Alterity." *The Wordsworth Circle* 18 (Winter 1987): 23–27.

Sturrock, John. "The New Model Autobiographer." *New Literary History* 9 (1977): 51–63.

Vico, Giambattista. *The Autobiography of Giambattista Vico.* Translated by Max Harold Fisch and Thomas Goddard Bergin. Ithaca and London: Cornell University Press, 1944.

———. *The New Science of Giambattista Vico.* Translated by Thomas Goddard Bergin and Max Harold Fisch. Ithaca: Cornell University Press, 1948.

Wasserman, Earl R. "The English Romantics: The Grounds of Knowledge." In *Romanticism: Points of View*, edited by Robert F. Gleckner and Gerald E. Enscoe, 331–46. Princeton: Princeton University Press, 1962.

Weintraub, Karl. "Autobiography and Historical Consciousness." *Critical Inquiry* 1 (1975): 821–48.

———. *The Value of the Individual: Self and Circumstance in Autobiography.* Chicago: University of Chicago Press, 1978.

Wheeler, Kathleen. *Sources, Processes, and Methods in Coleridge's Biographia Literaria.* Cambridge: Cambridge University Press, 1980.

White, Hayden. "The Tropics of History: The Deep Structure of the *New Science*." In *Giambattista Vico's Science of Humanity*, edited by Giorgio Tagliacozzo and Donald Philip Verene, 65–85. Baltimore: Johns Hopkins University Press, 1976.

Wolfson, Susan. *The Questioning Presence: Wordsworth, Keats, and the Interrogative Mode in Romantic Poetry.* Ithaca: Cornell University Press, 1986.

Woodmansee, Martha. "The Genius and the Copyright: Economic and Legal Conditions of the Emergence of the 'Author.'" *Eighteenth Century Studies* 17 (Summer 1984): 425–48.

Wordsworth, Dorothy. *Journals of Dorothy Wordsworth.* Edited by Mary Moorman. Oxford: Oxford University Press, 1971.

Wordsworth, Jonathan. "The Five-Book *Prelude* of Early Spring 1804." *JEGP* 76 (1977): 1–25.

———. "The Infinite I AM: Coleridge and the Ascent of Being." *The Wordsworth Circle* 16 (1985): 74–84.

———. *William Wordsworth: The Borders of Vision.* Oxford: Oxford University Press, 1982.

Wordsworth, William. *Letters of William and Dorothy Wordsworth.* Edited by

Ernest de Selincourt. Second Edition, *The Middle Years*, revised by Mary Moorman and Alan G. Hill, 2 vols. Oxford: Oxford University Press, 1969–71.

————. *The Prelude, 1798–1799*. Edited by Stephen Parrish. Ithaca: Cornell University Press, 1977.

————. *The Prelude: 1799, 1805, 1850*. Edited by Jonathan Wordsworth, M. H. Abrams, and Stephen Gill. New York: W.W. Norton & Co., 1979.

————. *The Prose Works of William Wordsworth*. Edited by W. J. B. Owen and Jane Worthington Smyser. 3 vols. Oxford: Clarendon Press, 1974.

————. *Wordsworth: Poetical Works*. Edited by Ernest de Selincourt. London: Oxford University Press, 1936.

————, and Samuel Taylor Coleridge. *Lyrical Ballads*. Edited by R. L. Brett and A. R. Jones, 1963. London and New York: Routledge, 1988.

Index

Abrams, M. H., 28–29, 49, 171, 172, 173, 175, 176
Allison, David B., 170
Anxiety of influence, 81
Apostacy, 129–30
Apostrophe, 56–57, 58
Arac, Jonathan, 174, 176
Auerbach, Erich, 186
Augustine, 115; *Confessions*, 28, 29, 171, 185
Augustinian model of autobiography, 172
Author-function, 15, 16, 26–28, 165–66
Authority, 133; textual, 124, 140–41
Autobiography: divided subject of, 39, 43, 48, 53, 108; doubling of subject of, 38; origin of the word, 35; poststructuralist theories of, 13; predicament of, 67, 76, 84, 106–7; strategies of representation in, 135, 156, 163; traditional concepts of, 18–19

Bahti, Timothy, 55, 170, 176, 181
Bakhtin, M. M., 180
Barnouw, Jeffrey, 172
Bate, Walter Jackson, 106, 119, 159,184, 185, 189,190
Benveniste, Emile, 24, 170
Bergin, Thomas, 172, 173
Bialostosky, Don, 188
Bible: Matt. 25, 14–30, 51
Bloom, Harold, 177, 180, 183
Bruss, Elizabeth, 23, 24–25, 168, 170
Buell, Lawrence, 184, 190

Cambridge University: Wordsworth's time at, 62, 63, 70; Coleridge's time at, 91
Carnall, Jeffrey, 187
Chandler, James, 175, 179, 181
Chase, Cynthia, 176

Christensen, Francis, 179
Christensen, Jerome, 14, 26, 31, 36, 108–9, 112, 122, 124, 168, 171, 172, 173, 185, 186, 187
Coburn, Kathleen, 185
Coleman, Deirdre, 186
Coleridge, Samuel Taylor: as reader of the Prelude, 37, 80, 81, 85, 92, 93, 96, 103–6, 136; critique of Wordsworth, 136–44; in *The Prelude*, 16, Youth, 91–92. Works: *Biographia Literaria*, 16, 17, 108–32, 135, 138–45, 154–55, 156–63; and *The Prelude*, 108, 111; as literary life, 111–16; as preface, 110; coherence of, 109; compositional history, 109; digressiveness of, 119–20; friend's letter in Ch. 13, 158–160; representation of Wordsworth in, 121; theory of imagination, 156–63; "A Letter to———," 146; *Conciones ad Populum*, 127; "Dejection: An Ode," 145, 146–54; *The Friend*, 16, 97–104, 121–23, 127, 130, 137, 141, 160; guidance to readers of, 97, 102; *Logic*, 17, 163–67; "Frost at Midnight," 83; *Lay Sermon*, 127–28, 166; *Notebooks*, 112; "Once a Jacobin Always a Jacobin," 130; *Sibylline Leaves*, 109, 134, 145, 150, 153, 154; *Statesman's Manual*, 17, 126, 127, 131–32, 166; *The Watchman*, 121–22, 127, 129; "To William Wordsworth," 86, 96–97, 104–6, 134, 145, 150, 159
Cooke, Michael G., 171
Courier, 117, 128

Davey, Humphrey, 183
De Man, Paul, 171, 175, 176, 177, 186; discourse of self-restoration, 51, 52
De Quincy, Thomas, 178

Derrida, Jacques, 19, 21, 25, 169, 185
Donato, Eugenio, 177

Eakin, John Paul, 168, 171, 175
Edinburgh Review, 128
Eisenstein, Elizabeth, 171
Engell, James, 119, 159, 190
Examiner, 126, 128, 130, 131

Fancy, 151–52, 157
Ferguson, Frances, 14, 168, 178, 179, 182
Fisch, Max H., 172, 173
Fleishman, Avrom, 22–23, 170
Fogel, Daniel Mark, 184, 185
Foucault, Michel, 15, 26–28, 170, 171
Fruman, Norman, 184, 190

Galperin, William, 105, 179, 184
Garber, Frederick, 171
Gill, Stephen, 173
Godwin, William, 87, 89
Good, James M., 173
Gravil, Richard, 188
Grob, Alan, 181
Gusdorf, Georges, 169

Haney, David, 174, 175, 176
Hartman, Geoffrey, 29, 53, 170, 174, 176, 177, 178, 179, 181
Hazlitt, William, 17, 126–32, 166, 187
Helvellyn, 78
Herder, Johann Gottfried von, 124
History, authentic, 117–18, 120
Howe, P. P., 188
Hutchinson, Mary, 146
Hutchinson, Sara, 151, 183

Imagination, 156–63, and Fancy, 152, 157, Coleridge's definition of, 160–61
Intertextuality, 15, 130, 133, 154

Jackson, J. R. De J., 190
Jacobus, Mary, 43, 44, 173, 174, 175, 176, 178, 181
Jay, Paul, 29, 172, 174, 178, 179
Johnston, Kenneth, 42, 68, 173, 174, 175, 176, 177, 178, 179, 181, 182, 184, 188
Jones, Stanley, 197

Kelley, Theresa M., 177, 178, 181, 184
Klancher, Jon, 14, 168, 186, 187, 188
Kneale, J. Douglas, 170, 174, 175

Lacan, Jacques, 19–20, 169
Lamb, Charles and Mary, 178
Language, propriety of, 167
Lejeune, Phillippe, 168, 169
Lingua communis, 143
Literacy, 137
Locke, John, 163
London: Wordsworth's experiences in, 71–77
Love, intellectual, 93

Magnuson, Paul, 15, 168, 180, 181, 189
Man of letters, 26, 30, 109, 121, 154
Marginal method, 108
Marin, Louis, 185
McConnel, Frank D., 174, 176
McFarland, Thomas, 82, 179, 180
McGann, Jerome, 185
McKusick, James, 190
Mellor, Ann, 171
Miller, J. Hillis, 181
Misch, Georg, 169
Morning Post, 117, 121, 122, 124, 145, 146, 147, 152, 153
Morrison, James C., 172

Newlyn, Lucy, 15, 168, 169, 179, 182, 188, 189
Nussbaum, Felicity, 171

Olney, James, 168, 169, 170

Parrish, Stephen, 173, 175, 188
Peterson, Linda, 171
Petrarch, 100, 134–35, 183
Poole, Thomas, 97, 183
Poststructuralism, 13, 14, 19
Print culture, eighteenth century, 18
Prophets of Nature, 96

Rajan, Tilottama, 171
Rationalism, Godwinian, 85, 88, 89, 90, 101, 181
Reader: as guest, 102; corrupted, 72; passive character of, 138; Coleridge's empowering of, 104; power,

15, 97, 98, 166; Wordsworth's desire to silence, 103, 133

Reading public, 16, 18, 80, 123, 126, 128, 131, 155, 166–67; compared to "the People," 70, 166

Reading: authority, 123; community, 68; demonstration of, 80; inward act of, 117; model of, 80, 126, 141; performance of, 107, 165; power of, 84, 136; process of, 62, 67, 80; promiscuous, 126, 128, 131, 166; scene of, 94; strategies of, 132; teaching of, 107

Reed, Arden, 170

Reed, Mark L., 189

Reiman, Donald H., 178

Robinson, Mary, 73

Roe, Nicholas, 181, 182, 183, 186

Rooke, Barbara E., 183, 187

Ruddick, Bill, 187

Ruoff, Gene, 15, 169

Rzepka, Charles, 68, 173, 177

Said, Edward, 173

Schelling, Friedrich, 160

Self-dividedness, 42, 44, 50, 51, 52, 57, 59, 60

Self-duplication, 161–62, 165

Self-presence, 42, 43

Self-representation, 111, Romantic, 15; strategies of, 158, 160

Selfhood, paradigms, 18–19

Shaffer, Elinor, 185

Shawcross, J. 184

Simpson, David, 73, 171, 178, 179

Southey, Robert, 98, 136–37, 139–40, 173, 157

Spectacle, 72–80

Spengemann, William, 169

Spivak, Gayatri, 170

Sprinker, Michael, 172

St. Bartholemew's Fair, 76

Starobinski, Jean, 23–24, 170

Stelzig, Eugene, 170, 180

Stuart, Daniel, 98

Sturrock, John, 168

Supplementarity, 23

Tagliocozzo, Giorgio, 173

Taylor, William, 173

Textual appropriation (reappropria-tion), 17, 122–24, 125, 128–29, 131–32, 133, 135–36, 141, 145, 154–55, 156, 161, 163, 165, 167

Thelwall, John, 186

Tristram Shandy, 132

Vallon, Annette, 146

Verb substantive, 17, 163–65

Verene, Donald Philip, 173

Verum factum, 33–34

Vico, Giambattista, 22, 30–35; *Autobiography*, 22, 30–35, 172; *New Science*, 31–35

Wasserman, Earl, 177

Watson, George, 184, 185

Weintraub, Karl, 169

Wheeler, Kathleen, 184, 189

White, Hayden, 172

Wolfson, Susan, 174, 176

Woodmansee, Martha, 171

Wordsworth, Caroline, 146

Wordsworth, Dorothy, 90, 93, 94, 146, 148, 178

Wordsworth, Jonathan, 173, 175, 177, 178, 182

Wordsworth, William: as reader, 138, 140–44, 152, 157; attitude toward *The Friend*, 98–100; attitude toward science, 86,89; poetic theory, 135; simplicity, 144, 152. Works: *Excursion*, 44, 45, 47, 50, 82, 159; "Home at Grasmere," 42; *Lyrical Ballads*, 138–39, 159; Preface, 70, 136, 138, 141–44; "Michael," 159; "Ode: Intimations of Immortality," 104–5, 146, 150; *Poems* (1815), preface, 156; *Prelude* (1799), 39, 41, 42, 47, 52, 53, 82, 84, 87; *Prelude* (five-book), 43; *Prelude* (1805), 37, 96, 150, 160; address to Coleridge, 43, 81–96; relationship between *The Prelude* and the *Recluse*, 15, 39, 40, 42, 44, 45, 46, 58–59, 60, 82–83, 108, 159; Book 1, 38, 40, 46, 48–49, 51, 53, 54, 57, 58, 60, 82–83; Book 2, 83–87, 88; Book 4, 63–70, 79, 88, Dawn Dedication, 64, 67, Discharged Soldier, 64, 67, 68–70; Book 6, 79, 86, 90–93, 102, Mont

Blanc, 93; Book 7, 70–77, 79, Blind Beggar, 76, Maid of Buttermere, 73–74, Rosy Babe, 73–74, St. Bartholemew's Fair, 76; Book 8, 70–72, 77–80, Grasmere Fair, 78; Book 9, 70; Book 10, 70, 87–90; Book 13, 93–96, Mount Snowdon, 94; Prelude (1850), 37, 90; Recluse, 37, 42, 44, 45, 46, 47, 58, 59, 60, 61, 67, 81, 87, 94, 96, 99–100